HIGH
PERFORMANCE
SELLING:

A PRACTICAL SYSTEM

FOR BECOMING

A MAJOR LEAGUE

SALES PROFESSIONAL

Cover Design: Marianne Young
Book Design: Practical Graphics, Inc.

ISBN: 1-886745-04-8

Library of Congress: 95-067242

Printed in the United States of America

A division of
Streamline Publishing, Inc.

Streamline Publishing, Inc.
Datura Street, Suite 718
West Palm Beach, Florida 33401
(407) 655-8778
1-800-226-7857

For information on Mr. Greenwood's speaking and consulting availability, phone (918) 747-1119.

To Marian, whose patience with a salesman and teacher,

and long hours at a word processor, made the ideas finally

find their way onto paper.

— K.G.

TABLE OF CONTENTS

FORWARDS
by B. Eric Rhoads
V

by Jim Rhea
I X

THE OPENING
Life Cycles Of Products, Businesses And Salespeople
1

CHAPTER 1
What Happens To Your Head As You Progress
Through The Stages
7

CHAPTER 2
Propelling Your Way To High Performance
1 7

CHAPTER 3
Competence, Commitment, Belief System And Experience
3 1

CHAPTER 4
Understanding a Little Something About Human Behavior
4 1

CHAPTER 5
Understanding Why People Don't Do Things
Can Help You Understand Why They Do Things
4 9

CHAPTER 6
Why Understanding The Belief System Concept
Is So Important To Selling In Today's World
5 9

CHAPTER 7

Positioning Your Product And Yourself
67

CHAPTER 8

No Help, No Benefit Or No Payoff
77

CHAPTER 9

Does The Concept Actually Fit Today's World?
85

CHAPTER 10

Adjusting Your Mind For Higher Performance
97

CHAPTER 11

How To Make It Bigger By Listening Better
111

CHAPTER 12

Understanding Powerful Phrases
125

CHAPTER 13

*Questions, And If You Don't Know Where You Are
Going It Really Doesn't Matter Much Where You Are*
139

CHAPTER 14

Now We're Ready To Think About Questions
159

CHAPTER 15

*Getting Ready To Position Your Product Or Service So The Buyer
Or Prospect Wants To Make A Commitment To Buy It*
175

CHAPTER 16

*Understanding How People Think Before You Put
Together Your Recommendation*
193

CHAPTER 17
*Presenting Recommendations And Understanding
The Four Possibilities Or Options*
203

CHAPTER 18
*Sometimes There Are Roadblocks To Complete
Agreement, How Do We Handle Those Objections?*
209

CHAPTER 19
*It Also Depends Upon The Personality Of The
Buyer Or Buying Influence, And Their Needs*
239

CHAPTER 20
*And If You Really Want To Be Successful In Sales,
You Will Focus On The Gap, Not The Goal*
249

CHAPTER 21
*How Closing, Getting A Commitment To Action
And Getting Decisions Are All Woven Together*
265

CHAPTER 22
"If You Ain't Been Throwed, You Ain't Been Ridin'"
277

EPILOGUE
281

CREDITS
287

INDEX
291

FORWARD

by B. Eric Rhoads

For years, many looked upon sales as one of the lowest professions on the totem pole. Selling has carried a social stigma equivalent to the lowest of positions, probably as a result of the tactics used in earlier times by car salesmen and door-to-door salesmen.

Today, it is a credible and respectable position, and one of the most lucrative. The profession of selling has become just that — a profession. Honor may not always be associated with every sales position, yet today most carry the badge of trust and honor along with their wares. Selling is no longer thought of as the high-pressure game with intimidation tactics, pressure and manipulation, although some, unfortunately, still practice these dishonorable and outdated tactics.

Salespeople are equipped with training in human relations and psychology. They understand their customers and have perfected the skills of listening, instead of living up to the old adage that people who can sell have "the gift of gab."

Selling in today's world is a delicate art, an exact science and a honed skill. Perhaps the sales profession would have continued tricking potential customers had it not been for a rare breed of individuals who saw the need to turn selling into the profession that it has become.

Ken Greenwood is one of those innovators who saw an opportunity to make selling a respected industry and an honorable profession. As a result, we rarely see the "winners" in the sales game selling by the seat of their pants. Those who are making the biggest dollars in the selling profession are doing so because they realize that, as circumstances change, so do selling tools and techniques. These high-test sales leaders know they must continually educate themselves, look for new ways to sell and investigate every tool and technique they can find.

This book is one of those tools. Its concepts are innovative, fresh and cutting-edge, yet they are combined with some of the most important selling basics, which never change.

I first encountered Ken Greenwood at a management seminar in Dallas. Though I had years of experience under my belt, I rapidly realized how little I actually knew. This seminar was somehow different. Unlike typical sales seminars, there were no motivation tactics designed to get me hyped up. There were no typical sessions to help us handle objections. It was low-key, extremely informative and focused on reading personalities and understanding how to meet the needs of individuals. It was my first experience with learning how to sell people individually.

Greenwood has a certain disarming quality. At the seminar I first attended, there was no indication I was dealing with a "sales type" person. In the past, I thought I could pick a salesman out of any crowd, and I fully expected another slick sales trainer. Ken was quiet, humble, reserved, thoughtful and very empathetic, thus changing my view of the selling profession and subsequently my view of myself.

Since that time, he has made thousands understand that they didn't have to be ashamed of being in the selling profession. He has individually lifted the self-esteem of many who were previously hesitant to admit they were in sales, because of the stigma the profession carried.

In my opinion, Ken Greenwood's training has set the standard for sales training in America. His wisdom is unparalleled in the area of selling. No one else I know has spent so much time studying the profession of selling and developing techniques and tools that are innovative and effective.

Interestingly enough, Ken is one of the most current mentors I've ever met. Although Ken has tried to curtail his heavy traveling schedule to allow time with his wife, dogs and extensive charity work with wildlife preservation organizations, he is still on the cutting edge. Most people opt for retirement once they've put in their years and made their nest egg. Ken is a rare breed. He continues to study selling, to refine his teaching to include the latest developments in research and to read vigorously to learn more about a profession he helped define.

High Performance Selling isn't just another sales book. It is the result of years of encouragement from those who have studied under Ken Greenwood. People have been begging him to put his selling system into print — because his system is one of the best ever developed, and because it is one everyone should have an opportunity to be exposed to. Humbly, Ken flat-out refused to write a book, because bringing attention to himself is just not what Ken Greenwood is all about. After much prodding and encouragement, he consented. The result is a phenomenal selling book by the mentor's mentor.

The Greenwood style in High Performance Selling will make the best salespeople better. In this book, you'll learn techniques and wonder how you ever lived without them. You'll be a better salesperson, your performance will exceed your highest expectations and, best of all, you'll be doing a service to all those people who need the product you're selling. I encourage you to read with a highlighter, make notes in the margins and put your personal revelations on the notes page in the back. Every time you get ideas that apply to you, turn to the back and write them there. Then put your ideas into practice immediately.

Since my first encounter with Ken Greenwood years ago, millions of dollars have passed through my hands as a result of the selling skills I acquired from Ken. I've since attended more of his seminars, even as recently as this year.

You'll see something in a Ken Greenwood seminar that you rarely see in other trainers' seminars — millionaires. The successful heads of multimillion-dollar corporations are still attending Greenwood seminars, knowing that each time they go back, Ken will teach them the latest techniques in selling, management and business operation. Most of these people are capable of writing volumes on their own, yet they still are turning to Ken Greenwood to teach them more.

You've stumbled onto a powerful book which will, if applied, make a huge difference in your life, your career and your income. Enjoy!

— *B. Eric Rhoads*

B. Eric Rhoads is an entrepreneur in book and magazine publishing. He has owned many businesses, including a group of successful radio stations. He currently owns and operates

Streamline Publishing, which is the parent company to Radio Ink magazine, Streamline Press and Airwaves Emporium. Rhoads was also the inventor of The Giant Boom Box, a giant radio studio on wheels which is used promotionally by hundreds of radio stations worldwide.

FORWARD

by Jim Rhea

When I first met Ken Greenwood, he was president of Swanco Broadcasting, a major broadcast group in the Southwest headquartered in Tulsa. He retired from Swanco to become head of the Department of Communication at the University of Tulsa. After leaving the University of Tulsa, he founded Greenwood Performance Systems. As founder of Greenwood Performance Systems, Ken created many of the intellectual properties which make up the Greenwood Performance Systems seminars and courses.

Greenwood Performance Systems was founded to train salespeople. Even though our original purpose was to bring a higher level of skill development to salespeople, we began to realize we must also provide managers with new ways to work with their people. We recognized the critical role managers play in supporting their sales people to reach these new standards and expectations.

In the last ten years, there have been dramatic changes in the competitive environment. One of the principal hallmarks of this new environment is the recognition that people are the key leverageable asset of business organizations. We think the sales force is the prime asset of an organization that will provide a business with a sustainable, competitive advantage.

When Ken discussed writing a book, I encouraged his efforts. The book is based upon the four levels of salespeople, material in the Sales Performance Systems and the Creating High Performance seminar. The book expands on the four levels, isolates the levels and explains what people do when they are at that level. Ken then offers ways they can advance their skills to attain a higher level of performance. He shares his experiences and creative thinking with energy and style. Readers will appreciate the road map Ken provides for High Performance Selling.

>   — *Jim Rhea*
>   *President and CEO*
>   *Greenwood Performance Systems*

LIFE CYCLES OF PRODUCTS, BUSINESSES AND SALESPEOPLE

LIFE CYCLES OF PRODUCTS, BUSINESSES AND SALESPEOPLE

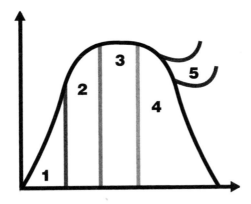

PHASE 1: Concept and development of the business

PHASE 2: Rapid growth and expansion

PHASE 3: Maturity and stability

PHASE 4: Decline

PHASE 5: Turnaround and diversification

The graph is taken from marketing. It portrays the life cycle of a product or an organization and shows that products and business have phases or passages.

These passages are fairly predictable stages: inception, rapid growth, maturity and stability, then decline or further extension. Coca-Cola would be a good example of this series of passages. At this writing, Coke is in the extension period, introducing new products and increasing its total share of the market.

As selling has moved into a new era and become more complex and competitive, the applications of the marketing cycle have become even more fascinating.

For instance, a salesperson goes through similar passages in career development. For the purposes of this book, we have changed the names of the stages or passages to Novice, Learner, Competent and Professional. But the concept of evolution is the same.

A salesperson has a career cycle that includes a beginning period, learning period, competent period and, finally, a professional period. Just as a product may not pass through all stages at exactly the same rate, neither do most salespeople. Some reach different levels sooner. Some never reach the upper levels, because they leave the profession or choose not to develop their skills to that high level of performance.

The idea of different levels of skill, expertise or development explains wide differences of opinion you'll hear expressed by salespeople. For instance, one salesperson goes to a seminar or workshop and comes away feeling it has been a very worthwhile experience.

A fellow salesperson goes to the same workshop and says: "There really wasn't much in that workshop that I feel I can use. It was all pretty basic stuff."

It's a good bet that if the material was basic, but good, one salesperson was at a different stage of development than the other. Had the material been more sophisticated, it is possible the two opinions might have been reversed.

MATURING AS SELLERS AND BUYERS

There is still another application for the cycle. At some time in their careers, salespeople say "AHA!" and begin to apply the idea to their buyers. Indeed, buyers go through a similar cycle. The more homes you buy and sell, the more experienced you become. A salesperson no longer leads you through the process. By the same token, a rookie real estate salesperson won't provide the expertise you need, because you have become a competent buyer of homes.

Many times, when salespeople are in the beginning stages of selling, they will locate a beginning buyer. Two novices hit it off and form a sort of bond. Many times we have seen a new advertising salesperson make that first sale to a brand new business where the buyer has never bought advertising. New real estate people often work with smaller, lower-priced homes. New office equipment people often begin by selling to smaller businesses, and are more comfortable with less-expensive installations.

Now add still another element. A necktie is not an exotic piece of clothing, nor is a handkerchief. With only a small amount of training, nearly any intelligent person can sell such an item. Translate the necktie into a highly stylized suit and the sale becomes more complex.

Another analogy to make the point might be that a hardware salesperson can handle a shovel, rake and hoe without a lot of problems. Make the equipment an expensive lawn tractor, and the salesperson needs more knowledge, more skill and more expertise.

Training becomes still another element that goes through stages. The Girl Scout cookie salesperson needs only marginal training to be able to perform. If she sells only one kind of cookie, the job is fairly easy. Give her a line of cookies and add some dietetic goods, and the process of selling becomes more complex, even for this young lady in her crisp uniform.

It has been said that selling is a complex process of persuasion. Some sage once told a beginning class of salespeople that the more he studied selling, the less he knew about it. It is a complex process because sellers and buyers are like snowflakes: No two are exactly alike. Already, we have the ingredients for a pretty fair snowball!

You can better understand selling when you understand the stages of development of a salesperson. This gives you a blueprint that allows you to determine where you are in your career, where you need to be and how to get there.

NATURAL-BORN

You may have heard the phrase (and you may believe it): "Oh, he or she is a natural-born salesperson!" You may also have heard some coach say: "He is a natural-born quarterback." There may be some truth to the idea that we are drawn to what we like, or seem to do well or think we can do well. Life may be a road of reward and punishment.

We won't argue that point. Our premise is that skill and ability are part of selling, and highly skilled salespeople are not all "naturals." In fact, some of them were rather unnatural. But nearly all of those highly skilled salespeople did have the ability to learn, and that was the ability they used! Some learned the hard way, by trial and error. Come to think of it, a lot of quarterbacks got to the top the same way, as did some scientists, teachers, musicians, lawyers and so on.

The point is that some salespeople have the ability to learn faster than others. That explains the speed with which they move through the four stages. It doesn't mean that others can't reach the top level — that of the high-performance professional — because they can.

If you believe the good Lord engineered us all for success, that we were designed to prosper, that we all have the ability to learn and grow as human beings, then anybody who wants to do it can climb to that top level of selling. They will just climb the hill at a different pace and may even use different paths (methods) to get there. They are able to do that if they are willing to make the effort.

So, if you're ready and you're willing ... read on. There is no question that you are able! And that takes us to the next chapter and what happens to your head as you go through the four stages.

::

WHAT HAPPENS TO YOUR HEAD AS YOU PROGRESS THROUGH THE STAGES?

WHAT HAPPENS TO YOUR HEAD AS YOU PROGRESS THROUGH THE STAGES?

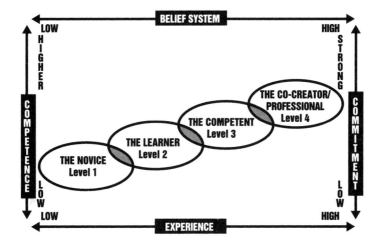

We asked salespeople, high-performing salespeople, what skills, attitudes and abilities it takes to be successful in the marketplace today. Through the years, it has been our good fortune to associate with high performers, the people who set records, who climbed the hills, who were regarded as top performers. So, we focused on those people.

There is an old saying that 20 percent of the salespeople do 80 percent of the business. We borrowed that point from Pareto, because he is no longer around to argue his point of view. Such people seem able to adjust to selling in a more competitive world. Larry Wilson talks about this in his book, *Changing The Game: The New Way To Sell.* It, like this book, focuses on the 20 percent who are winning with high performance.

We asked the high performers: "What do you need to be able

to compete today?" They gave us a list of skills which, in the drawing on the previous page, appear on the left as a dimension labeled COMPETENCE. We'll come back to that in the next chapter. The other abilities or characteristics of high performers were discipline, persistence and time management, and they separated these things from skills. "AHA," we said, "you're talking about things we can all do if we want to, if we're willing." We set those things on the right-hand side of the drawing and labeled them COMMITMENT. Now we have two dimensions, COMPETENCE and COMMITMENT.

"Anything else?" we asked. More discussion brought up what goes on inside your head when you're selling. We might call this THE INSIDE GAME of selling — how we think about and talk to ourselves. We determined it was highly important. We distilled this third dimension into BELIEF SYSTEM, including ego, ego strength and empathy. More on that later.

We suggested that experience is a part of selling, because it is not a classroom course, that until you actually closed you couldn't know what it was like. Until you had done a good question-and-listen session with a prospect, you couldn't know what it was like to guide a discovery stage of a sales call. It is like swimming: You can read a lot of books but until you get into the pool, you really can't learn to swim. So we added EXPERIENCE as the fourth dimension.

Now we have four dimensions: EXPERIENCE, COMPETENCE, COMMITMENT and BELIEF SYSTEM.

Somebody commented: "That's a little like ready, willing and able," and we wouldn't argue much with that point. In fact, one thing we've learned about selling is that you don't argue too much. Argument is for politicians, and that may be why most of them don't always wear well. Selling is seeing it from the other person's point of view. So much for argument. Back to our salespeople.

Then these salespeople said: "You know, I remember what it was like when I was first on the job. I didn't look at it at all like I do today." "Tell us about that," we said.

"Well, let's look at your drawing. You've got the NOVICE stage here and that is really true ... I was a NOVICE. I just hoped nobody noticed me the first couple of weeks. I was only interested in one thing. That was SURVIVAL! Money wasn't the issue the first weeks on the job."

So we took the dimensions out of the drawing and listened. Again, we heard similar stories and experiences, and again we did

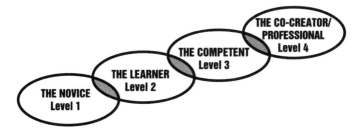

some digesting and heard them talking about money, survival, peer group acceptance, psychic challenge and focus. We tracked them through the four stages. Not every person fit exactly, but the pattern was amazing. This is the way it looked:

MONEY   For the novices, it wasn't part of the equation. Either they had a draw, or they were reconciled to starving.

               For the learners, it was more important. They liked the idea of selling something and getting paid. The pictures of dead presidents began to get appealing.

               For the competents, money was important. It may have been a driving force. Achievement was measured by how much they made.

               For the professionals, money was important, but not the driving force. They knew they could sell and make money. They had the security that goes with knowing they could sell.

(A pause here — if you're a sales manager, you may wonder why tenured sellers reach a "comfort zone" and don't need to jump tall buildings anymore. You want them to "make more money," and they tell you it isn't that important anymore. Money is no longer a motivator. They have it!)

SURVIVAL   The novice just wants this for now. Help me survive! Let me make it through the end of the month. Help me make it through this call!

               The learners also want to survive, but the question is less of daily survival and more of making it through the month. By now, there may be goals to be met, either personal or management-mandated. But at least they know the way to the comfort room, and that is encouraging.

               The competents are less concerned about survival.

They know they have skills and abilities. Prosperity is the issue!

The professional or co-creator has the security of knowing that skill and ability are commodities that can be sold to many companies. Survival is not an issue.

But look at the shift of what goes on inside the head of the salesperson. Look at how the priorities have changed as they have moved through the four stages:

FOCUS   The novices focus on activity. The more people they see, the more they sell. They learn to deal with rejection.

The learners begin to make some connections. Activity is important, but it needs to be the right activity. They begin to sort out suspects and prospects. They begin to make connections between selling skills and results. How many presentations they make is now a criterion for success.

The competent shifts to results. Where will the dollars come from? Who can spend big dollars? How much time do I invest to get a payoff? Sales in terms of dollars is now the criterion for success.

And the professionals or co-creators focus on solving client problems. They measure their success on how many customers they have helped. They are usually creative with solutions. Thus, they look at the concept of selling in a much broader perspective.

PEER GROUP ACCEPTANCE

The novices just hope nobody sees them make a mistake. Positive impressions of the group are not part of their thinking yet.

The learners like to be included in the group, but more often follow what the group does. Thus, the norm of the group members — how they see selling, how they sell, how they measure success — is very important to the learner. Often, they will find a mentor within the group who becomes a role model.

The competents want group acceptance, and the group may be wider than their organization. Consequently, many job shifts occur in this stage, because the competents are flattered by a job offer or they want to see if they can do it someplace else. Their idea of challenge is spreading a little. They may take to mentoring younger salespeople or, if they can't get this satisfaction on the job, they'll find it off the job by teaching or coaching. When the challenge flattens out too much, they come to a fork in the road. Often, at this point in their careers, they will consider management, because "this job isn't as challenging as it once was."

The professionals or co-creators usually have decided to remain in sales. They may even have tried management and found they didn't like it. Peer group acceptance is less important, but is replaced with social acceptance. They want to be accepted as professionals. They may join clubs or organizations. They look for challenge. They measure their success by the number of customers they have, not necessarily the number of sales they make.

PSYCHIC CHALLENGE

This seems to be another dimension that plays a part in the mindset of the high performer. If we reverse our order in this part and start with the co-creator or professional, it would surface in that need for challenge. The professionals seldom get swept up in competing against fellow salespeople. More often, their goals involve reaching new plateaus. They have their own goals. These may be to penetrate certain key accounts, to increase volume from present clients, to add lines, to find totally new business, to provide innovation in their sales approach. Maslow might put this level of salesperson in the "self-actualized" level on his hierarchy of needs. Usually, this type of salesperson is self-disciplined, sold on what he or she is doing and has managed to find a fairly balanced lifestyle. Far from the stereotyped Willy Loman, they are satisfied they have reached, and can maintain, a very professional life. They truly get turned on when a customer asks for their help.

The competents get psychic challenge by beating goals, whether personal goals or management goals are the objective. They compete less against other salespeople; they have a customer focus and have built good client relationships. They do a lot of repeat business. They know their products and other products in their field; they can sell with or against competing products. They look for that edge they can get when they sell their product as a concept or system, usually to produce benefits.

The learners get their psychic kicks from winning — winning sales, beating a competitor, getting the business. They know their product and sell lots of features and advantages and, as a result, are very product-focused. They often are strong presenters and measure success by the number of presentations they make. Quite often they are still generic presenters, not having learned to make that subtle shift to finding the benefits that fit the customer.

The novices are so focused on themselves they really don't have time for something like psychic challenge.

In a much broader view, the novices and the learners are focused on themselves and what's in it for them. They may even see the buyer as an enemy or antagonist and have a somewhat adversarial relationship. The competents and the professionals do not share this view. They have learned the skill of separating people and problems, and they tend to adjust to the people and find the problem. This adds another quality to the mix. The competents and the professionals or co-creators have been able to learn to adjust their social style to the expectations of the buyer. As a result, they are buyer-focused, not self-focused.

Now, add all these elements to the drawing (larger type indicates a greater level of importance), and you have a picture of what's happening in a salesperson's head during the four stages of development.

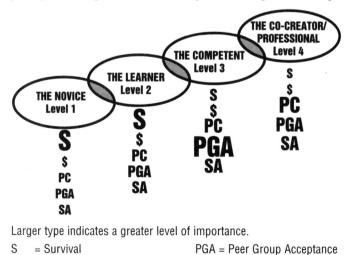

Larger type indicates a greater level of importance.

S = Survival	PGA = Peer Group Acceptance
$ = Dollars/Income	SA = Self-Actualization
PC = Psychic Challenge	

One other element needs to be added to the mix. Most top sales-people, that upper 8 percent to 10 percent, understand one other dimension. It is perhaps the most mysterious of the dimensions or elements in the mind of a salesperson.

If you are familiar with Abraham Maslow's Hierarchy of Needs, you have a word picture of a pyramid. At the bottom of the pyramid, Maslow put the basic need for survival: food, shelter, water, the necessities of life. His thesis was that as man satisfied one need, he would move to a higher need. His point was that a need satisfied is no longer a priority.

At the top of his pyramid, or the highest state of humankind, he put the self-actualized individual. Maslow described self-actualization as a state where a person loved what he was doing so much it was no longer "work." He was doing something so fulfilling, he lost all track of other needs. What he was doing, and his satisfaction with that work, was the reason for existence.

If this is true, self-actualization is a part of selling for the high-performance salespeople — the true professionals. Balanced people aren't myopic on the subject, but they sell because they love the challenge of helping people solve problems. If you aren't at the top level of selling yet, this may sound a little altruistic. If you truly are at the top level, you will have a feel for what we are saying. In its highest form, selling provides self-actualization. When a sale is right for buyer and seller, when both win, when both prosper, there is no finer feeling of achievement.

This dimension of selling is not much of a factor at the novice level. It is a powerful factor in the fourth, or professional, level.

If there is merit in our belief about the evolution of salespeople, their skills and belief system, then there would be every reason to believe this matrix would not be a constant. It isn't. Salespeople can move up in selling level. But they can also move down, and some-times they do. Often, when the level-three and level-four people go into a slump, they have allowed one of the three dimensions — com-petence, belief system or commitment — to slip down a level or two.

So, your place in this matrix may not be the same for each dimension at the same time; in fact, it may vary from day-to-day if your performance is inconsistent. The awareness of this possibility adds another element to the belief system of the level-three and level-four people: They must continue to learn and grow. They must find the time to "sharpen the saw" and keep their perspective keen and cutting.

The dynamics of this matrix become almost an ecosystem. There is the perception that each level can also evolve. Without learning and growing, the level-two person simply cannot make it, today, to the level-three stage of competent. For instance, in many types of selling, the salesperson who hasn't kept up with modern technology such as the computer can't make it to the third and fourth levels. Many industries recognize this need for continued growth and require a certain amount of training for everybody, every year, in order that they retain their jobs or maintain their positions. Otherwise, competence becomes obsolete; overall sales performance regresses.

And, in one other way, the matrix has changed at the top level. At one time, that level was described as a "sustaining resource" or a "professional resource" — the type of salesperson who really was regarded by the customer as "an unpaid member of the customer's team." In the past few years, we have seen that perception shift. To cover this evolution, we invented the term "co-creator" to describe that high level of selling. It is possible we may now have a fifth level.

At this level, the salesperson works as a creative source for the customer and his or her own company, service or offering. They use creative thinking and problem-solving ability or orchestrate solutions that benefit both parties to the agreement. They are negotiators, synergizers, team leaders who find new answers for tough problems. They create new methods, systems or structures for the customer; they do the same with or for their offering. To use an analogy, they are much less the standard, the ruler or the blueprint ... they are the compass that points in the right direction.

If you accept the concept of the matrix, it becomes a living thing. It is an ecosystem. No one single dimension can live alone. If one dimension changes, other dimensions may need to change, or adapt or modify.

But if you are in any form of selling, your four dimensions are someplace in the evolution of this matrix. If you are not at the level you want to be, then the matrix can provide you with a pathway that can lead you to higher levels.

Much depends on the choices you want to make and your perception of that dimension labeled "commitment." High-performance selling is not something you want to do. Rather, it is something you *decide* to be. The choice must be a conscious choice. It is yours!

::

CHAPTER 2

PROPELLING YOUR WAY
TO HIGH PERFORMANCE

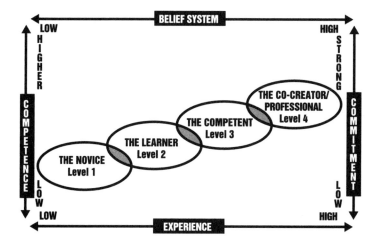

As selling almost anything has become more competitive and complex, sales managers have become more aware of the importance of the growth of their salespeople. We introduced them to the concept of the four-stage matrix and demonstrated using that matrix to help them identify stages of development.

Instead of judging or evaluating salespeople only by the number of dollars generated, they could look at the total salesperson and find out why, or why not, performance was there. By the same token, the use of the matrix enabled the salespeople to analyze their own performances.

How does the matrix work as a tool for analysis? Well, let's look at competence. This is the skill area. This is where a trainer or coach can help a salesperson. We asked salespeople to give us a list of the skill areas they thought were important in making it in today's marketplace. Again, as a composite, this is the list they put together. We dubbed them the CAN DO things. If you can do these things, you will prosper.

At the top of the list is listening. A good salesperson simply MUST be an excellent listener. This is followed by asking good questions, making a good presentation, providing creative ideas, handling objections and closing. Getting the contact the first time is high on the list.

In almost every group of salespeople, there was a long discussion of "people skills" and where they fit. Was this a skill that could be learned? The conclusion was that it definitely could be learned. In fact, the company we founded teaches the skill as Social Style, and this version is in the marketplace from Wilson Learning, David Merrill's company and several other legitimate sources.

So, we added "people skills" to this grouping, with this footnote: That people skills are also intertwined with empathy, and that empathy is intertwined with your belief system. People skills can be conscious or unconscious. Because of their importance in the matrix, we'll shift to that subject later in this chapter.

Competence, then, consists of CAN DO skills.

When we talked to people about COMMITMENT, or the WILL DO skills, the clear ideas got more misty. As one person expressed it: "I would put time management over there, because you can learn the skill of time management in an hour, but you may spend a lifetime really doing it, and that's commitment. It is not a question of 'can I manage my time,' it is a question of 'will I manage my time.' That's discipline!"

On the list we assembled, self-discipline and time management were mentioned often — staying organized, staying in shape, perseverance, persistence, will to do what you ought to do, staying on purpose, staying focused and completing your paperwork. Being accountable came up.

One very successful person, nearing retirement, put it this way: "If you are the kind of person who is focused on what you must do, one day you discover that what you *want* to do is what you *must* do, and then the job gets much easier."

Then the remaining two dimensions are added: BELIEF SYSTEM and EXPERIENCE.

Let's examine the belief system, without getting heavily into psychology. Belief system is how salespeople talk to themselves.

Good ones talk "good" to themselves. In fact, there is strong evidence that until salespeople think well of themselves, they can't make it into the area of high performance and stay there.

That doesn't mean an ego trip or acting like an egomaniac. It does mean having a good opinion of yourself, being confident, self-assured and self-contained. It says: "I'm OK." For many people starting in sales, this attitude is a little hard to understand, because our culture has often taught us to be humble, self-effacing and grateful for small favors. That is fine if you are teaching youngsters about Abraham Lincoln, but it doesn't fit selling.

Novices, especially, need to feel good about themselves. They need ego. They must tell themselves: "I can do it ... I can do it ... I can do it ... I'll make ...," and a good sales manager will reinforce that attitude. The learners must learn to visualize success, learn to rehearse mentally doing it right, learn to rehearse their questions, their presentations, their closes. Every one of these actions will build the feeling that I CAN DO IT!

That's ego, plain unvarnished ego. And you need it. You must have it.

You also need ego strength. Once, in a workshop, I raised the question of ego strength and asked the group for a possible definition. One lady responded: "That's how long you want to stay in the recovery room." Like many unrehearsed lines, that comes very close to describing ego strength. The professional salesperson MUST learn to bounce back from rejection. Selling is perhaps the only occupation that invites rejection! Other professions deal with it. A lawyer won't win every case. In fact, they may try only one case a day, maybe even a week. Salespeople may try as many as eight or ten cases in one day. They won't win them all!

So, two critical things the novice and the learner must find in their physical and mental storehouse are ego and ego strength. In the beginning levels of selling, these two ingredients will take the average beginner a long way. But, there is more to the story.

We have already suggested that the novice and the learner are inwardly focused, that they see the situation or the problem from their point of view. They are self-focused. That's ego and ego strength at work. But, as their careers evolve, as they move toward the third and fourth stages of selling, their belief system will shift, or it must shift, if they are to reach high performance. If ego and ego strength are what give them the "I'm OK" feeling, then empathy gives them the "you're OK, too" feeling. Ego and ego strength are my view; empathy is your view. Ego is what I need; empathy is understanding what you need.

Someplace between the learner stage and the competent stage, high performers make a transition. At first, they are much like the fiddler on the roof, scratching out a living and balancing on the ridgepole. On one side are their ego and ego strength — what they want. On the other side are empathy and an understanding for what the buyer wants.

At first, this is not an easy balance, and they may weave too far to one side or the other. But eventually, the competent learns that delicate balance. Now, their belief system shifts and matures. Now, it is not so much getting the customer to buy something as it is making them WANT to buy. It is not so much telling them what they need as it is listening to them express what they think they need.

Part of this transition from the ego-motivated salesperson to the empathy-driven salesperson is simple: They stop talking so much and start asking a lot more questions and listening more. In fact, our observation of high-performance, professional-level salespeople is that they listen 80 percent of the time and talk only when necessary. They really "see it through the eyes of the customer."

Competence, commitment and belief system are three of the four dimensions salespeople identified. We added experience.

Now, how does the matrix work? Can a salesperson be a novice in the belief system, being very immature, but still have the skills of a level-three person? In other words, can someone be level-one in some areas and level-three or even four in one area? Absolutely. You can have all the skill in the world, but if you don't have level-four commitment, you won't reach that total fourth level.

The matrix takes a rather complex process of evolution and breaks it into four stages of growth or four levels of expertise. It helps salespeople know where they are in terms of professional development, and it helps sales managers track the growth of their people.

That progression is really an adaptation of the marketing curve, the four phases a product or a service goes through, from development stage, to rapid growth, to maturity to extensions.

Any new salesperson begins in the novice stage. Even people who have sold previously, whatever and wherever, need to learn new things about a new job, or they should learn new things about a new job. Sometimes, this means they must "unlearn" old information or misinformation before they can learn a new knowledge base. They may be forced to break old habits, comfortable old connections, former ways of doing things. Confusion is part of this first stage. So is fear. If they are brand new to selling, there is the fear of rejection. If not-so-new, the fear of being wrong. There is the fear of not being liked. Every new situation requires a new set of emotional muscles.

Consider how salespeople have been trained. Suppose their previous sales training has been old line, high tell, creative advantage, overstated benefits and hard closes. To give this up and shift to a more counselor type of selling requires breaking many old habits and establishing new behaviors.

If we break our matrix apart further and list certain novice skills, certain habits of self-management or commitments, there would be two lists of basic things in this first stage. Those lists might look like this:

I. THE NOVICE STAGE

COMPETENCE / SKILLS   COMMITMENT / WILL DO

Presenting	Product knowledge
Features/benefits	Keeping records
Planning calls	High activity
Prospecting	Product beliefs

Closing

You might compile a different list for each, but you would hope the novice could learn to present decently, understand features and benefits, plan activity, prospect and ask for the order. On the other side is that misty area of education and commitment. You would hope they would learn their product, the industry in general, begin keeping good records, set a high activity level and believe in what they sell — all basic, fundamental things.

Look at the learner, or second phase of rapid growth:

II. THE LEARNER STAGE

COMPETENCE / SKILLS   COMMITMENT / WILL DO

| Qualifying | Managing accounts |

Questions/listening	Planning for a process
Handling objections	Understanding buying criteria
Explanations/recommendations	Service orientation
Developing people skills	Self-assurance

This is a slightly higher level but contains many of the skills or attitudes of salespeople when "they begin to take off." They tell a little less and begin to ask questions. They tend to focus more on the quality of the account and on whether they have a buyer. They begin to handle objections and can explain a presentation rather than just make one.

They also begin to develop some empathy and people skills. Instead of just listing accounts, they begin to manage those accounts in terms of return on investment. They don't try to close on every call, but see selling as a process. They understand buying criteria. They develop some appreciation for the value of service. They begin to feel good about what they are doing and lose a lot of the fear of selling.

However, they will still probably be more tell than ask, more product-oriented, and still require a good amount of counsel, coaching and guidance by the sales manager. They will still be more activity-oriented and less guided by results. But there is more confidence and a better understanding of the total process.

How do they reach that even higher level of performance?

Beyond the learner stage or passage, there begins to open up a third level. It is a combination of improved skills, a better or more mature belief system. The "competent" level is short of truly professional. Still, it means a very competent and rather skilled salesperson. Their levels of expertise have improved. More specifically, the attributes they would now have might be broken out as follows:

III. THE COMPETENT STAGE

COMPETENCE / SKILLS   COMMITMENT / WILL DO

Problem orientation	Develop complex accounts
Develop key accounts	React to buying criteria
Negotiation skill	High call proficiency
Tactical sales strategy	Value/benefit orientation
Interpersonal versatility	Strategic planning

Looking first at the competence or skill levels, there have been some shifts. They have become less product-oriented and more keenly aware of solving buyer problems. They have begun to develop their own key accounts and will have accounts spending major dollars.

They have begun to negotiate as well as sell. They are capable of finding options and alternatives. They are less rigid in their presentation. They see selling as a series of tactics and begin to know more people in a decision-making loop. There is more client contact.

And, finally, their versatility has become apparent. They can relate to people of all social styles and sell to all types of buyers.

On the commitment or "will do" side, they begin to find a challenge in handling complex accounts. They need less handholding and develop the ability to handle their own problems. They know how to react to buying criteria, to find ways around absolute buying criteria.

Buying criteria constitute an element of selling that is often left out of the equation. If a person were selling large trucks to a city refuse system and that organization released "specs," those "specs" would become the buying criteria.

But often a buyer has a set of buying criteria without realizing it. For instance, a couple enters the marketplace as buyers of a home. They have always rented and this is their first house or home. They have, spoken or unspoken, a set of buying criteria.

The couple in our illustration has a certain price range. They have an income level on what monthly payments can be. They have a dog. The man is handy, so a "fix-up" is not out of the question. She wants a certain neighborhood because she likes to be fairly close to work. They must have two bedrooms and two baths, and if the price is OK, wouldn't mind three bedrooms because he would turn one into a study. Now, a real estate salesperson can either find a house that meets these criteria or try to change some buying criteria.

In this case, because the criteria are personal, they are built into the belief systems of our couple. Each has a picture in his or her mind of what the house ought to be. Each believes he wants a certain type of home. Because a home is both a tangible and an intangible, the buying criteria will be a combination of actual criteria and belief system criteria. The actual criteria might include the number of rooms. The intangible criteria might be which way the kitchen faces because one of the buyers thinks every kitchen ought to be sunny.

Another illustration might be a restaurant. Often, we do not think in terms of buying a restaurant. We buy just a dinner, we think. Sometimes we do. We tolerate less than cuisine-type surroundings because this "place has great chicken fried steak." But the seller will tell you that today's customers not only buy food, they buy selection, service, presentation, atmosphere, table selection, hours of serving, special features and even how long they have to wait. In the opinion of some restaurateurs, some people really believe that if they don't have to wait, it can't be a very good restaurant. Other people believe the restaurant makes you wait on purpose so you'll buy a drink or two before dinner.

Can you describe what you believe is a "good restaurant?" "What is a superior restaurant?" You have an idea. And that idea is buried in your belief system. You will go to certain restaurants and won't go to others. You have buying criteria for restaurants. What's more, your criteria may change from day to day. If you are like most buyers today, you do have buying criteria, you are more sophisticated and complex than in times past and you might tell a salesperson what your criteria are, or aren't, and you might not.

Today, a good salesperson would dig and probe to find your criteria. Not long ago, I had occasion to dine at a nice restaurant with a companion. These were the questions that qualified my belief system that evening:

1. Good evening. Did you have reservations?

2. Would you prefer smoking or non-smoking?

3. Would you like a window table or something on this side?

4. Have you dined with us before?

5. Are you familiar with our menu?

6. May I bring you something to drink first? Or, would you prefer to see a wine list?

7. May I tell you about our specials this evening?

8. Would you like an appetizer?

At the time, I thought nothing of the questions. But when the waiter said: "I assume this will be a leisurely dinner," I realized he was a salesman disguised as a waiter. His service was excellent. His presentation was excellent. His attention was superb. He had sneaked into my belief system and had read me as something of a snob when it came to high-ticket dinners. He delivered a beautiful meal and a splendid tab. It was win-win. He has a satisfied customer who would recommend the restaurant to others. But, in the process, he had discovered what I believed about a dinner. He truly had taken the time to read my belief system. What a different type of selling than if he had walked up to the table and simply said: "Well, folks, whattal it be tonight?"

The novice and learner types seldom make any effort to get the buying criteria. If they're selling advertising, these salespeople take the criteria for the buy as absolute, seldom ask any questions and then try to deliver their offering to meet the terms of the "buy."

But, when the level of skill has reached the third or competent level, there is an exploration for what the buyers think, what they feel, what they imagine, the reasons they buy. There is a search, not only for why they buy, but also for how they buy! Consequently, there has been a change in the selling process. Not only have the salespeople matured and their skills improved, but the manner in which they search for information about buying criteria and the way they probe to learn of the belief system of the buyer has become more sophisticated.

By now, the sellers will probably be making fewer total calls, but will have better batting averages. Their call proficiency increases. They position their product more in terms of value and benefit. And last, but not least, they develop more strategic planning, making better use of every call and every opportunity. They also begin to know when to walk on a piece of business that does not result in a good return on investment.

Moving to the fourth level, that level of true professionalism, which some people call "the sustaining resource." Don Beveridge uses that term. We call it the "professional resource," or the co-creator, where the perception of the salesperson is one of high professionalism and really being a part of the buyer's team. This level has some shifts in skill and commitment.

In fact, "the sustaining resource" or "the professional resource" may be terms that describe a fourth level of selling, and the co-creator is still another type of selling. Originally, these terms had the connotation that the sellers became so close to the client or customer they were almost "an unpaid member of the customer's staff." They were often called upon when the customer wanted help. Or, they understood the customer's business so well, they could foresee certain problems in the offering and offer suggestions before the problem materialized.

But, as marketing continued to evolve, so did selling. Let's expand further on the way the top professionals may have evolved into co-creators. This development is especially true in marketing and advertising. At the very top level of selling, the salespeople often become orchestrators or co-creators. They develop one idea with one customer, but there are opportunities for a partnership or even partnerships. The salesperson takes the idea to other possible participants. The original idea is leveraged and expanded, and you have several companies involved in the final strategy.

For instance, in baseball you have events. A soft drink company prints a special offering on the side of the can. The can might be worth a general admission ticket. The ball park supplies the general admissions. They advertise the offering on their TV coverage of the ball games. The soft drink company advertises the offering on their radio and TV announcements. There is a salesperson or salespeople involved in all these contacts. It is a layered sale involving many points of contact. It becomes a cooperative effort among several parties. In this total mix, the salesperson pushing the final concept may be in contact with a dozen different buyers, advocates, financial people and marketing people.

This type of selling takes strategic planning. It demands the versatility to interface with many different types of personalities. It requires modeling or creating a concept that fits the buying criteria of different companies.

IV. THE PROFESSIONAL STAGE

COMPETENCE / SKILLS	COMMITMENT / WILL DO
High closing skill	Leveraging accounts
Focus on decision makers	High results-orientation
Develop customer relations	Manage business relationships
Prospect from present clients	Establish buying criteria
Superior people skills	Added-value perception

This level of selling will produce a very high level of closes. As an extension to that, it also produces a high level of renewals. There is contact at the client level, and the account is a customer, not a sale. This enables the salesperson to prospect and obtain leads from this type of relationship. Often, that information is volunteered. One satisfied customer tells another prospect they ought to call that salesperson.

And, finally, these salespeople usually possess a very high level of people skills. They wear well with any social style. They can work a loop of people without ruffling any feathers.

They have commitment to being a professional salesperson. They really believe they offer a service that is needed. They see themselves almost as a private businessperson. They are usually very secure and react poorly to fear tactics used by management.

They know their accounts well enough to forecast buyer needs, and often combine accounts in promotional activity. The term "promotional activity" is a reality of a changing marketplace. It is especially true in marketing, where products or services are advertised together. An example of this is a frequent flyer program. This combines the marketing of an airline with a hotel, with a rental car company. It is true in the high-tech field, where programs from several vendors are sometimes combined. It is true in the food industry, where snack food promotional activity is combined with soft drink marketing. All of this synergy was sold by some salesperson who combined products or services to produce a marketing concept. In real estate, it is no longer enough to know the housing market; the high-performance salesperson must also know the financial marketplace and be able to work with dozens of different financing approaches to make a "deal come together." They can leverage the needs of one client to provide a synergy with other resources.

This creates a different concept. Now, the salesperson establishes the buying criteria. Rather than filling an order, they create an opportunity and package that opportunity. By so doing, they reduce the emphasis on price and increase the emphasis on value and benefit, or a solution to a problem. Consequently, closing shifts from a focus on price to an evaluation of the solution. As a result, the salesperson sets the buying criteria.

Because of these skills and this commitment, they really do produce a perception of added value. Often, the buyer will value their opinion and ask for their input and help. They will often brainstorm with buyers and clients. They seem to work for the client or buyer.

As a result of this perception, they will rather consistently sell business that produces a good return on investment.

Any sales manager might turn to the East each day and ask Mecca for several of this fourth type of salesperson. We often joke in workshops about these people being the "eagles" who fly high and produce high returns.

The truth is, on most sales staffs, about 20 percent of the salespeople will achieve either level three or four. That rare combination
of competence, commitment and a good belief system is a valued
commodity.

::

COMPETENCE, COMMITMENT, BELIEF SYSTEM AND EXPERIENCE

CHAPTER 3

COMPETENCE, COMMITMENT, BELIEF SYSTEM AND EXPERIENCE

You have now been introduced to a matrix. It is a simple explanation of a complex process of persuasion, selling, sales growth, customer growth ... the many dimensions of selling. First of all, the salesperson is always in one of the four levels of selling. Not every call may be exactly the same. One time they may be at one of their peak moments and they perform "over their head." Another time they say, after a call: "Well, I botched that like a beginner."

By the same token, and to add another element, the buyer will always be in one of those four levels. If the buyer is the type who buys a lot, one who deals with a lot of vendors, goes to market often, then that buyer will also increase in skill level. And, again, growth will be based upon competence, commitment, belief system and experience. The more professional the buyer, the more demanding it will be for the salesperson.

If commitment is "will do," and competence is "can do," what elements are present in each? Let's start with competence. Two hundred top-producing salespeople had listening at the top of their list as a demand skill. This was followed by people skills — the ability to build credibility, to establish commonality fast. Third was questioning skills — knowing how to elicit information from the buyer, knowing how to make the buyer want to talk to them, openly and candidly. Then they listed, in various order, presentation skills, handling objections, closing and post sale implementation and service.

Years ago, that list was very different. Handling objections was the No. 1 request in a sales seminar, with closing skills following close behind. Of course, if a salesperson in those times didn't know how to open the sale, learning how to close wasn't all that important. You just pitched it, tried to close it and moved on. It was transactional selling.

In this material, we examine that list of competence priorities. The order will begin with listening, move to building credibility or people skills, then into giving and getting information. Then, we will develop questioning skills with our SEES model, using the model to position a recommendation, solution or plan.

The salespeople we did our research with listed the skills or competencies rather specifically. When we began trying to define commitment, as we said earlier, things got a little misty. One person described it this way: "Competency is your tool kit; skills are like tools for the craftsman. Commitment is whether you use them in a skilled way." Another person described it this way: "Commitment is doing what you have to do because you need to do it, even if you don't want to do it." Another person had this definition: "Commitment is attitude toward life and the hand you are dealt. Your belief system is your attitude about yourself. One is about your job, the other your relationship with your self-esteem."

The salesperson who gave us that last one gives you some idea of the quality of people involved in our study. She is an absolutely high-performance person who is a bundle of class and integrity. We asked her how you could have a relationship with your self-esteem. She explained: "I think self-esteem is something you aspire to. And you probably keep moving it up further and further. The better you set your values, the more likely you are to aspire to them. And I would put honesty, integrity, perseverance, being mature about delayed gratification, keeping a balance between work life and family life, I would put all those things in commitment. Those are 'will do' things you make a commitment to do. Self-esteem is the image I have about myself that says I'm OK and you're OK. I feel good about what I do and about myself. There is a little ego there, but you need a little ego to have any self-esteem."

Self-esteem is based upon three elements — ego, ego strength and empathy — which we outlined in the previous chapter.

One last point as a part of a road map of how our material will be presented: If our belief system is our attitude about ourselves, and commitment is our attitude about our task or job, then competence becomes the supply of skills or those things in our behavior that we can change and adjust to become better or improve. It is a blend of attitude and behavior that produces high-performance selling.

You can go to all the great motivators in the world and get so charged up you are ready to fight tigers. But, without skill, in today's world, you are likely to run into a brick wall. From the other side, you can have all the skill in the world, read every book on selling, know every technique and, unless you make the commitment to do it, nothing happens. And selling is a skill. The skill increases with practice and refinement. You evolve and go through passages. Different skills, different training, different modifications are elements that move through the matrix, forward or backward, at different times in the total development of a salesperson.

Here is another way to look at the belief system at work in this matrix equation. Suppose you put potential on one side of a line and achievement on the other. In the middle you draw a barrier:

POTENTIAL ———→ | **HABIT ATTITUDE CULTURE EXPECTATION** | ———→ HIGH PERFORMANCE

What keeps people with potential from reaching high performance? What self-imposed roadblocks do they place in their own way?

The first of the barriers is habit. Now, take notice, any of the barriers can be roadblocks, or they can be positives. It depends entirely on how we handle each element — what choice we make, what we decide to believe. You can have good habits and poor habits. The trouble with habits is they become unconscious habits, both good and bad.

Salespeople come in three varieties.

First, you have the UNCONSCIOUS-INCOMPETENT.[1] They don't know what they are doing and don't know why they do it.

Then you have the CONSCIOUS-INCOMPETENT.[1] They know what they ought to do but can't do it. For instance, they know they ought to close, probably know some closing techniques, but they never close. Sometimes that is fear of rejection, sometimes they don't want to appear pushy, sometimes they simply shrug and say: "If the prospects like it, they'll buy it."

Then there is the UNCONSCIOUS-COMPETENT.[1] They can sell and often demonstrate that fact by being high producers. But when you ask them why they do certain things at certain times, they are unable to explain their action. They might respond: "It seemed like the thing to do." Very often, these people are especially vulnerable to habit. They are often "streak" salespeople. They hit a lot of home runs, then they go into a slump. The odds are excellent they have fallen into some bad habits. They don't realize this, because they are UNCONSCIOUS-COMPETENTS, and sometimes they are highly resistant to suggestions that they may have fallen into bad habits. They take refuge in their bad habit and tend to justify and protect it.

How easy it is to fall into a habit pattern can be illustrated by professional athletes. Granted, their line between winning and losing is very thin. But then, the line between winning a sale and losing one is also often very thin, as the marketplace provides more options and alternatives for the buyer.

Still, the golfer who is shooting par will go to a teaching professional who will spot some small habit that is making a five- or six-stroke difference. A period of lessons, some advice, then some practice to ingrain the new habit into the belief system, and the pro is back shooting subpar golf. You can transfer the same analogy to nearly any sport that requires a combination of competency skills and a strong belief system.

The interesting thing about this situation is that it takes a certain attitude to go to the teaching pro. When playing, pros' egos get so huge they feel they don't need help or advice, so they keep repeating the bad habit. Furthermore, when they get the advice, if they believe it to be untrue, they continue in the bad habit pattern. So it is with drinking habits, weight habits or exercise habits, any of those habits with physical elements as well as attitude. So much depends upon what we choose to believe.

Habits ought to be recognized as part of our belief system. If we believe we can always learn, then changing a poor habit into a good one is much easier to accomplish. If we believe there is a connection between physical health and mental health, then our attitude toward exercise is much different and we have different eating habits, different training habits, different living habits.

I like to think that "attitude" is how I choose to look at something. Consequently, my attitude toward others is that they have the right to their attitude. It may not agree with my attitude, but they have the right to the space for their attitude. In fact, I further reserve the right to change my attitude. One day, my attitude is that rain makes it a lousy day. That was a day for golf. Another rainy day was beautiful. That was the day I had just planted grass seed. What's more, nobody can change my attitude. My attitude is loyal to just one person ... ME. Whether it is a bad attitude, a poor attitude or a naive attitude does not alter one bit who possesses it. My attitude is mine. Only I can change it!

It is the way I choose to look at things. That is perhaps where I have a slight edge over other animals. Some can see better than I can, some can smell more keenly and some can leap better. It is possible that other animals may have attitudes. I'm not certain of that. But I have attitudes and, by the eternal warthog, they are mine! I choose them, I decide what they will be.

Now, my culture ... my culture may blame my parents for my aberrations. But my attitude is mine. And having said all this in an attempted humorous way, I have mocked myself into accepting responsibility for my attitudes. Having done so, I would like to think I have taken one small step for humor and one giant step into maturity.

Culture is another thing in my wonderfully mystical, hard-to-define belief system. What I was taught, what I learned from my childhood friends, from early teachers, from mentors, from going to John Wayne movies to sitting in the summer on the front porch in the swing with my grandmother and hearing her explain: "If you want to eat fresh peas, son, you have to have the patience to shell them." My culture is embedded in my belief system.

And then, we have expectations. Disappointments are what we walk with on the road to expectations. You can avoid disappointment by having no expectations. In selling, different levels of salespeople start the day with different expectations.

The NOVICE begins the day with a focus on making calls. The LEARNER tends to have a focus on "pitches" or presentations or showings. The COMPETENT has a focus on sales or closes or culminations. The PROFESSIONAL or CO-CREATOR has a focus on getting decisions, including closing decisions. They may need several approvals or sign-offs before they reach the final decision and get the order. In each case, different levels of selling skills have different levels of expectations.

The belief system is not a simple thing. Our training, our experience, our culture, even our religion are all parts of this barrier that keeps us from achievement. To illustrate that point, you find an exploration of a cultural belief system in the work of John D. Kasarda, Director of the Kenan Institute of Private Enterprise in Chapel Hill, North Carolina. His work has dealt with cultural differences and why certain cultures will produce entrepreneurs and others will not.

His line of reasoning goes this way: "Cultures for which religion explains and justifies success are development-prone; those for which religion eases or explains suffering are development-resistant. Cultures which see wealth as something that is created by human initiative promote development. Those that see wealth as something that exists are likely to devote their efforts toward redistribution of wealth and thereby impede development. Cultures that see labor as a moral or social duty and as an important form of self evil, and who believe pleasure is attainable only outside the workplace, are progress-resistant." This line of reasoning leads Kasarda to a point that has great implications for salespeople: "The successful culture, or individual, sees life as 'something I will do'; for the unsuccessful, life is 'something that happens to me.' "

The beautiful thing about selling is that you can be a proactice person, depending upon how you decide to deal with the barriers that keep you from reaching achievement. Not want to .... but decide to!

The secret, it seems to us, is that you need to know where you are, where you need to be or want to be, and then determine a way to get there. Perhaps this material can be a flashlight that will enable you to see just a little more clearly where you want to be.

What you have in your belief system will determine how you approach your career in selling. Understanding your own belief system and how it works makes it much easier to understand the other person's belief system. Once we accept our own product features, our skills and our personal values and attitudes, we set the stage for understanding the other person's agenda. This understanding opens the door to much higher performance in selling.

A KEY BELIEF FOR HIGH-PERFORMANCE SELLING

Selling is a combination of how you use your "can do" skills or selling techniques and how you choose to use your belief system. Choice is the key word. You absolutely have that choice.

You begin to mature as a salesperson when you understand you can sell, if you choose to use your skills and keep learning from mistakes. YOU CAN WIN! YOU WILL WIN! You were not designed to be a loser. YOU WERE DESIGNED FOR SUCCESS!

I WAS DESIGNED FOR SUCCESS

but often in selling

I AM PROGRAMMED FOR FAILURE.[1]

The odds of selling are programmed against you. Rejection is built into the very environment of selling. But, you cannot win unless you play! You cannot experience success unless you also experience rejection.

How you handle success is important in becoming a high-performance salesperson. How you handle failure is even more important. Just remember, as the rodeo cowboy said ... "If you ain't been throwed, you ain't been ridin'."

::

UNDERSTANDING A LITTLE SOMETHING ABOUT HUMAN BEHAVIOR

UNDERSTANDING A LITTLE SOMETHING ABOUT HUMAN BEHAVIOR

Adults and young people learn things differently. Adults often believe they ought to know everything. When they learn they don't know something, they go on a short guilt trip. You'll see them slap their foreheads, swear or say something like: "Now that was really stupid!" They often say this just after they have learned their car jack has instructions in Japanese and they don't know how to make the jack work. They pause for some "education." They go through trial and error to change the flat.

Adults go through four stages of learning. The diagram illustrates those stages: First, guilt at not already knowing, then trying it a few times and feeling clumsy, then getting competent at doing it and, finally, having the action, skill or technique become habitual. That process looks like this. By the way, what happens to adults when old habits no longer work?

The pattern game[1] on the next page is a neat way to illustrate this, because it also illustrates how easy it is to get better at something. Give it a try!

1.   Put your index finger on #1, move it to #2, then #3, etc. Time yourself, or have somebody time you. Move your finger from number to number, always advancing to the next higher number, as fast as you can. Move as

far as you can in two minutes. At the end of two minutes, notice what number your finger is on and write that number down.

2.   Now, do it again. Concentrate on moving the finger from number to number just as fast as you can. Again, stop after two minutes and write your number down. Do you have a higher number? Good! You're doing great!

3.   Now, study the numbers a few minutes. Notice, there is a pattern. Right and up, down and left, now right, or across to the right, then up and to the right. Now, try again!

You may have noticed by now in reading this book that we try to avoid psychology. One selling trend of the past few years has been the introduction of psychology into selling. It is possible that there is a time and place for psychology. The word has a mysterious appeal. But our training has been more in the area of human behavior. In our opinion, understanding something about human beings

The Pattern Game

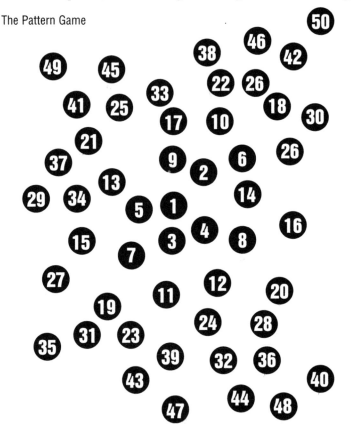

can be very helpful to salespeople.

When salespeople ask what sources we use for our material or what they should read if they want to really background themselves for selling, we steer them to Carl Jung, Albert Maslow and Maxwell Maltsby. At the end of this chapter, you'll find a list of possible reading.

The pattern game explains how adults learn. It also provides insights into how we may be using habits or paradigms of human behavior to find a selling style. For instance, the pattern game provides a new experience. Most people have never done it before. The first time they try it, they are a little awkward, maybe a little clumsy.

If they are challenged by it, they quickly lose their inhibitions and it becomes more like a game. Each time they try the new experience, the effort becomes a little easier. If they are told about the pattern, they explore that. Some people, by trial and error, discover the pattern. The pattern, or knowledge of the pattern, gives them still more ability. Finally, they become comfortable with the whole concept.

They have, in playing the pattern game, gone through nearly the same steps they go through when they learn to sell. At first, they may be a little uncomfortable. With practice, they get better. Somebody, or some source, tells them about a pattern or way to approach the exercise. They apply that new knowledge and their skill level goes up.

Or, they may disregard the suggestion that there is a pattern. But, they stick with the effort to do it better and, gradually, through trial and error, they do improve. They may even discover there was a pattern and involve that in the way they go about improving their ability with the game. If they had considered the advice, it might have increased their skill level faster.

The application of this process to improving your skill in selling is then evident. If you are proactive, and if you try new techniques, you can improve your skill. You can improve by applying advice or ideas, or you can improve through trial and error.

In either case, you must take a new experience or new knowledge, try it and determine what the consequences will be. The first step is the action of trying it. You must be open to a new experience. You must be proactive.

That provides another connection to another very simple

model. This model is the basis for much of the philosophy of selling found in this book.

This is the model:

Not very astonishing, is it?

Let's use you, right now, and try it out. We've suggested that this is a model for understanding human behavior. You say: "OK, that's an idea." So "A" is the idea, a bit of knowledge, a new technique. It is the starter or the stimulus. Now, you do something with that thought.

You filter that thought through your belief system, "B." If you automatically reject any new idea because you tried one once and it didn't work out very well, that new idea won't get very far. If we tell you about a new and better way to use the telephone, but you have taken so much rejection on the phone asking for appointments you've had all the pleasure you can stand, you will reject that idea. That's your belief system.

If you are a business person, and you really believe that seeing a salesperson is a waste of time, and you get a phone call, "A," you filter that call through your belief system, "B," you tell them "No," which is "C," because you just don't take phone calls. That's your belief system.

Your belief system is a combination and collection of training, culture, education, stories you have heard, peer group norms and what you have learned through experience, reward and punishment. If you believe that radishes make you burp, you've tried them and they did make you burp, it will be difficult to make you a radish fan. Now, take that analogy one step further.

Suppose I prove to you that radishes are an absolute cure for arthritis and you are badly crippled with that disease. Would the benefit of getting rid of your arthritis encourage you to tolerate a burp now and then? Would the consequences of eating a radish a day be worth it to you?

Now we have added "C," or the consequences, to the model. But we have modified those consequences to have more value to you, personally. What growth potential this book has for you will be sifted through your belief system. If you are a NOVICE in selling and don't have much of a belief system, you'll not filter every idea through a belief system. You'll try a lot of things because they might work, and then wouldn't the consequences be a wonderful payoff for you!

This model has two important purposes in selling. First, consider it from the perspective of making that first connection with a potential customer. Maybe they had a bad experience with a salesperson, or they bought once and were disappointed, or they don't like the advertising your company does, or they don't have time or they don't trust strangers. If any of these elements is present, you'll need to get through that belief system before you get an appointment.

In the next chapter, we will explore the reason people won't buy and suggest that the reason is NO CREDIBILITY with the salesperson or the product. What we call NO CREDIBILITY is also called a lot of other names. You may have heard it called "no trust," "no mutuality," or "no comfort"; all of these terms fit the idea. You may have called it rapport. It is usually the initial foundation or the basis to do business or communicate. What it really means is the ability of the salesperson to establish a more common buyer-seller belief system.

What we have also done with this model is establish solid ground for understanding objections and how to handle them. People object to an idea when it runs smack into their belief system. "Your price is too high" is really the belief that "I don't think it's worth that." That belief may be based on comparison with similar products or services, past experience or the belief that "there is always an asking price and a taking price, and I never accept the first price."

Benefits and advantages are ways the salesperson tries to modify the belief system. Consequences are really payoffs. Said another way, if the payoff is great enough, people find a way to modify a belief system. If the value is great enough, if the return on investment is high enough, there will be ways to justify the decision to buy.

But understanding the model has great value to a salesperson. It makes prospecting a little easier to understand. You are likely to focus more on the problem of prospecting and less on the people. And when the time comes to handle objections, you have a better understanding that you don't "overcome people," you handle their objections by appealing to their belief system or using it to show how the consequences justify changing their mind.

This understanding leads, then, into the reasons people won't buy.

DEEPER READING YOU MIGHT ENJOY EXPLORING

Toward a Psychology of Being, 2nd ed. (New York: D. Van Nostrand, 1968) Abraham Maslow

Psychological Types (Princeton, N.J.: Princeton University Press, 1971) Carl Jung

Personal Styles and Effective Performance; Make Your Style Work For You (Radnor, Pa., Chilton, 1981) David Merrill and Roger Reid

::

Understanding Why People Don't Do Things Can Help You Understand Why They Do Things

UNDERSTANDING WHY PEOPLE DON'T DO THINGS CAN HELP YOU UNDERSTAND WHY THEY DO THINGS

W e use that title carefully, because if it got too much expo-
sure some country songwriter might take it and make a
new hit record out of it. Country music has a way of
relating to people and to people's problems. That may explain its
great popularity. There is probably more commonality between
country music artists and their audience than other types of musicians and their audiences. Country artists build rapport with their
audience. People "buy" them because they are comfortable with
them.

We first ran into the concept of why people don't buy when we
visited Wilson Learning in Eden Prairie, Minnesota, and met Larry
Wilson. He had conceived the idea of four reasons people don't
buy. At that time he called them: no trust, no need, no help and no
hurry. He had used these for the insurance business where he had,
personally, been very successful and where Wilson Learning later
developed a program called "Sales Sonics," which was marketed to
the insurance industry. Out of this concept came "The Counselor
Salesperson," which is still one of the staples of the Wilson
Learning offerings.

We added the dimensions to the concept and made some
changes so the model fit more than the insurance business. Since
that time, Wilson Learning[1] has also done some modifying. We use
the model on the next page.

People don't buy because they are uncomfortable with the person selling or representing the product or service. Or, they are
uncomfortable with the product itself. This discomfort can be more
than "no trust," although that may be part of the relationship. But
previous dissatisfaction with a sales rep or a product can also be a
reason there is "no comfort" with the present situation. The real

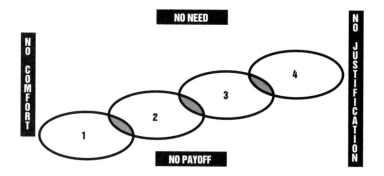

issue is the credibility of the salesperson or the product.

You can also include such terms as "mutuality" and "commonality" and say that the buyer and seller had nothing in common. In other words, there was no basis for a relationship. There were no things they shared. On the other hand, I may like the salesperson but not the product, or like the product but not the salesperson. When that paradox exists, I'm usually uncomfortable. I, the average human being, will buy most readily when I'm comfortable and see the seller as a credible source. What's more, there will be times when I buy only for that reason.

As an illustration, have you ever gone into a favorite restaurant? You're tired, it's been a tough day, and you want to relax and kick back. They give you a nice table and you reflect on the menu and your favorite waiter says hello and you ask: "What's good tonight?" He tells you and you have no idea what the concoction is, but it doesn't matter. The waiter has always treated you right, never steered you wrong, so you take the easy way out and say: "I'll try it." You might not have done that with another restaurant or another waiter, but here you felt comfortable doing it. You bought because of comfort and the credibility the waiter had established with you.

Now, track the circles and the dimensions and see how they apply. In any sale, buyers can be a 1 through 4 in readiness to buy. Their comfort level can range from very low to very high. If the comfort level is very high, at the 4 level, they may buy for that reason only. Interestingly, you often experience this when you turn your car over to the mechanic. You have a high level of need for a car to be repaired and you have been told you can trust this mechanic. If he did you right the last time, he has established credibility and you are comfortable with him. In fact, enough so that he may operate on your car and you won't know what the cost will be! But he has always treated you right before.

Each dimension, then, can have four stages. Need can range from 1 through 4. Payoff, value, help can range from 1 through 4, and justification can range from 1 through 4.

Sometimes, the strangest of all is justification. For instance, I don't suppose this has ever happened to you, but I sometimes buy something I don't need. I have a weakness for old, antique, beat-up duck decoys. I come home, trying to smuggle them into the house in a brown paper bag. The dialogue goes something like this:

HIM:	Aaaahh ... whatta trip. (Designed to encourage sympathy)
HER:	Whatcha got intha sack? (The word sack goes up, indicating suspicion)
HIM:	Uuhh ... something I picked up in New Orleans.
HER:	What kind is it this time? (Breakthrough question that cuts through mist)
HIM:	Teal. Beautiful example of Gulf Coast teal. Original state.
HER:	How many teal do you have already? (Cuts into possible value or need)
HIM:	Not one like this one. This is really a primitive. (Try to build need and payoff and maybe even justification)
HER:	How many decoys do you have now that aren't even on the shelf?
HIM:	But, you have to understand, I really got a super value on this one. (And this is followed by a long story about the arduous negotiation that resulted in a $20 saving)

THE PLAIN TRUTH IS, I DIDN'T NEED ANOTHER DECOY. This one wasn't all that valuable, and the good wife forced me to do some fancy footwork to find justification for having bought it. But, the salesperson knew his stuff on decoys, he was pleasant enough, the store had a good feel, the deal was OK, not sensational but OK, and what the heck, it had been a long time since I had come home lugging another decoy. I found a way to justify it!

I don't suppose you ever did anything like that?

Now, as the dollar value of the thing being sold goes up, the need for justification usually goes up, too. As the importance of the decision goes up, so does the need for justification. A body can buy a decoy for $50 without a lot of justification. But when I get ready to buy a new car, I'll ponder the variables very carefully. But, the four elements are always there in various degrees.

Looking at the fun side, you see how we can provide justification if we have to do that. Looking at the serious side, a high-dollar, well-conceived, well-executed sale will have buyer levels at 4 for all four dimensions. The buyer will be comfortable with the seller and the product, there will be a need, there will be a payoff or value or benefit and there will be justification for the payoff! It's a simple diagram, but it handles the complexities of most sales.

How often has a major sale been blown when a seller didn't like a buyer or vice versa? How often has a major presentation failed because all of the buyers in the decision-making loop couldn't or wouldn't see the same degree of need? Or of value? How often has a big sale fallen because one of the buying influences couldn't justify spending that much money?

The real story in this disarmingly simple diagram is that it makes a handy checklist for the salesperson. It is a barometer of customer readiness. The salesperson can check that barometer from time to time to find how the wind is blowing. Do I have good comfort and credibility established? Have I clearly established the need? What is the state of the need? Is it immediate, delayed, lots of urgency, no urgency? Have I really positioned the payoff, or benefit, or help? Does this recommendation really provide the solution? Finally, you can check for justification. If I were sitting where they are, could I justify this? How would I do that? Is there a clear and objective payoff for the decision?

The beauty of the concept is that it is simple. This may be part of the skill of selling — to keep the simple simple and help make the complex simple. The diagram fits the most complex sale you might want to try it on.

So, there are four reasons people buy. Or, four reasons they don't. Or, four dimensions present in any sale. If you have a four level on all four dimensions, you have a sale. High comfort – high need – high payoff – easy justification.

Do all four always need to be present? No. You've bought something when you had a great need and didn't like the salesperson. You've bought when you couldn't justify it. You've bought something you thought you needed, only to discover it had no value or didn't help a bit. But, such instances only strengthen the concept.

If you have a four level on all four dimensions, you have a sale! What's more, the odds are excellent you have a satisfied customer.

Now, let's add another insight to the dimensions. Let's say you work in an industry where you have a buyer who represents the customer or client. We'll use advertising as the example, but the concept can fit anywhere a buyer represents a third party. In advertising, the "buyer" is usually a person in an agency. Many fields have buyers who see the "sales reps."

Sellers dealing directly with the customer or client will be dealing with the variables in the left column below. If they are dealing with a "buyer" in the agency, they will be dealing with the variables in the right-hand column:

THE CUSTOMER	THE BUYER
Wants impact, action, response, something good to happen!	Wants efficiency. The best buy for the dollars invested based upon their specifications or system of buying.
Wants results, a solution to a problem, to take advantage of an opportunity.	Wants justification. Wants to be able to prove they bought the right thing. May never know what the results were.
Wants return on investment, a bang for a buck, a feeling or actual proof, dollars well-spent.	Wants no hassle, no afterburn, no challenges, no post-buy analysis.

Two very different-looking lists, aren't they? In media selling, many people sell both a direct customer and the agency buyer the same way. The NOVICE uses the same information, the same brochures, the same package with both types of buyers. The second-level or LEARNER will add some bells and whistles to their "pitch" and might even throw in a few ratings, but essentially pitches the same idea the same way. Price is often the deciding factor. The third-level, or the COMPETENT, has taken the four dimensions of why people do buy or don't buy, and concluded that two different types of sales processes are at work.

For instance, in both cases, you would hope the salesperson had built comfort. Second-level salespeople often try to "kill the agency with kindness" or establish themselves as deserving the business because they are more comfortable to work with. In other words, they focus on getting the buyer to like them so much the buyer perception of them is at level-four or above and this will offset low marks in other areas.

Because, when they deal with the buyer, be it agency or a vendor situation, the buyer will tell them ... "Look, I don't need you, I've got plenty of people who will sell it to me at my price." And with the buyers, the ultimate result or payoff is not really the issue. Their payoff comes in justification. Price is their primary criterion.

Actually, in this type of selling, the rules of the game have changed. The "buyers" are really not buyers. They are negotiators disguised as buyers, and their primary goal is efficiency. They want a buy that is so efficient they can justify it to anybody who asks what they did or why they bought.

Many fields of selling have this type of disguised buyer. In some selling scenarios, the salesperson becomes "the supplier" or the "vendor" and is regarded as the carrier who brings in the offering. He becomes the product peddler. That perception of the salesperson is further enforced when the buyer has many options and alternatives.

The fourth-level salesperson is generally not involved in the "efficiency" sale, because that sale essentially focuses on price. In nearly every field of selling, the beginning salesperson is focused on the WHAT of their offering. WHAT their product is. WHAT the product does. WHAT the price is ... and here they need the lowest price, the cheapest house, the lowest-cost pickup truck.

As expertise evolves in their selling skills, the shift is more to WHY. And this, of course, introduces features and benefits selling. They will often help the buyer justify the buyer's decision.

By the time the evolution reaches the fourth level of selling, the emphasis shifts to HOW. For instance, in real estate the sellers have the expertise to lead the buyers through the steps of buying the house. They show them HOW they can afford it, HOW it can be financed, HOW to complete the transaction. In a sense, they present a plan for buying.

For many years, in media selling, salespeople focused on the WHY of their offering. WHY print was better than radio. WHY radio should be used instead of TV. There was a great deal of selling against another product. In essence, their message was ... "Buy us, and here's WHY you ought to buy us." This was also true of insurance selling.

Today, high-performance salespeople tuck this information into a total presentation focused on HOW. Today, the buyer usually wants a certain result. Certainly that is true of the decision makers in the marketing process. The process looks something like this:

This chapter has made two important points about selling. The first is that people choose not to buy because of the absence of one or more of four reasons: NO COMFORT, NO NEED, NO PAYOFF, NO JUSTIFICATION.

Comfort can be a variety of reasons but, essentially, as the importance of the buying decision increases, credibility becomes more of a key part of comfort with the seller and the offering.

Need may be just that. "I don't need it." Or, "Who needs it?" Or, this just doesn't fit my priorities at this time. Urgency, timing and priority are all part of need.

Payoff usually means the buyer does not see a value, a benefit or an advantage.

Justification can be a logical or an emotional process and can come at either end of the action of buying. Some people buy, then justify; some justify it thoroughly before they buy.

Another way to look at the concept is to use a scale of 1-4. A well-handled sale would be at the 4 level for all elements.

The second important point about selling is this: As salespeople evolve during their careers, as their skills and expertise increase, and as they move from the novice level to the high-performance level, several changes take place or several things evolve.

1.   Their focus changes from WHAT to WHY to HOW.

2.   The perception of them changes and they become less a product peddler and more a partner in the search for a solution.

3.   At levels 1 and 2, selling is more an adventure; at levels 3 and 4, it is more a joint venture.

4.   They interface less with buyers, tire kickers or shoppers and more with decision makers.

KEY TECHNIQUES FOR
HIGH-PERFORMANCE SELLING SUMMARIZED

Following most of the chapters of this book, you will find what we call KEY TECHNIQUES. These are "how tos" reduced to the very basics. Study these techniques carefully. They work! Practice them, try them; we believe you'll find they will help polish your selling skill.

The first of these is more than a technique. It is more nearly a philosophy to be used to build selling credibility. It is based on three phrases that will demonstrate sincerity and honesty. They are helpful in prospecting, leveraging from one account to another and in customer service where a client is upset.

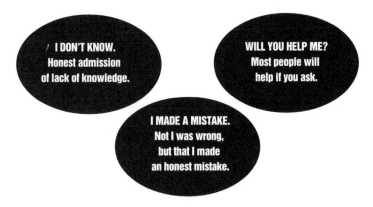

THE POWER IS IN THE TECHNIQUE. MODEL THE TECHNIQUE TO FIT YOUR STYLE. PRACTICE IT UNTIL YOU ARE COMFORTABLE WITH IT, USING YOUR WORDS AND YOUR PACING.

Why Understanding The Belief System Concept Is So Important To Selling In Today's World

WHY UNDERSTANDING THE BELIEF SYSTEM CONCEPT IS SO IMPORTANT TO SELLING IN TODAY'S WORLD

Because this concept is so central to high-performance selling, let's take the dimension of "comfort" or "no comfort" and focus on the "B," or belief, circle. You have ABC, the model:

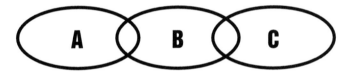

There is a knock on your door. It is early evening and you're relaxing and visiting or glancing through the mail. The knock on your door is the antecedent. Now, your belief system goes to work. You think: "Who would that be at this hour?" or "Probably a door-to-door salesperson." You might even be frightened because there has been trouble in your neighborhood recently. Still, you go to the door and open it.

Standing is front of you is a young lady. She is dressed in her Brownie uniform and she has a box in her arms. This is another "A" or antecedent. Your belief system changes gears. She is probably selling cookies, she is harmless because she is a Brownie (that's a good cause), cookies are usually good, etc.

What will be the consequences? If you're like most people, you listen, you tell her to wait, you get some money and, probably, in spite of meaning to eat fewer sweet things, you buy one or more boxes of cookies. Did she sell you, or did you buy? And, if you bought, did you buy for her reasons or for your reasons?

What did she do or say that gave her credibility or comfort with you? She told you her troop was working on a special project. Do you remember what that was? Or, did you buy because you just sort of think Brownies and Girl Scouts are a good idea and you like to help good causes? You may even give the cookies away (you say to yourself) and, besides, a couple of bucks is not a big deal and she was a sweet kid. What were your reasons for buying? If you took your reasons and put them on a list, that list would probably have two sharply different sets of items on it, but each list would involve comfort and credibility.

Might your lists look something like this?

Product	Personal
Nicely packaged	She was a sweet little lady
Choice of flavors	It's a good cause
Good quality	People used to help your kids
You've had them before	You'll find some way to use them

Really, you had two agendas working in your head: One involved the product, and the other was associated with the person selling it. The odds are excellent that you didn't buy because you were desperate for a cookie, had them on a shopping list anyway, had been waiting for some cookie kid to come to the door or you have a cookie fetish.

You bought the cookies for your reasons, and those reasons involved a whole lot more than just cookies. The product, in this case, was a small part of your belief system at work. Did the cookies have credibility? Did you need cookies? Two different issues. Let's start with credibility.

Suppose you had been undecided and the cookie kid starting pitching you on the ingredients in the cookies, how they were made from whole milk, real eggs and rushed into the package so they were absolutely fresher than fresh. Untouched by human hands, these cookies are the finest you could possibly buy. Would that have changed your mind?

Or, to get you to buy, would the youngster have needed to help you figure out how to use them? Oh, you're on a diet? Well, we have diet cookies. Perhaps you're having a party soon and these could be used at the party? Perhaps a friend at work loves sugar cookies? We have that kind.

Now, is the cookie kid working on the product pitch or the reasons you might want to buy? Isn't she working, in the latter case, on your belief system and aligning her product to fit something in your image of cookies? She is POSITIONING HER PRODUCT TO FIT YOUR BELIEF SYSTEM. Whether you buy will be based only partially on her product. It will also be based upon what you think about Girl Scout cookies and the whole idea of worthy causes.

Selling today is not a one-course meal. It is at least two courses. The customer or the buyer may be served one course and not buy it. That's the product course, the product sell, the product sale. Usually, the product sell becomes the sellers' reasons the buyer ought to buy. The sellers are convinced they have a good product or service. That is their belief system. That's their "B," and they tell you what that system is based on. "Now, look at this ..." and they give you:

Product specifications

Product implementation

Product bangles, bells and whistles

Product descriptions

Product packaging

Product capabilities

Product demonstrations

Product features and benefits

If you don't believe that list, they'll try another tack, along the lines of: "Look what others say about that list."

This is WHY selling. For many years, in times where there may have been shortages of options and alternatives, WHY selling would work. You bought a lawnmower because it had a longer blade, more horsepower, was red, used less oil, had an electric start motor and the seat had 11 tungsten springs. Features and features and WHY, WHY, WHY. Today, there are all types of products and services that offer why.

Selling today is based more upon HOW. For instance, how does a longer blade help me mow? What if I have lots of trees in the yard and I really need a shorter blade and shorter turning radius? How does more horsepower help? Not a lot if I have a small yard and limited storage space. How does the color relate to the job unless I want the mower to match my hair!

When I buy something, I want to know HOW it will help me,

fit my needs, fit my image of what the product or service is really intended to do. It is no wonder the marketplace has become littered with niche products and services. Each one can be positioned to do a rather special HOW. The product or service is positioned to fit a particular belief system.

What about the second course of the meal? The cookie kid was able to build credibility fast. You recognized her uniform, her product and her organization. Her manner was respectful. She was sincere. She was able to position herself quickly as credible.

But, more than that, she positioned herself to fit into your personal reasons to buy. Yes, she provided lots of product reasons. Her organization, her uniform and her cause gave her credibility. But you probably bought for personal reasons in your belief system.

The good cookies were her benefits. But she also gave you a small personal win, made you feel like you had done a good thing! Remember those two words — personal win — because we will come back to them.

Each of us probably has a different definition of "comfort." Depending upon our "belief system" or where we are coming from, we tend to filter our perceptions of others — how we see them — from our point of view. An old piece of sales advice goes: "You model the buyer." If you are on a formal business sales call, you better look and act like "formal business." If you are calling on a country feed store, such an appearance might not be appropriate. In fact, you might want to wear an old hat.

Appearance, competence, intent, sincerity are all factors in this equation. At the beginning level of selling, the seller doesn't do a lot of adjusting. By the fourth level, the salesperson has learned to model the selling situation. This may include such subtle things as body language and rate of talk or level of enthusiasm. If the buyer is rather cool and laid back, the seller will be cool and laid back. The seller takes the cue from the buyer.

We focus on the word credibility because it is the result of building comfort with the buyer. As we have attempted to illustrate, credibility is a two-pronged objective: credibility of product and credibility of the salesperson. Both images are mirrored in the perception of the buyer and filtered through the buyer's belief system.

If we use our box again and chart the evolution of the stages, they look something like this:

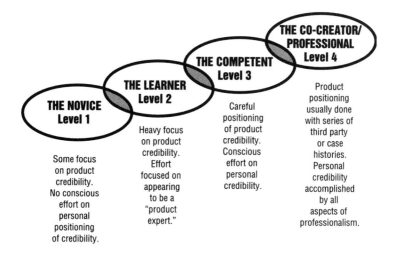

Track through the levels and evolution now. Keep in mind, we are isolating only one aspect: "no comfort" or credibility. Suppose people at each of these levels called on you. You filter their behavior through your belief system. These perceptions might be your reaction:

Level 1:   ... really didn't make a very good appearance ... didn't really listen to what I said ... didn't know their product very well ... seemed to use almost a canned pitch. RESULT: Not much credibility.

Level 2:   ... seemed to know their product pretty well, but were sure proud of that knowledge ... kept trying to get me to agree that what they had to sell is what I needed ... weren't very interested in me personally, but did seem to know what they were talking about. RESULT: Not a lot of personal credibility, but some product credibility. Can you sell out of this posture? Sure! One engineer sells another engineer who is only interested in the technical abilities of the product. Sure! If you have what they want and at the best price.

Level 3:   ... asked about what I thought I needed, listened carefully to what I said ... related my needs to their benefits ... knew their product and what it could do for me ... seemed eager to help me.

Level 4:   ... came highly recommended from a highly regarded company ... seemed very professional ... got along well with everybody ... did their homework in terms of

research ... understood how their offering fit my conceptual needs ... used satisfied customers to prove their
benefits ... provided added value in terms of expertise
and service ... showed how they could help us.

If the purpose of the salesperson is to establish credibility, there
are — tucked into each synopsis — clues that represent "how to"
build your credibility. Those clues can help you grow your skills and
polish your abilities.

Their value becomes more evident as you move toward higher
performance, because then you are moving toward bigger dollar
sales and higher-level decision makers. This begets an even higher
level of performance. Just as in the Good Book chapter where there
was all that "begetting," so it is in selling. If you choose to move up
in skill level, that begets more opportunity, which in turn begets new
challenges, which in turn begets new opportunity, which in turn
begets the need for higher-level skills.

This just doesn't happen. You must decide to make it happen. It
is a matter of choice, not happenstance.

::

CHAPTER 7

POSITIONING YOUR PRODUCT AND YOURSELF

POSITIONING YOUR PRODUCT AND YOURSELF

S tep back a moment, in your world of selling whatever you sell, and look at the marketplace. It is a marketplace of options and alternatives. What car will you buy? You have 850 different models to choose from. What computer will you buy? You have hundreds of different versions of technology from which to choose. Now, let's go out for a hamburger. Where would you like to go? What kind of burger do you like? Talk about choices! What else can they do to ground-up beef? Now, if you worked for BMW, IBM or McDonald's, you would have definite answers for the questions we have posed. But, looking through the eyes of the buyer, you honestly don't see a lot of difference in products.

Let's again isolate one dimension of the matrix and focus on need. The question buyers ask is: DO I NEED THIS PRODUCT/ SERVICE? Their need, or perception of need, is also in their belief system.

We would suggest that in selling or marketing, the seller has three edges[1] to consider. The first of these is THE CRITICAL EDGE. This gives the seller such a margin of superiority that there is no question. Obviously, if you are the only one of your kind, you have a monopoly or you are brand new and no other product or service is like yours, you have a CRITICAL EDGE.

Not many products enjoy such an edge. The world moves too fast. A new product is introduced and there will be imitators or like versions on the shelf within weeks.

The second, or COMPETITIVE EDGE, is possible when a product or a service really does have a clear-cut advantage in features, technology, packaging or implementation. When two items stand side by side and any customer can clearly see the superiority of one, there is a COMPETITIVE EDGE. Few products or services in the marketplace enjoy that edge. That edge is more often in the eye of the seller than the eye of the buyer.

That brings us to the third edge, or the PERCEIVED EDGE, which includes those products or services that may not be clearly superior but for some reason we think they are. Somebody asks why we think or feel as we do. We're not sure, but for some reason this model or brand or product just blows our socks off. That's why we bought it. We had a perception, someplace in our belief system, that this was the one for us. That item enjoyed a PERCEIVED EDGE for us and, by golly, that's why we bought. We had our reasons!

If I were the seller and you were the buyer and I wanted to reach you and get you to want to buy, I would need to position my offering in terms of your perception, not mine. I would need to get "inside your head" and see the reasons you were going to buy through your eyes, not mine. If I could locate your reasons, within your belief system, I could align my offering to fit in the boundaries of your perceptions. We took that "B" of the "ABC" concept and divided it into two parts: the product part and the personal part.

Positioning is based on perception. The seller takes the perception the buyer gives them and, within the buyer belief system, positions the product to give the offering the personal PERCEIVED EDGE.

If we go back to the matrix and the four levels of selling, we find that the novices usually make the product sale first. They pitch the product, or the package or the house or whatever. They "tell, sell and give it hell," as we've heard it described. The perception sell is never considered.

By the second level, the sellers are usually so proud of all their product knowledge, so happy with their silver-tongued ability to do their shtick, that again the perception part of the sale is pushed into the background. Second-level sellers focus on the product and what, in their opinion, the product or offering will do for anybody. Not just this buyer, but anybody can use these features and advantages. This is WHY selling.

By the third level, the process of selling is nearly reversed. The sellers are more sensitive to the buyer belief system. They have grown wary of the product sell and all the objections they run into in the later stages of the process. They like the advantages of the perceptual sale.

First, by learning more about the customers and their reasons for buying, they really get closer to the customers and can figure out "where they are coming from." They find that by taking this approach, they are much less likely to get compared head-to-head with competition. Price is less an issue, because the focus in the recommendation is on the solution and not necessarily the product. They have also found that by taking this approach, they often have a much better idea of who the real buyer or buying influence will be. This is HOW selling.

Let's illustrate that last point. We were working with a group of high-performance salespeople with Northwestern Mutual Life Insurance, which is a superior, marketing-driven company. It was a fast-track group.

By late afternoon of the first day, we had established some credibility and they were getting more comfortable. We got on the subject of locating the decision maker or buying influence in a two-income family. One of the old pros leaned back and said: "Yeah, the dinks ... how do you deal with them?" That created a good laugh about Double Income No Kids families ... DINKS. One of the new people, a woman who had been selling only a short time, but who was half of a DINK family, said: "Well, I don't know if this would fit or not, but early in the discovery or questioning phase, when I am probing for need, I ask a question. Most DINKS love to travel; it is sort of a social status thing. So I ask them if they travel, which I have a good idea they do, and then I ask them who decides or how do they decide where they will travel? This often gives me a clue on how they make decisions or who is the buyer in the family for an insurance plan."

Needless to say, pencils went to work on scratchpads and there was some murmuring about "good idea," "yeah." The point was made. If that young woman had merely been pushing product, she never would have understood the belief system of the DINK when it came to making decisions.

Another advantage of focusing initially on what the customers want and their reasons for buying is that it allows the seller to focus on results. They can focus on product advantages that fit the solutions or the results the buyer wants. They position their benefits in terms of the buyers' perceptions. They search for the perceived edge. They see it through the eyes of the buyer.

Still another advantage of this focus on the selling situation, rather than on the product, is that the job of qualifying is speeded up. If the salesperson is trying to establish what the buyers have now and what they want, and how the product can fill that need, then focusing on the reasons the buyer will buy provides early evidence of a fit or, as some people call it, WIN-WIN. In other words, what I have to offer can fit you and this is how you get the results you want with what I have to offer. We both win.

To summarize the idea, we need to understand that people buy for their reasons and not ours. Their reasons for buying are to be found in their belief systems, in what they perceive our offering will do for them, what results or solutions they will be provided. Until the seller understands those reasons or the buyer belief system, he will be pitching product aimlessly.

Our focus in this chapter is on need. Does the buyer, within his belief system, have a perception of need? The search for this need can be with one person. If the sale is a complex, organizational sale, it becomes the search for the corporate or organization need. To add complexity, that may mean any number of buying influences with different ideas of the need.

Is there a model for this search for the buyer's perception of need? In workshops we often tell the story of a wonderful unconscious-competent.

There was once a young salesman in Kansas City. He had the good fortune to find a mentor. Today, we would probably call him a coach.

One day, while they were having a hamburger lunch together, he asked the coach the broad question: "Why do people buy advertising?" The coach took out a piece of paper and drew four circles. "I don't know if this idea has any value," he said, "and it's just something I worked out for myself. But I put my prospects or customers in four different groups." He put a word in each circle:

"I think of this as that old pea game. Under which shell is the pea? And the pea is their need. Let's suppose a car dealer has just had a poor month and is determined to get sales back up. The regional office is on his back and he has trouble in river city. He wants to move and move fast to sell some units. In his case, the pea is under the urgency shell."

He paused, asked for some catsup and continued. "Now, this second shell is potential or gain or good news. The buyer is thinking of making it better. He hopes to make the situation better, improve it, bring in more traffic, get a better floor turn of goods, whatever. If that is the need, we can help him."

He dipped his hamburger in the catsup. But the young man was entirely focused on the circles of need. "In this case" — the coach pointed to the word "maintenance" — "this may not be the right word, but it describes a situation where somebody wants to maintain their present market position. Or their market share. Things are good and they want to keep them good. Now, in this position, it's easier to keep them sold than it is to switch them to something different, like from one station to your station or from newspaper to radio. You might think of this as preserving the status quo. OK?"

Another catsup dip. Lordy, he loved catsup. "This one over here, I call euphoria. This is the guy who tells you he has all the business he needs, things are just wonderful, couldn't be better and don't bother him about advertising. Of course, that's a fool's paradise. Another sign of this is when the owner of the business has bought a big ranch, a condo in Florida and is only at the business about half the time. They are also headed for the rude awakening."

"So," asked the young man, "you're saying in this analogy to the pea game that everybody is somewhere under one of the shells." "Well," the coach responded, "I'm saying it works most of the time for me. Now, understand, I'm not saying for you to think this way. We all got to think the way that fits us. I'm just saying the pea game has worked for me most of the time."

Keep in mind, this man had never taken a course in selling, never had a nickel's worth of training or read what few books there were on the subject in those days. He was, in all respects, an unconscious-competent. He couldn't always tell you why something would work but, boy, could he do it! Then he added this thought:

"You see, it isn't always people under the shells. Too many salespeople, in my opinion, put labels on people. What they ought to be looking for is the selling situation. They ought to know what the situation is. When you have an agency involved, they may have one idea of the situation. They are wrapped up in what they need ... how many announcements, how much reach, what days they will run, what is the cost per announcement? That's their need. For the automobile dealer, going back to my illustration, his need is to move some iron off the lot. Now, you try to fill the needs of both parties and it's a little more complex. But, you understand the selling situation a little better."

We've told this story many times in workshops around the

country. People have told us later they have changed the words around a little to fit their particular style of selling or their type of selling. And they tell us how they now consciously try to move the selling situation from one position of readiness to another. They understand their greatest hope for a positive selling situation is to find the pea under the urgency shell or the gain shell, or to get the buyer to move their pea, their belief system, to one of those two shells.

As time has passed, we've modified the analogy to explain that need is either the push of discomfort or the pull of hope, and those descriptions give the word picture a little broader interpretation. It also has implications for motivation and what encourages people to be proactive. There are some nice fits from that perspective. In that case, the questions still relate to the pea game, but now the search for need becomes the location of the discomfort or the hope.

Can the salesperson help the buyer move from one stage to another? Absolutely! But that comes in the sales process. The purpose of this chapter was to explore the dimension of need or no need and the buyer belief system that created that stage of need.

To summarize the main points of this chapter:

• At level 1 and 2 of selling, the offering is presented by the seller and the buyer must locate the fit with their need. That connection is too often buyer-motivated.

• At level 3 and 4, the salesperson locates the need before presenting the offering.

• Urgency and gain represent better selling situations than do maintenance and euphoria.

• Urgency and gain can be translated into the push of discomfort and the pull of hope.

KEY TECHNIQUES OF HIGH-PERFORMANCE SELLING

Too often, salespeople fall into the habit of being reactive. They wait for clients or customers to take the lead in meetings or discussions. The technique or key skill is to CONTROL THE DIRECTION OF THE DISCUSSION ... not necessarily to control the buyer.

There are three questions to ask yourself before every buyer encounter:

1.   What is the purpose of this meeting? (Call?)

2.   What plan will I follow or develop to guide the encounter?

3.   What will be the payoff? (Both for me and the buyer?)[1]

Purpose?
Plan?
Payoff?

    To move from learner to competent, try putting the word "special" or "specific" in your opening statement of purpose. "My special reason for wanting to see you this morning was to review our last meeting and see if you were ready to make a decision."

THE POWER IS IN THE TECHNIQUE. MODEL THE TECHNIQUE TO FIT YOUR STYLE. PRACTICE IT UNTIL YOU ARE COMFORTABLE WITH IT, USING YOUR WORDS AND YOUR PACING.

::

No Help, No Benefit Or No Payoff

No Help, No Benefit
Or No Payoff

W e have examined in some detail two of the four dimensions of why people buy or don't buy. They buy when there is product and personal credibility and when they have a need. No credibility results in no buying, either for product or personal reasons. No need is another reason for not buying.

The buyer belief system contains another dimension in the selling situation. That dimension is benefit, payoff or result. We use the term payoff. We reason that not every result may be positive, but a benefit is usually positive and will provide a payoff.

Again, if the seller is dealing with only one buyer, this idea of the benefit is somewhere in that buyer's mind. It is what the buyer sees as the answer to a need. If the sale involves several parties or buying influences, each buying influence will have a different mental picture of the payoff. In a very complex sale involving an organization, that mental picture may go so far as to involve the corporate image.

For instance, it is our understanding that McDonald's buyers have two cultural requirements of their vendors. It is the McDonald's "way of doing things" that they seldom have a written contract with their vendors. They believe that as long as the agreement is win-win, to the mutual benefit of McDonald's and the vendor, there is no need for a written contract. The second part of their culture is their desire to be partners with their vendors. They put the concept of a joint venture (our term) into practice in the form on an ongoing relationship.

They encourage vendors to search constantly for improvement in the supplied product or service. They want to be involved with their suppliers in the research and development of improvements to the product or service. There is no such thing as the status quo for your offering with or to McDonald's. You must be part of the constant search for better or improved. If you were making an initial call on a McDonald's purchasing agent, you would need to understand this uniqueness of the buying situation. You would need to understand that McDonald's would see any of their needs, and the benefits for those needs, in terms of no written contract and the willingness to be part of the constant search for improvement.

Bama Pie in Tulsa, Okla., supplies biscuits in at least two McDonald's regions. They maintain a research department that constantly looks for ways to improve the biscuit itself. The marketing department at Bama Pie is constantly looking for ways to facilitate better delivery to ensure freshness and inventory control.

Because they are, in essence, partners with McDonald's, they provide a unique benefit to McDonald's. The benefit to Bama Pie is that because of the McDonald's volume, the company is able to engage in other types of marketing. It is a win-win arrangement.

In the selling situation, benefits are what the offering will do to provide answers or solutions to the need, either the push of discomfort or the pull of promise. Simply stated, benefits or payoffs are the positive results provided by the offering.

If, in the selling situation, those payoffs or benefits can provide advantage, the salesperson's position becomes stronger. For instance, in advertising, the salesperson might be able to show a strong benefit as a result of the reach of the medium. As a benefit, that would be positioned as "our station (or any medium, depending on what you were selling) can give you greater reach than any of our immediate competitors." If the buyer wants reach, that is a benefit or a payoff.

If the seller can then add: "and that reach is 60 percent greater than this competitor and two times greater than this other competitor," he has added an advantage, provided he can prove it. In this illustration, that proof would probably be a mathematical proof using circulation figures or ratings.

Too often, when we talk about selling the benefits, we lump benefits and advantages together. They are not the same. The advantage is the result of the benefit. Usually, this competitive edge will be positioned as both a benefit and an advantage. You hear this in competitive advertising now. A car is positioned as "more economical (benefit) than Ford, Chevrolet or Dodge (direct competitive edge) because it gets 32 miles per gallon on the highway, which is 60 percent better than these rival cars. Actual highway tests prove it (advantage)." And then they may name the highway test or the source of the advantage as additional proof.

When we get to presenting, or making a presentation, in this book, we will come to the P-A-P-A Model.[1] That model is a positioning tool that enables the sellers to think in terms of their promise (solution), which is followed by the amplification of that promise or the benefits and advantages, then the proof of the promise and finally the action. The action may be positive approval of the entire offering, or it might be positive approval of a particular aspect of that offering. The P-A-P-A Model positions the need uncovered by the salesperson with how the solution or promise will be delivered.

In most sales, someplace in the buyer belief system there will be BUYING CRITERIA. Someplace between need and benefit, buyers establish what they will buy, how they will buy it and what they will pay. In technical sales work, when there is a technical buyer or an evaluator, the buying criteria will be a system of buying. Again, in advertising, the technical buyer will have criteria for reach, frequency and price. The system may be based on "cost per point" or gross rating points delivered. The buying formula becomes "the buying criteria."

When the buying criteria are very rigid, the sellers must position their offering in terms of the criteria, or specs, that are being used. They have two choices: Meet the buyer's criteria or not. There is no room for qualitative selling. The criteria will be based on quantity. The lowest price usually wins. Thus, the selling situation becomes commodity buying and transactional selling, because the buyer sees no difference between your offering and any other. They have plenty of options and alternatives. For the seller, it becomes a matter of haggling over price. At best, it is a very tight box that often produces a poor buy.

If you look at our matrix, about the only place the seller can be in such conditions is at the first or second level of selling. Then look at it from the other side. Hasn't the buyer also placed himself at that level? If price is the compelling factor and the only benefit is the efficiency of that buy, isn't the buyer ignoring other values that might be important? If that buyer is truly a good buyer, won't he look at other values? And, in adding other criteria to the buy, won't he, in effect, move to a higher level of buying?

Going back to an earlier illustration, let's assume the seller is at level two. She really knows her product. Give her most any buy and she can figure out a way to manipulate the offering into the buying criteria. As a last resort, she trims the price a little here and there.

The buyer has a myopic fixation on the buying criteria. She sees it only from the vantage point of the specs involved. We used the illustration of one engineer selling another engineer, not to be disrespectful to engineers, although their breed has a tendency to focus on the specs. Small wonder seller and buyer vibrate together. Of course, it is possible there is another person in the company who has a broader view and adds elements to the buying criteria not known to the salesperson. The salesperson had never discussed the buy with that person, and her buyer-engineer was not aware of those additional criteria.

Our matrix also fits this scenario. Suppose the salesperson wants to change or modify the buying criteria? One way to do this is to present valid reasons to the technical buyer for changing the buying criteria. Perhaps the salesperson turns to one of the popular concepts in selling today: "added value."

If the technical buyer insists on the buying criteria, then "added value" becomes an addition to the offering. In advertising, that would be more announcements; in outdoor selling, additional billboards; a 13th issue in a 12-month campaign in a magazine at no charge. The technical buyer or negotiator simply adds this "added value" into the system and reduces the average unit cost. The objective of efficiency has been achieved.

Put all these variables into the mix of who sets the buying criteria and you add another evolution in the skills of the salesperson. The level-four salesperson offers a total system, solution or promise of resolving the urgency or achieving the gain. The unit cost is now clouded in many other values. But clouding is not the point. The point is that the buyer sees the need for a total solution, sees the benefits and the advantages, sees the payoffs in terms of results and return on investment.

A story to illustrate this point: A calling officer at a bank was working a rather large potential account. She had visited the business manager of the account and they had discussed CD rates, interest rates for loans and all the technical aspects of moving the company account. The business manager wanted the assurance of the lowest interest rates in the event the company had to borrow money to cover late receivables. The business manager also intimated the head of the company would be involved in any final decision.

The calling officer felt this account could be an important piece of business for the bank. She went to a senior officer in the bank.

The senior officer was slightly acquainted with the head of the company being solicited. They agreed upon a strategy where the senior officer would call the head of the company and suggest having lunch at the bank. They would invite the business manager of the company, and the calling officer would also be present. In the meantime, the calling officer would do a little research and make a list of banks that had failed in the past ten years and how many of these had ended up having their loan portfolios worked out by the Resolution Trust Corporation.

The purpose of this strategy was to change the buying criteria of the company, if they could get the company to change it. If the lowest interest rate was the sticking point, they had to modify that part of the belief system of either the company or the business manager.

At the appropriate time during the lunch, the senior officer made a point of the stability of the bank, how in spite of tough times, it had been able to continue to serve the needs of its customers. He pointed out the sense of security that developed. Customers knew they could always count on the bank. One reason the bank had been able to maintain that consistency of performance was fair interest rates, not necessarily the lowest, but always fair in that the rate represented a reasonable rate of return based on the risk.

Turning to the calling officer, the senior person said: "In fact, Alice has worked up a list of banks that failed in this area in the last ten years, which, of course, have been very turbulent times for banking. Beside those names is an asterisk if that bank was known for the lowest interest rate and for making imprudent loans. You'll notice nearly every name has an asterisk beside it." And the calling officer passed the list, not to the head of the company, but to the business manager.

The end of the story is that they were able to change the buying criteria for this company. And they accomplished that without getting the nose of one of the buying influences out of joint. Their selling strategy had moved them to the fourth level of selling.

In this chapter, we have suggested thinking of "no payoff" in terms of no benefit. We have defined benefit and attempted to show the relationship between benefits and advantages. We introduced the concept of buying criteria and how this element often bridges the space between the buyers' image of the need and their image of the payoff or benefit. And, finally, if you track the matrix, you see how the level-one salesperson is often suspended on the

petard of price as defined by the buyer, while the level-four salesperson often sets the buying criteria.

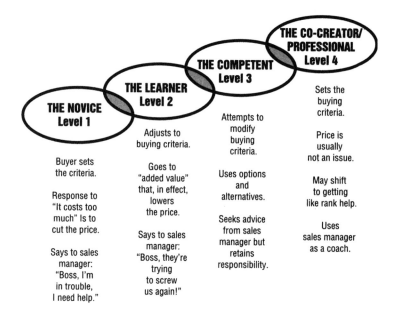

THE NOVICE
Level 1

THE LEARNER
Level 2

THE COMPETENT
Level 3

THE CO-CREATOR/
PROFESSIONAL
Level 4

Buyer sets
the criteria.

Response to
"It costs too
much" Is to
cut the price.

Says to sales
manager:
"Boss, I'm
in trouble,
I need help."

Adjusts to
buying criteria.

Goes to
"added value"
that, in effect,
lowers
the price.

Says to sales
manager:
"Boss, they're
trying
to screw
us again!"

Attempts to
modify
buying
criteria.

Uses options
and
alternatives.

Seeks advice
from sales
manager but
retains
responsibility.

Sets the
buying
criteria.

Price is
usually
not an issue.

May shift
to getting
like rank help.

Uses
sales manager
as a coach.

DOES THE CONCEPT ACTUALLY FIT TODAY'S WORLD?

DOES THE CONCEPT ACTUALLY FIT TODAY'S WORLD?

L et's take this concept of the four stages of selling and see if it fits "no justification." Let's begin with the subtle idea that, in most cases, buyers have a reasonable idea of their buying criteria. Certainly that is true when a salesperson is dealing with a professional buyer, one whose job is to buy equipment, office supplies, parts, oilfield supplies, advertising, trip accommodations. These people usually have buying criteria, which may be policies, specs or set ways of evaluating products or services offered them.

Novices are not aware of these buying criteria. They are focused on their offering. They have no benefit of past experience with the buyer. They may have limited knowledge of other products in their field, but basically they are working blind.

Learners begin to suspect there are buying criteria. As they learn to ask questions, they find it pays to ask who, what, when, where and how. They often find the "rules of the game" seem to be very rigid. Very often, they hit the price objection. They are subject to the other person's buying criteria.

Competents find ways to challenge the buying criteria and may even begin to establish new criteria. Because they focus more on solutions, specific criteria become less important and less rigid. They may even become a part of establishing the buying criteria by showing the ultimate value of their solution. This skill is especially true in insurance selling, where point-by-point comparisons are often made by a group health and hospital insurance buyer.

Professionals may, by the nature of their approach and their solution to the need, actually set the buying criteria. This is often true in high-tech selling. The sellers provide solutions so unique that no comparison is possible. They actually establish a critical advantage for their offering and, by so doing, establish the buying criteria.

Price is less important. Results provide the payoff.

Buying criteria are a part of "how this buy is made." Who makes the buying decision may be part of the question that sellers must know before they can make an intelligent call. When we speak of buying criteria, we mean the numbers of the buy, in a rather narrow sense.

But buying criteria can actually be much broader. That's why we use the term "the selling situation." For instance, there may be a person in the total selling situation who will never make a buying decision, but who will be involved in approval of that decision.

In workshops, when we bridge into the "no justification" part of the matrix, we go back to the ABC diagram hanging on the wall.

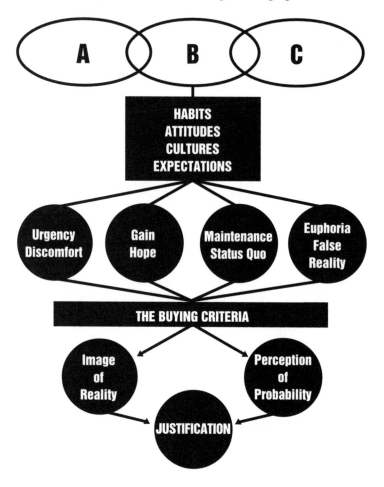

We make sure the barrier reef is on the drawing and explain that it can be the belief system of a single person in the selling situation, a number of buying influences, a committee or even company culture. The concept of need is filtered through that belief system and emerges in one of the four positions of buyer readiness. These are: urgency or discomfort, promise or hope, maintenance or status quo and euphoria or false reality. We stress that these stages are not absolute; they can change and evolve.

What's more, if it is a complex sale, not all buying influences may have the same view of the position. They are intended to provide four positions or possibilities that enable the salesperson to identify an important part of the selling situation — the position of readiness — which now becomes part of the buying criteria.

The buying criteria may also include specifications, which are a form of need. You will often hear a technical buyer or evaluator say: "I need to bring this buy in at 'X' dollars." Let's switch the type of selling to further illustrate this point.

A couple is looking for a new home. They give the real estate agent a list of needs. "We need three bedrooms and at least two baths, a large lot, a certain school district, a pool would be nice and a large kitchen or eating area. Oh, yes, and a family room, and we don't want to go over $200,000." This is the wife talking. Then the husband adds: "We have $15,000 to pay down and we don't want to pay over $90 per square foot." Suddenly, the purchase of the home — the selling situation — becomes a blend of conceptual needs, actual need and buying criteria.

Then they add: "We want to sell our present house because it is too small." And if they add: "We would like to be settled in before school starts," then the selling situation has added the positions of urgency and gain. The salesperson now has an evaluation of the selling situation.

But all these reasons for buying belong to the couple. They will buy for their reasons. The salesperson will need to position the offering of homes against this selling situation. So the search for the fit will begin.

How will the couple justify any decision they make against any offering made?

They have a position or evaluation of the selling situation from their viewpoint. It is based on two things: their IMAGE OF REALITY and their PERCEPTION OF PROBABILITY.[1]

Their IMAGE OF REALITY is their view of the buying situation. Their needs and buying criteria produce what becomes their IMAGE OF REALITY. Eventually, they will position their IMAGE OF REALITY against the offering under consideration. Each benefit will be positioned against the IMAGE OF REALITY. In a complex sale, each person will place the solution or the promise against his or her IMAGE OF REALITY. Does this fit? Is this what I wanted? Is this what we need?

The second part of this equation is the PERCEPTION OF PROBABILITY. What are the odds it will work? What are the odds this car will perform as the salesperson said it would? What are the chances of success for this advertising campaign? What is the degree of risk?

If the offering fits the IMAGE OF REALITY, and the PERCEPTION OF PROBABILITY is favorable, they will justify the decision to move forward.

At first glance, this progression of thinking or feeling may seem very complex. It may be clumsy for salespeople to use initially, because it forces them to break old selling habits. Instead of labeling the buyer, or buyers if there are more than one, with useless labels, the sellers asks themselves: WHAT IS THE SELLING SITUATION? What are the needs as they have been described? What are the specifics? What will be THE BUYING CRITERIA? That is step 1 of the sales strategy.

Step 2 becomes the offering, the solution or the PROMISE I will recommend. How does this fit the buying criteria? What benefits will this provide? What advantages? Where are the strong points? The weak points?

Step 3 becomes seeing it through the eyes of the buyer. The salesperson says: "If I were the buyer and I took my view of the SELLING SITUATION, what are the odds this will work? What are the odds of success? What is the possibility this will help ease the position of urgency? Or, what is the probability of gain? Is it worth the risk?"

If the offering fits the buyer's IMAGE OF REALITY and is favorable to the PERCEPTION OF PROBABILITY, the buyer can justify the decision.

Let's look at this concept from a slightly different view. How does the marketplace deal with the PERCEPTION OF PROBABILITY? Why are we rather secure with a guaranteed national name brand and less comfortable with an item that has no guarantee?

What happens if you buy something at Wal-Mart? Isn't their policy that if you take it back, they give you your money back or another like product and there are no questions asked? How, then, has this adjusted or modified your PERCEPTION OF PROBABILITY? Hasn't a lot of the risk of the decision been taken out of the justification?

When a quality organization puts great emphasis on service, when the buyer is convinced that "if it is broke, they'll fix it," hasn't this benefit influenced the PERCEPTION OF PROBABILITY? When you buy the same tires again and again because you have always had a good experience with them, aren't you inclined to go with what has been proven? Isn't that your PERCEPTION OF PROBABILITY at work?

Now, up to this point, our illustrations have been with tangible products or services. Switch to the intangible. Advertising offers no guarantee. Seldom, when you buy advertising and it doesn't work do you get your money back. Consider life insurance. As the fellow said: "I'll never know if they paid off because I won't be there. I can only believe they will honor their contract."

Yes, there are rich payoffs for those salespeople who can sell intangibles like advertising and life insurance. But those salespeople who have done well, in our observation, have the expertise to locate the customer's IMAGE OF REALITY and position their offering in such a manner that it fits the customer's PERCEPTION OF PROBABILITY. They are, indeed, high-performance salespeople!

Perhaps the matrix on the following page can help justify that statement. Let's track it through.

If you followed the matrix through all the levels, you will notice one final line in level four. "Provides a win." The concept of "win" is almost another subject, and yet it is an integral part of the level four selling expertise. We'll come back to "win."

It is the rare person who doesn't like to win. Winning is part of the American culture. We love games we can win. We love to see the underdog win. We even label people "winners" and "losers."

One of our clients tells a wonderful story about a personal experience from his early days of selling. He had been assigned to work with a more senior salesperson for a week. The office nickname for the senior person was "The Hawk." The joke was that he flew into high-commission territory that none of the other birds had ever seen and pounced on business with a furious style of selling. Myth had it that he would sharpen his talons every night to be ready to pounce

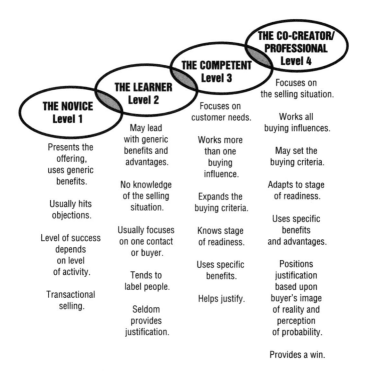

the next day. Well, it seems our storyteller had a series of experiences the first day or so and, as he got into the routine at the dinner table, as he was inclined to do at times, he soon had the dinner party in tears from laughing so hard. Which brings us to his story of the third day.

They were calling on a customer who was very upset. Their last delivery had been messed up and the customer was three notches to the north of irate. To paraphrase the story: "Well, the customer started out strong and then shifted to high and pretty soon was pounding on the desk. WHAM ... WHAM ... WHAM ... and the next thing I know The Hawk is on his feet and he is pounding on the desk, too, and now it's WHAM WHAM ... WHAM WHAM ... WHAM WHAM ... and The Hawk is hollering that he didn't blame the customer ... he would be mad, too ... and would be insisting on his rights ... WHAM WHAM ... WHAM WHAM ... and you would have thought there was a war going on. Pretty soon, things quieted down and The Hawk said he would personally take the responsibility for straightening out this unbelievable mess, and the next thing you knew, he walked out with a big order.

"Well, we got out in the car and The Hawk was just as calm as if nothing had happened. "WOW, that was really something!" I said. "Aw," said The Hawk, "that was really nothing. Murray just likes to win once in a while, and so I give him a win now and then. You know, you should always give the buyer a win. That's a feel-good, a justification for buying. Notice I told Murray I wished we had more customers that bitched like he did because then we would have a better product? That's a win for Murray. He likes to think he keeps us on the ball. And he does, in fact."

Always give the customer a win! Later in this book we touch on the concept of Social Style, where people are divided into the four quadrants: Driver-Expressive-Amiable-Analytical. The premise of this material is that each social style has a want. The Analytical wants to be right. The Driver wants results. The Expressive wants recognition. The Amiable wants to be liked.

Level-four salespeople, with or without formal training in social style, work with wins. You'll hear it in the way they position benefits: "It would be very difficult to challenge the efficiency of this buying decision. You have efficiencies here that are at least 30 percent improved over the other options on the table. Certainly, you could defend your decision if you needed to do that and could show very clearly where you made the right choice."

Take that positioning apart a little and you will hear benefit (efficiency) and then advantage (30 percent better) and then the personal win (you could prove you were right).

This concept of adding the win is based on the model that looks like this: BENEFIT — ADVANTAGE — (to you personally) WIN. Said another way, after using a benefit and an advantage, the salesperson may think but doesn't say out aloud: "Which means you," and they then add the personal win for the buyer.

Anytime you are involved in a complex sale where there are several buying influences and THE SELLING SITUATION requires approval, tacit or otherwise, from several people, every one of those buying influences will have a need for a personal win. It might be they are recognized for seeing the merits of your proposal. It might be the proposal allows them to get the results or achieve the control they need in their department or district. It may be that it will provide a sense of security or a degree of safety. It may be they can prove the merit of their logic.

Wins fit with personal interest. The product or service benefits and advantages provide the payoffs, they fit the job or the task to be accomplished, they address the urgency or help the hurt or discomfort, or they provide the gain or the hope. That's product or service. They hook to benefits or advantages. Wins are the hooks for self-interest of the people involved.

WINS provide the justification for the self-interest involved in the IMAGE OF REALITY and the PERCEPTION OF PROBABILITY. This chapter can be summarized by reviewing the matrix on page 90.

BELIEF SYSTEM EXERCISE

Below is a series of 16 faces.

Imagine you are a headline writer for a newspaper or magazine and each of the faces is an ad. Your job is to write a four-word headline — no more than four words — for each of the ads or faces.

When you have finished, if you are working alone in the book, think about why you chose the headline you did. Do this after you have written the headline. If you can, think of the event or the experience or the belief that caused you to write the headline you did.

If you are working in a group, or with a partner or another person, compare your ad headlines. Have them tell you why they wrote what they did, and you tell them why you wrote what you did.

If you are in a group of several people, pass the headlines around. First, you'll find it really is a funny or fun-filled experience but, more than that, it will give you a deeper understanding of different belief systems.

We are willing to bet that in a group of any size, no two pages will have the same or similar headlines for the 16 faces.

The message is very simple: PEOPLE BUY FOR THEIR REASONS, NOT FOR OURS. If I want to reach them in selling, or in an ad, I need headlines that fit their belief systems, not mine.

∷

ADJUSTING YOUR MIND FOR HIGHER PERFORMANCE

ADJUSTING YOUR MIND
FOR HIGHER PERFORMANCE

"What are you going to do on this call?" How many times have you said this to yourself? When you've made sales calls with a sales manager, have you ever been asked that question? "What are you going to do on this call?"

Just the way we say it tends to put some bad information in our heads. The question we would raise is: Just what is a call? That word "call" can produce a poor mindset, because it raises pictures of a social visit, a nice chitchat, just stopping to see if anything is going on right now.

Again, let's go back to the idea that salespeople go through those four stages of development. In each stage, their concepts of their activity ought to change. Hopefully, it does change.

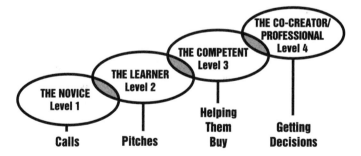

Novices really believe in activity, and they do "go out and make some calls." Or, they get on the phone and "make some calls." And because they measure their success by the level of activity, the word "call" can fit rather well. The trouble with the word is that it can get ingrained in the head game salespeople play with themselves. We use that word so many ways in selling. "It was a good call." Or, we refer to making "cold calls." We tell the sales manager: "I called on so-and-so today."

Truly, the word can get rather deep-seated and become almost habitual.

To break out of this mind trap, salespeople can use a simple three-step model.[1] They can simply say: What is the purpose of this call? What plan do I want to follow? What is the payoff going to be? Purpose ... plan ... payoff. To illustrate:

The purpose of this call is to propose a use of our full line of printed services. I'll open the presentation using what they told me last time about their needs, especially the seasonal variations. Then I'll be prepared to show samples of ideas that have worked well for others. Then we will talk about a next step, perhaps trying one of our services on a pilot basis. That's my plan.

Now, you have a purpose, a plan and a payoff in mind. It is no longer a "call."

This novice stage of selling is tough to handle. First, if the emphasis is on activity, and novices measure their success by the level of their activity, they will make a lot of calls. More than likely, they will not be well-planned calls, nor will they be highly productive calls. The novice will experience a lot of rejection. If you have ever sold anything door-to-door, you know the meaning of this analogy. Selling is an adventure!

The second level of selling usually has a different focus. By the time sellers emerge from the novice stage, they have a different perspective. First, they should have learned their product or service. They feel comfortable with what they are selling. They have learned how to secure appointments, and their quality of call goes up. In more instances, they are seeing the same buyer a second or third time. Either consciously or unconsciously, they have done a little mental qualifying, though not a lot and probably not in much depth.

So now, they start pitching or presenting. Their calls are focused on giving the facts about their product or service, the features, the advantages and even a few benefits. They begin to measure success by the number of presentations they make. Again, activity counts. There is a certain truism in selling. When you tell your story to enough people, you'll find a few who want what you're selling and you'll make some hits or some sales. The focus is on the sale.

You've probably seen the sign that reads: "Babe Ruth struck out 3,000 times, but he hit 1,000 home runs." The idea is that if you go to bat enough times, if you keep swinging, you'll get some hits. And, there certainly is truth to that adage.

Can you sell this way? Certainly! Thousands of people do, and in many instances they are successful. They have that natural ability to sustain a high activity level, rejection doesn't bother them much and they just keep swinging. Do they go into slumps at times? Yes, they do. Because again, their batting average programs them for failure more times than it does for success. If they have the mental maturity to sustain this, they come out of the slump and start hitting again. Quite often, if they examine their performance, they focus on their presentation and closing techniques and increase their activity in both areas of the sales process. In other words, they revert to what they perceive as their strengths and do more of those things they believe they are good at.

Interestingly, their prospecting may sound as though it includes their "pitch." Have you ever heard something like this: "Good morning. I'm trying to reach the person who decides what advertising to buy. Can you tell me who that is? (Now, the odds are pretty good they hit a gatekeeper who says: 'Can you tell me what you're selling?') Yes ... I'm with _____ and I have an idea I believe they might be interested in hearing about."

Or, it might be: "I'm with _____, and we're running a special promotion this month," etc.

In the effort to get the appointment, they pitch their idea, their promotion and whatever. It isn't just advertising people who get appointments like this. Rug cleaners, cemetery plot salespeople, even stockbrokers get appointments this way. The stockbrokers work on credibility in their openers: "Good morning, Mr. Greenwood, I'm so-and-so and I'm with Lehman and Stern. You've heard of us, I'm sure."

The third-level sellers do a little homework before they try for the appointment. They have a third-party reference and they bridge into this. It might go: "Good morning, Mrs. Dodson, I'm so-and-so with (company or service) and I got your name from (reference). We have been working with them and in a recent conversation (reference) gave me your name as a person who might benefit from our services."

The letter asking for an initial appointment might use a similar approach, using a reference to establish credibility.

The third step at this level of selling, or the payoff, is usually a letter confirming this call, the date and the time and the seller's purpose.

In the third level of selling, there are several mind shifts and technique shifts. In the first two levels, salespeople focus on the sale. Since both levels sell very much from a transactional sale posture, both levels are high talk, high present and high close type calls. By the time salespeople reach the third level of sales skills, they have a different attitude, a different mindset at the beginning of the call, and they use a different set of selling skills. They prospect for opportunity.

They have learned the value of questions. And, in fact, questioning skills have been evolving as they progress to higher skill levels. Consequently, they talk less, present less and make greater use of questions. By the same token, they begin to see buyers less as opponents they must overcome and more as customers or potential customers. Selling becomes less an adventure and more a joint venture.

Consequently, on the first call, their purpose is to qualify customer needs. The process is a series of discovery questions. The payoff is to determine if customer needs can be met by their product or service.

Let's skip to the fourth level and prospecting. These sellers prospect almost entirely from references, but their reference is a two-part reference. Some customer suggests a name they might see. That's a product referral. The fourth level adds the personal referral. They ask about the people they will be calling on, their personalities, their hobbies, how the referent knows them. They get the personal book on the prospect as nearly as they can.

When they call or write for the appointment, they can now personalize their request in the bridge portion of the opening line. "I got your name from (your referent) and he/she tells me that (use a fact you learned from the referent)." Then comes the power. The word "promised" is used in some way.

The full introduction or request for the appointment might go this way: "I got your name from George Roberts. We were talking about start-up companies that were growing rapidly and people who are gaining a good share of their markets. I promised George I would contact you with the idea that our services might have an interest to you. Would there be a time next week that we might arrange an appointment?"

After the phone call, the letter confirming the appointment again mentions Roberts and your promise to him. The letter also includes something of added value. It could be a trade article about this business. It could be an article from one of your trade magazines. Its purpose is to add credibility to that first appointment.

Quite a difference from the level-one effort to get an appointment. You probably can't make 15 efforts like this every day to secure an initial appointment, but there is every bit as much activity involved. In truth, it is working smarter.

Many factors have compounded in today's world to make prospecting more difficult: More options and alternatives, more security, more people in telemarketing.

That's the negative side of the marketplace today. On the positive side, somebody will make an appointment, somebody will present a product or an idea and somebody will sell something, or the business won't be in business. Opportunity just knocks more softly these days.

Zig Ziglar tells a wonderful story in one of his books about a salesman who had experienced a broken appointment. He had an hour to fill. He walked into the office of a man who had not taken his calls and spoke to the secretary. "I would like to see Mr. So-and-So," he said. The secretary replied that Mr. So-and-So was busy and didn't see salesmen without an appointment. "Could you ask for me, please?" he said. She picked up the phone and asked. The man's voice could be heard from the other room. "Tell him I'm busy," he said. The salesman persisted. "Tell Mr. So-and-So I just want to ask one question."

The voice could be heard from the other room: "Tell him it better be an awfully good question." And Mr. So-and-So walked out of the office and faced the salesperson. "What do you want?" he said. The salesman looked him in the eye and said: "Mr. So-and-So, what do you tell your salespeople to do when they tell you somebody is hard to get to see?" Mr. So-and-So stood there a minute and then replied: "You've just asked the right question. Come in."

The story has a double meaning. First, it illustrates that there is a way to get to see even the people most difficult to meet. But the second point is this salesperson saw it through the prospect's eyes, and that Mr. So-and-So had probably told his salespeople: "Don't take no from somebody who can't say yes."

Again, to review within the context of four passages of selling, the novice, the learner, the competent and the professional all prospect differently.

Novices play the odds. They make lots of phone calls. They make a few connections. They knock on a lot of doors. They make some connections. They take a lot of rejection. But their skill begins to improve. Their percentages begin to improve. High activity helps them beat the odds. They learn to deal with rejection.

Learners begin to learn that creativity is possible in getting appointments. They begin to write good letters to request appointments. They learn to drop in names of satisfied clients. They may even send a prospect who hasn't returned their call a dead plant. Attached to the dead plant is a card. The card reads: "Look what happened to my plant while I've been waiting for you to return my call. I would like to meet you." By the way, that salesman got the appointment, and today that car dealer is one of his large accounts.

Competents learn to work the buffers or the screens. They treat the secretary or the receptionist as a friend and an ally. They are honest and straightforward with that person. They use benefits for an appointment with the target person and persuade the buffer they ought to get in. After all, the person who can keep them out probably can get them in. This level of salesperson sees the appointment as a small sale. They follow up with a letter, confirming the appointment.

Professionals use a still more advanced technique and one that is even more powerful. They prospect from their present clients! They ask for opinions of present clients. They ask about the present clients' business friends or suppliers who might be needing similar services. High-producing automotive salespeople use this feeder technique. Real estate people use it. Office machine people use it effectively. Insurance salespeople live by the technique. Always, when they call that fresh prospect, they have a name, the name of a reference, and they use that name as bridge to get the appointment.

Salespeople tell us there is another reality in the marketplace today that must be recognized. Let's say they have done their homework. They have developed a strategy for a particular sale. They have outlined their tactics. They believe they have identified the various buying influences and their respective roles in the selling situation.

They have an appointment to make a preliminary presentation and ask a few more questions. They ask for their party and the voice on the phone says: "Mr. So-and-So is no longer with us." Or, the voice says: "Angela Tippet has been transferred to the Atlanta office."

The truth is that the time span of the selling situation has been extended in many instances. Selling a house takes longer. Getting a decision on a group insurance plan takes longer. Selling an advertising schedule tied to a promotional event takes longer.

The adage "if something can go wrong it surely will" has more opportunity to come into play. And, in this interim period, the buying criteria, the "who buys it and the how they buy," are more subject to change.

If the mark of the novice is to focus on one buyer, one contact, one set of rules for the game, then the professional has had to learn to focus on the possibility that the selling situation today is a very fluid one. Consequently, the fourth-level sellers work more contacts on the same sale, they are faced with more appointments, they are faced with developing a relationship with one person without alienating another.

Level one and two salespeople prospect for sales. Level three and four people prospect for opportunity.

Instead of finding ways to sell the buyer, the level three or four salesperson searches for payoffs or benefits that will make the customer want to buy. If we took this sequence and put it in real estate, it would look like this: The novice would show the prospect a lot of homes, letting the prospect narrow the choices. The second-level salesperson would have pre-selected homes that are good values or good homes and would "show" the houses or present the homes. Fewer numbers, but each house with a valid reason to buy. Third-level salespeople would have rated the buyer carefully, would have a good idea of needs and expectations, and would fit homes to the buyer. They would show fewer homes, but in more depth, matching buyer needs to the features of those particular homes. Their goal would be a satisfied customer who might, at some future date, decide to list with them or buy another home from them.

Now, as you follow this sequence, it might seem that the activity level is dropping. It is, in the sense of shotgun selling, but quality of activity is increasing. Now we see the possible evidence of the saying "You ought to be working smarter, not harder." The truth is, this third-level selling is hard work and requires a high level of effort. To be successful, the salespeople simply must raise their closing ratio and sell bigger dollars. If the pattern is right, that happens as a natural process.

But, the process begins in the salesperson's head. Is she making calls, making pitches or helping a customer want to buy?

This leads to the fourth level of selling and the mindset of the true professional. The true professionals meet with any prospect or customer with a different mindset. Their goal is to get a decision.

That goal may be of several different types. It might be to qualify a prospect and get that prospect to decide to see them or work with them. It might be a closing decision.

Let's explore this important concept further, looking at the decisions a buyer or prospect makes along a series of steps the buyer goes through:

1. THE APPOINTMENT.

    Do I want to see the salesperson?

    Do I have the time?

    Do I have the money at this time?

    What does this salesperson really want?

2. THE QUALIFYING.

    Is this salesperson credible?

    Is he competent?

    Is the company trustworthy?

    Can he help me?

3. THE DISCOVERY.

    Do I want to take the time?

    Do I want them to know about my problems?

    My needs?

    Will all these questions provide a payoff for me?

    Is this worth the trouble?

4. THE ALIGNMENT.

    Does this fit my needs?

    Do we have something in common?

    This is what I have now, but is this what I want?

    How does this compare to other offerings?

5. THE CONSIDERATIONS.

What is the value to me?

What is the cost?

Do I want to shop for other offerings?

Did I want to change what I'm doing now?

Is there a payoff?

6.   THE COMMITMENT.

Do I do it now?

Or later?

How does this compare?

How do I justify this commitment?

7.   POST-BUY

Did I overlook something?

Was I treated fairly?

Will it work out?

How long do I wait for results?

Did I make a good decision?

Would I recommend this to others?

You might want to read this list again. It represents a fairly accurate chronology of what goes through the mind of the buyer. And, more importantly, every step of the way requires decisions by the buyer. Long before the salesperson gets to the close, the buyer has already made a number of conscious or unconscious decisions. The fourth-level salesperson understands these steps in the buying process.

Let's take this concept out of the context of selling and put it into something less complex. Let's say somebody asks you how to work the copy machine in the office, how to tie on a bass plug so it won't come off or how to start a lawnmower. You've never really thought about this because you're good at it. You learned how to do it some time ago. You've done it many times. You feel comfortable explaining how to go about doing it. Think about this experience.

How many times did you ask them if they understood? How many times did you say something like: "Are we OK so far?" How many times did you say: "Have you got that part?" "How do you feel about this? Pretty good?" And they said thank you and then did it. Now, how many decisions did they make in that process?

Let's say that along the way they said something like: "Boy, that's tough, I'm not sure I can do that." What did you do? Probably went back to something they didn't understand and started the decision-getting process over again from that point. Maybe you said something like: "Now, are you clear on that?"

Examine your own mindset. You make the decision right now what level of mindset you have in your daily selling. Do you make calls? Do you make pitches? Do you help the customer want to buy? Or, do you get a series of decisions that lead to a successful customer relationship?

Here's the test for the fourth level of mindset. If you have led customers along the path of good decisions, then, when you are in that post-buy posture with them, they will provide you with the names of other people who need your product or service. They provide your references. They will coach you, if you ask.

So, you decide. At the very beginning of the sales process, what is your mindset?

KEY TECHNIQUES OF HIGH-PERFORMANCE SELLING

A key technique in moving from the novice stage of selling to the learner stage is to visualize the call before you make it. Take a pad and write down questions you would ask. THINK PURPOSE. What is the purpose of this call? What do I need to know about the selling situation? What is their objective? What do they need? Who makes the buying decision? Can they utilize my offering? What is the buying cycle? What is the state of buyer readiness?

Step two is to organize these questions into a logical order. Remember, the plan must make them want to talk to you.

IN THINKING ABOUT
THIS MEETING, I WROTE
DOWN SOME QUESTIONS.
WOULD YOU MIND IF WE
WENT OVER THEM NOW?[1]

This technique can be modeled many ways. For instance: "In thinking about our last visit, I recall you raised the issue of timing. Could we begin by reviewing your points on that?"

Remember, when they say "yes ... go ahead" or give you permission to follow your plan, you have your first decision.

THE POWER IS IN THE TECHNIQUE. MODEL THE TECHNIQUE TO FIT YOUR STYLE. PRACTICE IT UNTIL YOU ARE COMFORTABLE WITH IT, USING YOUR WORDS AND YOUR PACING.

::

How To Make It Bigger By Listening Better

HOW TO MAKE IT BIGGER BY LISTENING BETTER

What are your prospects' needs? What do they like? What do they dislike? How do they feel about you and what you are saying? Do they have an opportunity? Or a problem? Do they want more information from you?

All the skill in the world at asking good questions, to learn the answers to those questions, won't serve much purpose unless you can do what? Unless you have that skill of good listening!

Listening is a funny subject. For most of our lives, most of the emphasis of our training has been on talking. Father comes home from work and mother says: "Guess what, Sarah said her first word today." Mother picks Sarah up at nursery school and the person in charge of the school tells her: "Sarah said her little stand-up speech today very well. Excellent! She showed a lot of poise." Sarah grows up, gets through high school and becomes valedictorian. By now, we have a single-parent family, but united for this important event, and both parents take great pride in Sarah's speech.

In each sequence, you can bet father didn't ask how Sarah was listening, but he probably praised her for her first word. And mother didn't ask if Sarah was listening at nursery school, only praised her for "doing your part so well." And you can guess what happened after the speech at graduation.

Probably, Sarah, in her entire life, was never praised for listening. In fact, in her teens she probably heard that great line: "Now, listen to me, young lady!" She was then accused of not listening, and she probably wasn't, because there was no payoff for listening. So, Sarah got a job selling print advertising and one day her sales manager suggested that she didn't listen very well.

Why should she? She had never been praised for listening,

probably went to sleep as a youngster listening to a bedtime story and just had never had many payoffs for listening. Then, she found herself in sales and, suddenly, there was a payoff for good listening. Except she didn't know how. Oh, she could hear. But all the speech courses didn't help much with the skill of listening. In fact, in her framework of experience, people described as "good listeners" had always been thought of as being rather unassertive people. A "good listener" was just somebody you took for granted — unless you were describing a good friend!

By now, you have some sense of the four stages, or passages, all salespeople go through as they attain the different levels of selling. Let's bring you into the equation here and ask you to think about how people listen, or don't listen, in those four levels. Here are some clues:

At each level, does it look like they are listening? What sort of feedback do they provide the speaker or talker? How do they respond? Whose world do they seem to be in? You have the four levels. You have four boxes with some space to write in your observations. Take a minute and see if you can match certain levels of listening to the passages of selling.

When you finish the work below, consider this question. Where would you put yourself most of the time in your selling experience? Then, look to the next page and we'll give you some thoughts about the kind of listening each of the four levels does.

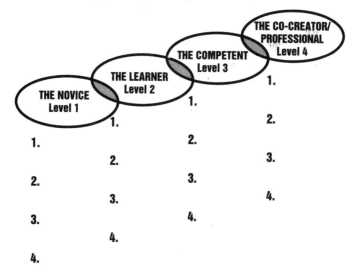

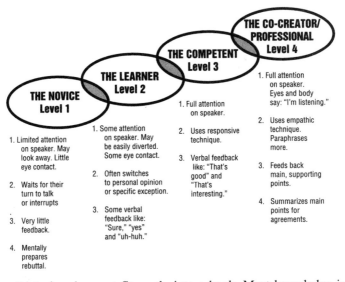

1. Limited attention on speaker. May look away. Little eye contact.

2. Waits for their turn to talk or interrupts

3. Very little feedback.

4. Mentally prepares rebuttal.

Listening does not fit neatly into a book. Most knowledge in schools is passed along in books. But listening is not knowledge. Listening is a skill, and until you practice a skill, you never really learn that skill. Some steps, however, can be taken to improve your listening skills.

Good listening requires that you focus on the other person. You can't listen to the radio with one ear, wait for the phone to ring and really hear what someone is telling you. You become a good candidate for the first kind of listening: Selective listening.

In our noisy world, we hear what we want to hear. If we listened to everything, we wouldn't have time for anything but listening. So, our ears get to be like push buttons, and we push the button when we really want to hear something. We sift out the rest of the noise. But when we do this, we judge immediately what we want to hear and what we don't want to hear. In so doing, we miss important points.

Salespeople who are good listeners focus on the other person, really give them their full attention. Thus, the novice salesperson is likely not to pay attention. They merely wait for their time to talk. They provide the other person very little feedback. Their eyes send the message that they are not really listening, and sometimes they forget to tell their face they are supposed to be listening. Mentally, they are getting ready to speak.

Good listening requires that you try to get the other person's main point. What are they trying to say? Few people ever tell you: "This is my main point." They expect you to dig it out of talk that is sometimes disorganized and rambling. So, as a good listener, you need to do a little organizing. When you hear the main point, you grab hold of that. In fact, a really good listener may ask: "So, you're saying the main point is ..." and repeat what they thought the speaker was saying.

In so doing, that person has used the second type of listening: Responsive listening.

Now, the listeners, because they are focused on the person talking, begin using some feedback. It may be nothing more than an occasional "I see" or "That's interesting," but they punctuate the dialogue now and then with a message that they are really listening. Parents sometimes use this listening style by tossing in an occasional "uh-huh" at the same time they are watching TV. As the little girl said on such an occasion: "Daddy, you're not really listening. You're not listening to me with your eyes." Responsive listening can help you get the main point. It can also help you with the second step in good listening, and that is to organize what the other person is saying so you better understand it.

Good listening requires an open mind. You need to put your own belief system on hold and avoid making judgments about what the other person is saying. You hold the rebuttals and the exceptions to what they are saying and try to understand the message. You hold off on how they are saying it and why they are saying it. You reserve judgment.

When you have a good idea of the "what," you start filling in the supporting things they are saying, why they feel that way, the reasons they give to justify their main points. And, again, you avoid making judgments. You simply file their points in an order that completes your understanding. At this point, you may move to the third type of listening: Empathic listening.

Now, listeners may begin to do a little paraphrasing. They feed back exact lines or main points and try to determine the feelings behind those main points. An example might be: "So the production costs seem to be important to you. I think you said that was your main reason for not using our services. Did I understand that correctly?"

Empathic listening is the highest level of listening skill because, in order to paraphrase back what they said, you really need to pay attention to them. Your mind can't wander, and you can't be getting ready to argue with them. You are truly listening! And quite often you will find you didn't hear what they said or thought they said. They might reply: "No, that isn't exactly what I said." Now you and the person talking have the opportunity to get on the same wavelength.

The highest listening sales skill is the ability to summarize the main point, or points, of the conversation. Some few professionals have the ability to do this without taking any notes. They can ask a series of questions and summarize the answers without referring to their notes. Those steel trap minds are rare. A better technique may be to make a note of main points. A good listener might say: "That seems to be important to you. Let me make a note of that." And, the conversation moves along.

On a recent trip to South Africa, we had occasion to watch a top salesperson in that country. He was very disarming person, very British, hardly the slap 'em on the back type. He had only two accounts on which he worked regularly. They were the two largest banking organizations in South Africa.

His great skill was making you feel that what you were saying was very important to him. We watched him and listened to his use of STIMULUS-PAUSE-RESPONSE. Someone would make a comment. Gordon would pause a moment and say something like: "Yes, yes, never thought of it quite that way. But, of course, it makes good sense from that view." Then he would go on to make his point or piggyback onto the speaker's statement.

Level one and level two salespeople are in a hurry to talk. Sometimes they interrupt, sometimes they are waiting to speak before it is really their turn. There is no pause between what the other person says and what they say. They send a message, loud and clear: "I really don't care what you just said ... and now this." Level three and level four salespeople have learned the skill of listening. And, quite often, you hear them pause after the other party has made a point. They pause, then they respond, often with a comment on what has just been said. Then, they agree or disagree or build on that point. Stimulus, pause, response. The pause that enriches the listening.

These listeners are always in constant alignment with the speaker. They are building empathy. When they hear the stimulus of that other voice ... THEY PAUSE ... then they respond. STIMULUS ... PAUSE ... RESPONSE. A great skill that can enhance the richness of listening.

In what follows, we outline some conversations. You might want to read the statement in quotes out loud so you can hear it.

Then make a note or circle your response. Each exercise gets a little tougher. See how you do with them. Then check the last page for the recommended answers.

EXERCISE ON LISTENING

#1. Salesperson: "Sure you can send letters and printed material to your customer. That's helpful. And I know a lot of people who do that. But not me. I make all my calls in person. I think customers like that and it works well for me."

Check the main point.

A. A lot of people send letters and printed material.

B. It's helpful to send letters and printed material.

C. This person makes calls in person.

D. Customers like personal calls.

#2. Salesperson: "I had to learn the hard way to hand people my calling card with my left hand. I'm right-handed and it was more natural to do it that way. But now that I've learned that little secret, I'm ready for any eventuality like a handshake or whatever."

Check the main point.

A. This person is right-handed.

B. It was hard for them to break an old habit.

C. They now hand their calling card in their left hand.

D. They are ready for any eventuality.

#3. Salesperson: "I've had this briefcase for what seems like years. I've jammed it in elevator doors, dropped it, had it rained on. It has been almost indestructible. And the beauty of it is that the dear old thing really didn't cost very much."

Check the main point.

A. The briefcase was inexpensive.

B. The person was attached to it.

C. It has been almost indestructible.

D. They have given it hard wear.

#4. Customer: "You don't seem to understand me. Your production costs are just too high and your competitors don't pass those costs on to me. And, besides, I enjoy doing my own layout work. It takes time, but I do it almost like it was a hobby. And I'm getting better at it the more I do it."

Put an "M" beside the main point and "S" beside supporting point(s).

A. I enjoy doing my own layout work.

B. I'm getting better at it.

C. You don't seem to understand me.

D. I like to do my own work.

E. Layout work isn't easy.

#5. Customer: "Today is really a dismal day, isn't it? Rainy days like these really get to me. You know, I don't even like to drive on days like this because people bumper-hug you and the roads are slick. Getting around on a day like this must make it tough on you."

Put an "M" beside the main point, and "S" beside supporting point(s).

A. They don't like to drive on days like this.

B. Today is a dismal day.

C. Rainy days get to them.

D People bumper-hug you and roads are slick.

E. Days like today make it tough on salespeople.

RECOMMENDED ANSWERS FOR LISTENING EXERCISES

#1   The main point is "C." This person makes calls in person.

#2   The main point is "C." They now hand their calling card in their left hand.

#3   The main point is "D." They had given it hard wear.

On the next exercise, you were asked for the main point and then to organize the support points.

#4   "A" would be the recommended main point. I enjoy doing my own layout work. To add supporting points:

D. I like to do my own work.

B. I'm getting better at it.

E. Layout work isn't easy.

C. You don't seem to understand me.

#5 "A" would be the recommended main point. They don't like to drive on days like this.

To add supporting points:

D. People bumper-hug you and roads are slick.

C. Rainy days get to them.

B. Today is a dismal day.

E. Days like today make it tough on salespeople.

HOW WELL DO YOU LISTEN?

Here are three tests that rate you as a listener. There are no correct or incorrect answers but, rather, responses that will extend your understanding of yourself and your listening. The tests will also highlight areas in your listening where improvement might be welcome. An analysis of your test results appears on page 120.

This material was prepared by Dr. Lyman K. Steil for the Sperry Corporation and originally appeared in Sperry's booklet *Your Personal Listening Profile*. The information is based on Dr. Steil's copyrighted material and is reprinted by permission of the author and the Sperry Corporation.

QUIZ 1

A. Check the term that best describes you as a listener:

__Superior   Excellent

__Above Average   Average

__Below Average   Poor   Terrible

B. On a scale of 0-100 (100 = highest), how would you rate yourself as a listener? _____

QUIZ 2

A. How do you think the following people would rate you as a listener? (0-100).

Your Best Friend   _____

Your Boss   _____

Business Colleague   _____

A Job Subordinate   _____

Your Spouse   _____

QUIZ 3

As a listener, how often do you find yourself engaging in these ten bad listening habits? First, check the appropriate columns. Then, tabulate your score using the key below.

	Almost Always	Usually	Sometimes	Seldom	Almost Never	SCORE
1. Calling the subject uninteresting						
2. Criticizing the speaker's delivery or mannerisms						
3. Getting overstimulated by something the speaker says						
4. Listening primarily for facts						
5. Trying to outline everything						
6. Faking attention to the speaker						
7. Allowing interfering distractions						
8. Avoiding difficult material						
9. Letting emotion-laden words arouse personal antagonism						
10. Wasting the advantage of thought speed (daydreaming)						
TOTAL SCORE:						

Scoring: Almost Always +2, Usually +4, Sometimes +6, Seldom +8, Almost Never +10

PROFILE ANALYSIS

This is how others have responded to the same questions you've just answered:

QUIZ 1

A. 85% of all listeners questioned rated themselves as Average or less. Fewer than 5% rated themselves as Superior or Excellent.

B. On the 0-100 scales, the extreme range is 10-90; the general range is 35-85; and the average rating is 55.

QUIZ 2

When comparing the listening self-ratings and projected ratings of others, most respondents believe that their best friend would rate them highest as a listener. And that rating would be higher than the one they gave themselves in Quiz 1 — where the average was 55.

How come? We can only guess that best-friend status is such an intimate, special kind of relationship that you can't imagine it ever happening unless you were a good listener. If you weren't, you and he or she wouldn't be best friends to begin with.

Going down the list, people who take this test usually think their bosses would rate them higher than they rated themselves. Now, part of that is probably wishful thinking, and part of it is true. We do tend to listen to our bosses better — whether it's out of respect or fear or whatever doesn't matter.

The grades for colleague and job subordinate work out to be just about the same as the listener rated himself — that 55 figure again.

But when you get to spouse — husband or wife — something really dramatic happens. The score here is significantly lower than the 55 average that previous profile-takers gave themselves. And what's interesting is that the figure goes steadily downhill. While newlyweds tend to rate their spouse at the same high level as their best friend, as the marriage goes on ... and on ... the rating falls. So, in a household where the couple has been married 50 years, there could be a lot of talk, but maybe nobody is really listening.

QUIZ 3

The average score is 62 — 7 points higher than the 55 that the average test-taker gave himself in Quiz 1. This suggests that when listening is broken down into specific areas of competence, we rate ourselves better than we do when listening is considered only as a generality.

Of course, the best way to discover how well you listen is to ask the people to whom you listen most frequently: your spouse, boss, best friend, etc. They'll give you an earful.

10 KEYS TO EFFECTIVE LISTENING

The keys below are a positive guideline to better listening. In fact, they're at the heart of developing better listening habits that could last a lifetime.

10 KEYS TO EFFECTIVE LISTENING	THE BAD LISTENER	THE GOOD LISTENER
1. Find areas of interest	• Tunes out dry subjects	• Takes advantage, asks: "What's in it for me?"
2. Judge content, not delivery	• Tunes out if delivery is poor	• Judges content, skips over delivery errors
3. Hold your fire	• Tends to enter into argument	• Doesn't judge until comprehension is complete
4. Listen for ideas	• Listens for facts	• Listens for central themes
5. Be flexible	• Takes intensive notes using only one system	• Takes fewer notes; uses 4 to 5 different systems, depending on speaker
6. Work at listening	• Shows no energy output; fakes attention	• Works hard, exhibits active body state.
7. Resist distractions	• Is easily distracted	• Fights or avoids distractions, tolerates bad habits, knows how to concentrate
8. Exercise your mind	• Resists difficult expository material; seeks light, recreational material	• Uses heavier material as exercise for the mind
9. Keep your mind open	• Reacts to emotional words	• Interprets color words; does not get hung up on them
10. Capitalize on fact; thought is faster than speech	• Tends to daydream with slow speakers	• Challenges, anticipates, mentally summarizes, weighs the evidence, listens between the lines to tone of voice

LISTENING SUMMARIZED

There are three types of listening. Selective listening is a process of sifting information that seems to be important. Responsive listening is more "tuned in," where the listeners send messages that they are listening. Empathic listening is "feeding back" key thoughts for complete understanding.

SELECTIVE

>"If it doesn't seem to be important to me, I probably won't hear much of it."

RESPONSIVE

>"I understand what you saying."
>
>"That's interesting." "Uh-huh."
>
>"Tell me more about that."

EMPATHIC

>"So, what you are saying is ... (feedback)."
>
>"Let me see if I understand your point ...
>
>you believe (feedback)."

THE POWER IS IN THE TECHNIQUE. MODEL THE TECHNIQUE TO FIT YOUR STYLE. PRACTICE IT UNTIL YOU ARE COMFORTABLE WITH IT, USING YOUR WORDS AND YOUR PACING.

::

CHAPTER 12

UNDERSTANDING POWERFUL PHRASES

UNDERSTANDING POWERFUL PHRASES

A salesman in a larger city in the Midwest always seemed to find time to do a little coaching with the younger salespeople in the organization. He had the skill of never telling them anything directly. He never used the phrases "Let me tell you something" or "Let me show you something." Instead, he would tell short stories to make his point. This was one of his stories:

"There was this priest in this small town and, boy, it was a poor parish. But this priest had the uncanny ability to always get people to contribute to the church when the parish needed something. He would have made a beautiful salesman. Well, one day I was feeling kinda low. I was visiting in that town and ran into the priest as he was on his way to a call.

"He asked me how things were going and I told him, sparing no detail. Then I asked him how it was going in his line of work and he told me things were going quite well. I asked him how he could say that when I knew things weren't always that good when it came to raising money. Then I asked him how he was able to get people to give. Well, he smiled and looked at me and said this. Never will I forget it.

" 'When you are in sales, son, you remember the three most useful phrases that we have to reach the other person. The first one is: "WILL YOU HELP ME?" Most people will. The second is: "I DON'T KNOW." Most people will give you directions or instruction. The third phrase lets them know you are human. It is: "I MADE A MISTAKE." Not that you were wrong, because that is a moral issue. Just that you were mistaken, which makes you human.'

"You know, I've found myself using those three phrases more than you could ever imagine in selling. I guess the priest had time for a lesson that day without me ever knowing it, because things sure turned around after that."

Let's focus briefly on the use of this concept in making a connection.

NOVICE salespeople are in an interesting position. More times than not, they start from scratch to build a customer base. But the reality is this: They must learn to make that customer connection!

We recommend they focus on the appointment. That's the purpose. Getting the appointment becomes the sale in this case. And, in this case, there is no substitute for initial activity. The fastest, most efficient way to generate that activity is to learn to use the phone in a simple, focused way.

YOU FOCUS ON GETTING THE APPOINTMENT!

Here is a structure that can start you on the road to winning. Notice the theme: I don't know and I need help.

1.   You identify yourself and your company.

2.   You state the purpose of the call.

3.   When you reach the right person, you ask for an appointment and, without pausing, suggest two times. You use an alternate close.

4.   You confirm the time and the place and thank them.

5.   You follow up with a note or a letter.

Here is the model "fleshed out" to fit a temporary hiring service.

"Good morning. I'm (your name, your company) and I'm wondering if you can help me? Could you tell me who in your company is responsible for hiring part-time workers when you use them? (You get a name and a title, if possible.) Would you connect me, please?"

"Good morning, (their name). I'm (your name, your company) and I've been advised you are the person who handles temporary hiring at (their company). My special reason for calling you is to arrange an appointment to determine if our services would fit your company. Would tomorrow at 1:30 be convenient for you, or would sometime Wednesday be better for you? (You arrange the time and day.) I appreciate this opportunity. I'll see you at (time) on (day), and thank you very much."

Your question now might be: "Will this work for me?" Yes, it will. It will improve your averages. You will be pleasantly surprised. The reason it works is the focus of the call. Your purpose is to get an appointment. The technique is assertive, but not aggressive. You use a specific time first. (Example) Would 1:30 tomorrow be convenient for you, or would sometime on Wednesday be better? The specific time puts some pressure on the other person. Most of the time they will decline that, but will negotiate a later time with you. In other words, you have shifted from a specific request to a general request. You let them choose. The appointment is the payoff.

SKILL PRACTICE

In the space below, write down your own model. Do it now. Your first draft may not be exactly what you want. Polish it. Keep it simple. Follow the outline. Make it your words and you'll be comfortable with it.

Good morning. _____

_____

_____

_____

_____

_____

_____

OK? You like it? Now copy it on a 3 x 5 card and put it by the phone when you make your calls so you can follow along with it.

LEARNER salespeople have learned to handle the rejection that goes with working the phone or just walking into a business and attempting to secure an appointment. They have learned something else about selling, and that is simply that it is easier for most folks to say no than it is to say yes. Someone has said we are living in a world of "push-button attention spans, fast forgetting and tentative commitment." And that all ties into using the telephone today in selling.

We made the point to the NOVICE about that final step in getting an appointment. It was to "tie it down." A sales rep in Florida said that she would do this with a person who had stood her up several times. In the tie down step she would say: "Now, Larry, I'm

writing this in ink this time. Is that OK?" She needed some way to
get the point across that tentative commitment wasn't good enough.
She wanted an appointment!

People aren't really bad. People aren't naturally cruel. People
don't intend to dish out rejection. But people are people. They have
short attention spans, they forget fast because one crisis replaces
another and they tend not to make firm commitments. That's just life
in the fast lane these days.

Think about your own life. How many times are you offered
the opportunity to buy each day? How many times does some person ask you to do something every day? How many offers you
can't refuse do you get every day? How many different items do
you have on your agenda today? And if you have focused yourself today, how many times will you say no? And aren't there
times when you reconsider that first reaction, then work out some
sort of compromise?

Some possible responses to the first turndown follow. They are
models[1] that have proven very useful to learners. They help the
learner give the other person a second chance to respond favorably.
Not all of them work every time, but most of them work a surpris-
ing number of times!

PLACE A COPY OF THIS SHEET IN FRONT OF YOU WHEN YOU MAKE TELE-
PHONE PROSPECT CALLS.

OBJECTION	POSSIBLE RESPONSE
No!	That might be a good decision. Let me ask — was there a reason you responded that way?
Possibly.	That's good. Could we check the calendar? What day are you looking at? (If you are already booked full that day, ask for an alternative date.) That date looks good. Now, would you like to pick a time?
I don't have time to see salespeople!	That's a very understandable statement, since we've had no opportunity to get acquainted. Sounds to me like that's final. Do you feel that's the case?
We aren't interested!	I can appreciate your response. Could I ask how you know that?
I'm not the person you want to talk to.	No problem. (VERY IMPORTANT LINE) Would you be kind enough to tell me who I should be talking to?

I don't have time today.	It sounds like I've hit you at a poor time, and I apologize for that. Could I call you early tomorrow, or could you tell me when it would be more convenient to call?

SALES LETTERS

THERE ARE SOME BASIC ELEMENTS FOR BRINGING SALES LETTERS ALIVE AND INCREASING THE EFFECTIVENESS OF YOUR EFFORTS.

1. Use an effective, attention-getting and personal opening whenever possible.

2. Put key selling points in short paragraphs. Make them stand out.

3. Use narrow margins when possible.

4. Use present tense when possible. Use vivid words when possible. Keep sentences short.

5. Present proof or evidence of your statements.

6. Ask for some type of action at the end of the letter. Make the final paragraph "move the needle" if you can.

Writing effective sales letters can increase the odds of selling. Here are five specific payoffs that good sales letters can get for you:

1. Increase the odds you will get an appointment.

2. Increase the customer perception they are dealing with a professional.

3. Provide written agreement after a discovery call.

4. Provide tangible evidence of your interest in the customer.

5. Convert a sale into a customer relationship.

AFTER YOU HAVE WRITTEN A LETTER, EDIT IT. TAKE OUT UNNECESSARY WORDS. ASK YOURSELF THE FOLLOWING QUESTIONS:

1. If I received this letter on a busy morning, would I read the opening paragraph?

2. Would receiving this letter make me want to do business with the writer?

3. Does the letter contain an important message?

4. If I received this letter, would I act on it or would I throw it away?

WHEN CONSIDERING THE SUCCESS RATIO OF YOUR SALES LETTERS, CONSIDER THIS POINT: MOST DIRECT MAIL PRODUCES A RESPONSE RATE OF ABOUT 2 PERCENT. WHEN YOU SEND 100 LETTERS, YOU CAN EXPECT A RESPONSE FROM 2 PEOPLE. THAT SAYS RESPONSE TO AN ORDINARY LETTER ISN'T GREAT!

But don't be discouraged by this ratio. Letters can penetrate where you sometimes can't. Letters can reach people who might not return a phone call. Remember, we're talking percentages and odds. Small percentages can often turn into big sales.

SOME SMALL THINGS THAT CAN PAY OFF BIG

1. Remember the power of the other person's name. Use it whenever you can in your letter.

2. Remember the power of "you." Write the letter to them.

3. Use a P.S. when possible.
    P.S. Don't forget the P.S. is the second most read part of a letter.

The COMPETENT sellers understand that the focus on making a customer connection is getting that first appointment. They have learned to use any means fair and ethical to meet the "hard-to-get-to-know" person. But they also understand there is a place for basic technique, and that includes the business letter.

They will often use a version of the short, punchy letter below.

APPOINTMENT LETTER MODEL

You are, (name)

… difficult to reach by telephone, according to your secretary. I can appreciate that.

It also tells me something positive. You are a busy person.

I'm wondering, would you help me?

My special reason for wanting to arrange an appointment with you is to explore the possibility that the services and concepts we at (company) have developed for other successful businesses like (name of client) could have a value to you. I would like to get your opinion of this possibility.

My call early next week will be to arrange an appointment for later in the week. I would appreciate your consideration.

Sincerely,

REFERRAL LETTER

Name of Prospect

A few days ago, (name, being careful about Miss, Mrs. or Ms.), I was with (name of your referral) completing some plans we had developed for their advertising campaign at (company name).

(Name of referral) was very pleased with the manner in which our organization had been able to provide (company) with some enhanced values. We demonstrated we could provide more advertising impact.

(Select a brief description of what you did for your referral. We used "provide more advertising impact.")

I asked him/her about names of other businesses that might profit from our advertising ideas and was given your name. I promised I would contact you.

The special purpose of this letter is to introduce myself and ask for an opportunity to meet you personally.

I will be calling you for an appointment and would appreciate your consideration.

Sincerely,

(The key line in this letter is "I promised (contact name) I would contact you." "Promise" is the key word.)

Now, when you call, you can say: "I promised (contact name) I would be in contact with you." You are keeping a promise.

ADAPTING THE REFERRAL LETTER

Using the previous model letter as a guide, this is the way that letter might look if it were adapted to real estate selling.

A few days ago, (name, being careful about Miss, Mrs. or Ms.), I was with (name of your referral) completing some details on the sale of their home.

(Name of referral) was very pleased with the manner in which our company had been able to provide them with special service. We had demonstrated to them personal attention that allowed them to sell their home quickly.

I asked him/her about names of people in their circle of acquain-
tances who might be selling or buying a home in the near
future and they suggested your name. I promised I would contact you.

The special purpose of this letter is to introduce myself and ask for
an opportunity to meet you personally.

I will be calling you for an appointment and would appreciate your
consideration.

Sincerely,

SKILL PRACTICE

In the space provided below, list the last two sales you have made
and fill in the other information called for.

SALE #1

Name of company

Item purchased

Decision maker

Advocate

Things you did to support this sale.

a.

b.

c.

How might you ask the persons involved for other referrals,
either within that organization or similar organizations? Write out
how you might phrase your request for their help.

SALE #2

Name of company

Item purchased

Decision maker

Advocate

Things you did to support this sale.

a.

b.

c.

> How might you ask the persons involved for other referrals, either within that organization or similar organizations? Write out how you might phrase your request for their help.

ASSUMED CONSENT LETTER

Date _____

Dear Mr./Mrs. _____,

On Tuesday, February 16, I visited your office to share with you systems, programs and concepts we developed to increase productivity and improve performance at (name of your reference or present successful client).

Your secretary suggested you were in a meeting. (REASON YOU COULDN'T GET IN)

We believe these same or similar systems are important to your company (agency/department). I'll return to your office the morning of (DATE). I look forward to meeting with you at that time.

Sincerely,

ON USING SMALL JEWELS FOR BIG CALLS

Let's say you are a NOVICE and you're calling on a business and you don't have any names. You meet the receptionist or secretary.

Good morning. I'm hopeful you can help me, please. I'd like to speak to (the manager of the company) (the administrator of the hospital) (go to the top). Could you tell me who that would be, please?

THEY GIVE YOU A NAME.

Thank you. Would you please tell (the name) that (your name) (from your company) is here to see him/her.

THEY ASK FOR A REASON: WHAT DO YOU WANT?

The purpose of my call this morning (this afternoon) is to meet (their name) and discuss some possible mutual interests and arrange an appointment. Would you please tell him/her (your name) is here to see him/her.

YOU ARE PUSHING. BUT YOU ARE PUSHING TO GET IN AND SET AN APPOINTMENT. THERE IS A SENSE OF PROFESSIONALISM AND URGENCY IN THIS APPROACH.

The key part of this technique is that you avoid questions like:

Are they in? Are they busy? Would they have time to see me?

It's "Good morning. Would you please tell (your target) that (your name) from (your company) is here to see him/her?"

Your purpose is to meet them. What you will do is quickly determine if you have mutual interests. You will then set an appointment.

Suppose they want to know more. Have it neatly ready for them. "We're working closely with other companies very similar to this one. We use a (system) (product) (an approach) that (have the benefit ready: cuts costs, improves morale, increases traffic, reduces costly delays). I believe (name of target) could quickly determine if this had a value for your company. Could you tell him/her I'm here, please."

Examine this technique. The purpose is to get into see somebody. But, the stated purpose is not to sell them; rather, it is to allow them to make a decision, to get their opinion. It is a slightly different type of positioning. Suppose they want still more information.

"Well, perhaps you could help me. Let me ask you a few questions, please." (And you ask questions you would have asked of your target.)

They refer you to another person.

"Before I meet them, could I ask you this? Assuming that (your new name) would be favorably impressed with my idea, would he/she be the person who would make a decision?"

Please understand when we suggest models like these, we're not suggesting you use them verbatim. They contain some key words for your consideration. But they are meant to be conceptual. Take the concept and adapt it to your use. The concepts will work!

KEY TECHNIQUES OF HIGH-PERFORMANCE SELLING

"Would tomorrow at 3:30 in the afternoon be good for you or would <u>sometime Wednesday fit better?</u>"

Then, tie down the agreement.

Try using this key technique for getting appointments: Ask for an appointment by using a specific time and a general time.

This is a power technique because:

1. The use of the specific time will tend to increase tension.

2. The use of a general time will tend to reduce tension.

3. A repeated statement about the appointment will tie it down.

THE POWER IS IN THE TECHNIQUE. MODEL THE TECHNIQUE TO FIT YOUR STYLE. PRACTICE IT UNTIL YOU ARE COMFORTABLE WITH IT, USING YOUR WORDS AND YOUR PACING.

::

QUESTIONS ... AND IF YOU DON'T KNOW WHERE YOU ARE GOING IT DOESN'T MATTER WHERE YOU ARE

CHAPTER 13

QUESTIONS ... AND IF YOU DON'T KNOW WHERE YOU ARE GOING IT DOESN'T MATTER WHERE YOU ARE

F ew people ever started out to be in sales. We taught sales for several years in a college. First, the curriculum committee handled the suggested course like it was some social disease. Only after considerable discussion did they allow it to be offered.

If you check course offerings at most colleges, you will find few schools offering courses in selling. We sometimes ask in a large workshop: "How many of you planned to be in sales when you went into high school?" No hands go up. "How many planned to go into sales when you entered college?" Maybe seven or eight hands go up.

Which explains, to some small degree, why sales training companies and sales consultants have prospered these past few years. Add to this lack of formal training the tremendous changes in selling, plus the awesome pressure of the marketplace on marketing and selling, and it's small wonder that selling, as a profession, has enjoyed increased interest and popularity.

Say "selling" to the average person and they will respond with Harold Hill and 76 trombones, or Willy Loman from *Death of a Salesman*. Despite this misconception, salespeople in the United States today are the highest-paid profession. More people in the high-income brackets are in sales than any other profession. Yet the image of the "product peddler" or the "pitchman" persists.

Sometime in the 1970s, the idea of the "product peddler" or of pitching product began to get a little less stylish. There was a nagging suspicion that this style of selling just wasn't as effective as it once was. Major companies began to inspect their return on investment in this type of selling. They began to change and adapt their selling efforts. Out of this quiet change came a new hula hoop. Questions became the answers. All you had to do was ask questions!

Now, we had a whole new array of questions.

We had open questions and closed questions, permission questions and checking questions, fact-finding questions and feeling-finding questions; we had customer needs analysis; we had "Tell Me" questionnaires. We may even have had questions to ask when you couldn't think of a question.

Let's go back a step and look at what is in the customer's head, or the prospect's, before we step up and ask if we "could just ask you a few questions." If the end result of the sales process is to get buyers to want to commit to some sort of action, to agree to purchase, to install a pilot program, to try the machine for two weeks, to take it to the buying committee, to take it to the client, then before we get to the question stage we need to see it from their point of view. They make several commitments *before* we ever get to questions.

For instance, they usually make a commitment to time. Even the telemarketer selling rug cleaning must get the person on the phone to hear the pitch. That is a brief commitment of time. Second, the buyer makes a commitment to reveal information when you start asking questions. This is perhaps the toughest part of selling insurance. The bigger a proposed policy, the more intimate the questions an insurance counselor must ask. Your present income, your marital status, your health, what insurance you already have — all questions that must be asked so a recommendation can be positioned.

And, third, if you ask for an appointment, the buyer has made a commitment to look and listen. The reality of selling today is that often the sellers must give information before getting it. They must position themselves, sometimes in a minimum amount of time, as being credible enough to deserve a buyer commitment to take time, to reveal information and to look and listen. In short, that buyer has made three decisions before you really earn the opportunity to ask questions in great detail.

This ties back to your mission as a salesperson. Is it to make calls? See some prospect? Go make a few pitches? Or is it to get decisions? In the end, obtain a decision that will result in a commitment.

High-performance selling requires a different mindset. A salesperson must have this to make appointments. We have been using the words "comfort" and "credibility" because they work together. If you can establish credibility, there is a feeling of comfort on the part of the buyer. You must have "comfort" and "credibility" to establish "mutuality" — that feeling that you have something in common or something of mutual benefit. Sometimes, this is called "building rapport" or "gaining confidence." Actually, it is building a base of knowledge quickly about the other person so you can understand their belief system and align your style of selling and product with his or her belief system.

We call this step "positioning," and it is simply taking what they give you — the views, the information, the opinions — and aligning yourself and your product or services with those beliefs.

In our definition of "credibility," we include trust, mutuality, comfort and the result of these three items. This allows you to do your positioning. It looks like this:

Again, let's look at this issue through your belief system. How

CHARACTERISTICS	RESULTS IN ...	FOR THE GOAL OF:
		Positioning your product or service and
1. Honesty	1. Comfort	yourself so the
2. Sincerity	2. Mutuality	prospect wants to give you:
3. Courtesy	3. Trust	
		1. Time
	All of which build	2. Information
	CREDIBILITY	3. Look and Listen

did you choose your doctor? Did you ask somebody? Did one doctor send you to another? Did you learn of a doctor through a health club? And how did you select your health club? What about your mechanic? When your car was ill, how did you select the place of treatment? An authorized dealer? Did a friend tell you of a good mechanic? You needed help with financial planning. Did you just thumb through the Yellow Pages? Or did you locate somebody who was credible? You needed life insurance, so you thought of the rock, or the cavalry, or the good hands — somewhere in your belief system you had a reason for making the choice you did. And the more important your decision, the more you depended upon your belief system.

Something, someone, some idea, made you believe one of the following would happen:

1.   You could trust your source, so the name you got was credible.

2.   You could solve a problem.

3.   There was a new offering, a new product or new service.

4.   There was a creative way to provide a solution to your need.

5.   There was an event that you wanted to be part of.

6.   There was something that provided a payoff or benefit you wanted.

Six clues, then, for your consideration on how to position yourself as deserving a favorable response to those first three buyer decisions. Six credible reasons for an appointment.

1.   You have a third-party reference.

2.   You position yourself as solving problems.

3.   You have a new offering, a new product or service; you have new information.

4.   You provide another possibility, a creative way to accomplish a goal.

5.   You offer participation in an event, a plan, a concept.

6.   You can provide a payoff or benefit.

These are not listed in order of preference. We can tell you that, in our opinion, the sixth one is perhaps the toughest to work with, because you are shooting blind. Your payoff or benefit must fit the perceived needs of the buyer. For instance, if you were selling a landscaping service, any benefit you could offer would be of little interest to an apartment dweller.

The fourth question in the buyer's mind, whenever you approach, is "why choose you?" The reality of our world today is that, as buyers, we are offered a wide variety of choices and options. When we lived in a world of more scarcity, we could not be as discriminating. Said another way: When housing is scarce, we must be less selective in what we choose as a home. When we think an offer ends tonight, we may be more likely to decide to buy. When a play is presented only three nights, we are more likely to go one of those nights. Scarcity has a value of its own. But there is no great scarcity of salespeople, except those who really are professional resources. And they do their prospecting almost entirely by using the third-party reference.

When you are making that first call, getting that first customer connection, you need to position yourself as credible. You need a credible reason to ask for time, to ask questions, to get them to look and listen.

Some salespeople believe they can manipulate their way into the first call. Some companies use a survey of some sort. Some sales-people take the social way by asking for luncheon appointments. We believe there is no substitute for opening with a credible business reason for wanting to meet with somebody. Inspect our list again. Every one of those six reasons we gave you is completely credible. One of those, possibly more, could be applicable to what you sell. A straight-forward phone call, a letter to introduce yourself, a letter with a piece of information of value to the prospect — all or any of these can contain a credible business reason for making the connection. There are no substitutes for honesty, sincerity and courtesy.

In this regard, we can learn something from advertising. Many advertising people believe that a positioning statement says very clearly what a product does. In other words: "This is the product that _____." You've heard that line completed in many ways: "Gets dishes clean faster." "Prevents cavities." "Relieves headaches faster." If we adapted this to selling and positioning ourselves, it would be: "I am the person who _____" or "We are the company that _____" or "I represent the product that _____." All of these answer the question: "Why you?"

Salespeople have only a few ways to establish credibility. One is to earn it. That is hard to do when you have never done business with a prospect. That is why the third-party reference is effective. You use the credibility you have established with another customer to establish it with the prospect.

The other way you gain credibility could be the reputation of your product or company. Using this in your opening statement can have validity. The only other way to have credibility is to position yourself properly.

The credible business reason for wanting an appointment goes back to your purpose. If you have that clearly in mind, and state it briefly and clearly, the other person is more likely to decide in the affirmative. Remember, credibility, or lack of it, is one of the four basic reasons people don't buy.

Let's take this concept of credibility one step further. When you have it with a customer, how did you earn it? Think of present customers. How have you earned your credibility? We submit you earned it by using the following:

Your associations. Groups to which you belong, the company you work for, the people you work with, the professionalism of your support people, if you have those.

Your knowledge. Your technical background and expertise, your ability to solve problems, to be creative, even your educational background or continuing education. Real estate and life insurance both provide advanced training that enhances your image and knowledge base.

Your experience. Other companies or organizations you have as clients, letters of reference, teams with which you have worked, projects you have successfully completed. Often, outstanding community work can enhance your business credibility.

Your image. Everybody creates an image. All human beings judge other human beings. Usually, this judgment is based upon our own belief system. Even on the telephone, we create an image. If we are well-spoken, polite, speak clearly, even businesslike, we create an image. We create a better image of credibility than if we are crude in language, rude, mumble and ramble in our opening statement. Propriety is certainly a part of building credibility. How we present ourselves, our mannerisms, our tone of voice, our body language, how we dress — all these, if done properly, build our case for credibility.

Credibility also goes through the four passages. Let us trace those and see if they fit your experience:

THE NOVICE

> Those on the first level of selling are short on experience. They are short on self-assurance. They are willing to try different techniques, not always their own. Consequently, they may often open the phone call sounding mechanical or unsure of themselves. There is only one way out of this level of selling. Keep your opening positioning statement simple and straightforward. Clearly state who you are, who you are with and the purpose of your call.

MODEL   Good morning. (use their name, if possible). I'm Nancy Smith with Southside Realty. My special reason for calling this morning is to arrange an appointment with you to discuss listing your home should you decide at some time to sell. Would that be possible?

THE LEARNER

> The learning level of selling can often be where selling skill begins to dip and desire begins to wane. The companies who have studied the progression of their salespeople tell us that the end of the first 90 days in selling is a crucial time. The company is convinced it hired people who were ready and willing, but they

aren't yet able. That is, the people still want to succeed, so the company takes great care to program its
salespeople for success.

MOST SALESPEOPLE ARE PROGRAMMED FOR FAILURE, BUT THEY ARE
DESIGNED FOR SUCCESS.

Let's study that statement. If you are in sales, think about how
you got started. In real estate, you had no prospects. You worked
your circle of friends, maybe even your relatives. You sold some of
these. Then you got to meet the world. It wasn't as friendly as your
close circle. You began to get more rejection. You had to learn to
handle that. Perhaps you went into advertising sales. You had no list
of customers, only some discards from other salespeople. You had
very little training. You were literally programmed for failure. But,
if you wanted to be in sales, you believed you were designed for
success.

You decide, within 90 days, whether sales is for you. You may
stay with it a while longer, but you've made that unconscious decision. But wait! If you go into social work, you'll be in sales. It's very
subtle, but you'll sell ideas and concepts. If you are a parent, you'll
be in sales. You will mold and develop children, and that is a subtle
kind of selling. If you go into teaching, and you're good at it, you'll
be selling ideas. And if you aspire to management and leadership,
you'll really be in sales! And, as the preacher said to the frightened
passenger on the airplane when the passenger requested a prayer for
safety: "I'm not the Lord, I'm just his salesman."

Learners begin to experiment with different techniques. They
get a little more comfortable. They learn, often through trial and
error, what works for them. They learn that people don't reject them
personally. The prospect's belief system just doesn't include talking
to salespeople. They begin to look at different ways to position
themselves in that initial contact. If you are in that learning passage,
you'll go back and consider our list of six ways to position yourself
for credibility. You'll see some ways to adapt one or two of those
methods to your style.

THE COMPETENT

The Competents have learned to position themselves
for credibility by adapting to the situation. They have
learned to find out as much about the prospect as possible before they call or write. They have learned to use
bridging articles from trade magazines, and they
bridge from a general subject to a specific idea. They
have good self-talk by now. They feel they are OK and

that there are people out there who genuinely need what they sell. But they have also learned that salespeople are like snowflakes. No two sell exactly the same. They have taken good ideas and sound techniques and adapted them to their style of selling.

MODEL   Good morning, (name). I'm Boyd Caldwell with (name of insurance company), and I see by the business news that you recently moved into management with (their company.) We have been working with a number of young businessmen, like you, helping them with a sound plan for personal investment. I'd like to send you an article on this subject, written by one of our senior people, that would allow you to decide if the time is right for you to consider such a plan. An appointment with you would be our next step. I'll ask a few questions and, after 10 minutes, you can decide whether you want to continue our discussion. Does that sound like a reasonable approach to you?

If you are at that third level, inspect this positioning statement. It is brief, businesslike, not assumptive, states a purpose, a process and a payoff; and it calls for a decision. In short, it builds credibility!

THE PROFESSIONAL

Professionals usually work with a third-party reference. They let their clients open doors for them. Often, they have a very good idea of what it costs them to develop a new customer. They know the "cost of the new customer," and they realize a fully leveraged present customer may be the best way to get more business. So they are constantly upgrading present customers, selling additional items from their line, installing new systems, improving the customer position, anticipating needs and opportunities for the customer. But they also realize there is always some attrition of accounts. People move, customers go out of business. So there is always a need for a certain amount of prospecting for new business. They will spend a certain amount of time acquiring new customers, and it is not unusual for them to give that percentage in a number, like 15 percent. That's part of their self-discipline, part of their business plan, part of their return on investment of time and energy.

MODEL   (Use client name), I got your name from D.P. Davidson in (another city.) I'm (your name) with Bateman Earth Moving Equipment. I was told by Mr. Davidson you had just successfully bid several large contracts and might have a need for equipment. From what he told me about your operation, it would seem logical that some of our lines, especially some of our new equipment, might have a particular use for you at this time. I'm going to be in your area next week and would like to see you early on Tuesday morning or perhaps some-time Wednesday, if that would work for you. Could we arrange a date?

In this model, you'll hear several subtle ways the salesperson has built credibility. First, he has used a respected third-party reference. He knows something about the "operation," which is using their language. He teases a little about "new equipment" and uses more trade talk with "lines" to indicate size or range of choices. He pushes a little for a date, but that works with people who are in a world of push, especially if it's moving dirt. He uses a request for an early appointment, because he knows that contractors usually start early. In short, as nearly as possible, he has aligned his initial call into the belief system of that prospective customer. He has positioned himself as credible in a very short period of time.

Moving one step further, let's assume that your letter or call for an appointment results in a contact with the buyer. That person wants to do a little screening or sorting. So he begins by asking the salesperson some questions. He wants a little more information before deciding to see you in person. Some people are like that. They use the telephone as a safety instrument. Others are simply busy and they want information that will help them make a decision. Again, we come back to that question of "why you?" They are evaluating you, so they open up a little and seem to want to talk. Here are some general guidelines that can help at that stage of the process, if you're working on the phone.

1. *Stay focused.* Don't ramble. If you ask questions, use specific questions that are easily answered. Stick to who-what-when-where-how. Remember, your purpose is to get an appointment so you can develop a customer. You may want to draft some questions ahead of time to be ready for this eventually. Focus on the buyer's present situation.

2. *Don't be an instant expert.* Don't push the credibility by sounding like you know it all, and above all be careful with arrogance. Be careful with name dropping. If mutual business connections come up, acknowledge them in a businesslike way. Think like a trout fisherman. You don't use the biggest fly in your collection, and you don't splash it in the water. You present it as enticingly as

you can. The idea is not to sell your way in, it is to make them want to see you.

3. *Listen intently.* Listen for negatives. Listen for positives. Don't be reluctant to put some pauses in ahead of responses. You may want to take some notes and tell them you are making some notes for possible future reference. Remember, you have no visual to work with, so you need to increase your feedback to them. Use more "that's a good point" ... "that's an interesting view" ... "I can appreciate that" ... "that's helpful information" than you might in a face-to-face call.

4. *Stay Win-Win.* That's a Larry Wilson phrase, Win-Win, and it implies a partnership of sorts. It's a good negotiation technique and, quite often, getting that appointment is a negotiation, so some adaptability and flexibility can be helpful. Phrases like "what's a good time for you?" ... "I'll fit your schedule" ... "whatever works best for you" help build the idea that you want the call to be of benefit to them as well as yourself. And remember, if they are human, they will be wondering what's in it for you.

5. *Sometimes there is a place for a turnaround.* You aren't making much progress with the call, so you simply ask for help. It might be something like this: "It sounds to me that you really aren't sure of a mutual benefit here. Help me, if you would. What could I do, what information could I give you that would help you decide to see me?"

On the following pages, you'll find some exercises intended to help you design credible business reasons for getting an appointment. Select two possible calls you might make in the next two weeks. Write down the name of the account, the name of your buyer or buying influence, then take the list of six credible business reasons we have provided. Put down your positioning statement.

We have provided a guideline to help you get started:

FOR AN APPOINTMENT

1. You have a third-party reference.

2. You can solve a problem.

3. You have a new product, service or offering.

4. You provide a creative way to accomplish a goal or solution.

5. You offer participation in an event or a concept.

6.   You can provide a payoff or a benefit.

NAME OF ACCOUNT

BUYING INFLUENCE _____

WHAT WILL BE YOUR CREDIBLE BUSINESS REASON FOR CONTACTING THIS PERSON? _____

DEVELOP YOUR POSITIONING STATEMENT IN SUCH A WAY THAT IT WILL MAKE THEM WANT TO SEE YOU IN THE VERY NEAR FUTURE.

_____

_____

_____

_____

NAME OF ACCOUNT _____

BUYING INFLUENCE _____

WHAT WILL BE YOUR CREDIBLE BUSINESS REASON FOR CONTACTING THIS PERSON? _____

DEVELOP YOUR POSITIONING STATEMENT IN SUCH A WAY THAT IT WILL MAKE THEM WANT TO SEE YOU IN THE VERY NEAR FUTURE.

_____

_____

_____

_____

Most of the foregoing would be true under the proper circumstances. Not all circumstances today are exactly proper. When we visit with level three and level four salespeople, we find that in their perception they are making fewer sales to just one decision maker. More often, they are faced with a loop of people who are part of the decision-making process. In some instances, those people really can't say "yes" and make a buying decision. But they can say no, or stall the process, or delay the decision making. They may be influential in some way in the selling situation.

For lack of a better term, we call this a sales loop, from the phrase: "I'm trying to keep everybody in the loop." This is used more in communication circles (you'll excuse the pun) and less in sales circles, unless the salesperson is going around in one, and then you will hear them mumble something about "sure wish I could figure out who is doing what to whom and where." Some salespeople may refer to it as "figuring out the pecking order."

The group decision is a tough one to get. The odds that you can handle this type of sale go up when you do learn to "work the loop." Call on a single buyer and you deal with one person, one person's perceptions, one set of objections, one person to close, one person to make the buying decision. It's all wrapped up in one person.

Once upon a time there was a wonderful phrase in selling. The man who used it quite often was one of the most enthusiastic, dedicated and high-energy salespeople I have ever met. He would say: "Never take no from a person who can't say yes." And there was a time in selling, and in management, when that was probably very good advice. There were more single decision makers in those days.

Today, however, you have something in management called "empowerment," and top management is passing decision-making power down the line. In selling technology or machine equipment today, if the salesperson hasn't sold "the line" to those people on the line who will use the actual product, he isn't going to make the sale. In selling advertising today, if the store manager hasn't been sold on the value of the idea, corporate isn't going to make a move. It isn't a case of not taking "no" from somebody who can't say "yes," it's a case of finding all the people who will be part of the decision-making process.

This means today's high-performance salesperson must learn how to "work the loop" ... "touch all the bases" ... "find out who the players are" ... "penetrate the system." Call it by whatever name, it is group selling.

Information must be gathered from a number of sources. This takes what is often called a sales strategy. In some selling systems, the sales team is taught to focus on the roles people play. Who is the advocate, the person who can help you, aid your cause? Who is the gatekeeper, the person who controls the budget? Who is the user, the person who will actually use the product or service? Who is the implementer, the person who starts the ball rolling but may not make a final decision?

The way to improve selling skills is to keep the simple simple, and make the complex simple. Let's go back to where we started with the sales call and the suggestion of a three-step mindset. The salesperson says three things to himself: "What is my purpose?" "What is my process?" "What is the payoff?"

Now, in "working the loop," or strategic selling, what changes?

Certainly, the purpose is still to get a decision or make a sale. As a prelude to that purpose, you may have a lot of appointment calls, penetration calls and information-seeking calls.

Certainly, the payoff is the ultimate sale. But, along the way, salespeople have a lot of picnics before they get to the banquet. Good information is a payoff. A statement of support is a payoff. A statement like: "I'll recommend it" is a payoff. The little payoffs are picnics. They indicate progress. Enjoy them! They build success.

So, let's keep it simple. Let's focus on the process, because that's where the game really changes. The focus of the salesperson must be expanded. You really need to mind your Ps and Qs, to borrow from an old childhood phrase. Qs are the questions. You mind them. In the Ps, there is a need to pay attention to at least three.

There must be a focus on the Players. Who are the players? There are a lot of people in this loop. Who will help me win this game? The salespeople start with an inventory of the players. They work from player to player; they collect names, what the names do, how they fit into the loop, what can they do for or against the possible proposal.

Now, think in terms of questions that establish authority, territory and roles within an organization. Let us give you some examples. The quality of question can reveal the level of expertise. Tell us what level of salesperson would use each of the above questions:

QUESTION	LEVEL OF SALESPERSON
What does Mark over in marketing do?	_____
If something for this department cost over $10,000, who would make that buying decision?	_____
You folks recently bought a whole new computer system. How did you go about making that decision?	_____
How much stroke does Lonnie have over in accounting?	_____
Your organization has a seemingly sophisticated way at coming about making a buying decision on insurance.	_____
Would you be in a position to help me on that?	_____

Your line people tell me they
buck their recommendation to
you. Would that be a fair way to
describe the system?

This leads to the second P of our Ps and Qs analogy: the way each player sees the position. Not every person may have the idea of the position. In fact, management may see the position one way and the line may see it another way. Accounting may see it one way; sales will see it another way. Not every person will agree; is it urgency, gain, maintenance or euphoria?

Now, questions must be stated to leave room for opinion, feeling and intuition. Again, play the game with us. These questions fit which level of selling?

QUESTION   LEVEL OF SELLING

In your opinion, then, it is really a
matter of poor field follow-up?

Without laying any blame, where
do you think the old point of sale
material broke down?

Would you say, then, it was a
matter of timing or of execution?

So, you're telling me things just
sort of got screwed up?

Let's look at the previous
approach from an objective view.
Suppose you were to do it again,
what might you do differently?

By now, you're getting pretty good at the game, aren't you? You can say to yourself: "I said that once and I lived to regret it." Or, on the other side, you might say: "That's a neat way to phrase that. I'll just try that."

So, you start with questions that will give you the players, then you use questions that will help you determine their perception of the position or positions. In the general context of this approach, you are ready to use questions that will locate the priorities of the players, which produce buying criteria.

To the third P of this analogy: All people, in whatever walk of life, have discomforts and hopes. Some have big problems, some have insurmountable problems, some have nagging problems, some have in-law problems. All of what they describe as problems, real or perceived, have values. It is a question of priorities. And, for most people, their priorities of their discomforts or hopes are opinions, feelings, perhaps even views shared with the group or the crowd.

The salesperson who probes for priorities will use opinion questions — soft, feeling-finding questions — and will have a careful list of priorities of the involved players when they are selling the group or working the loop. Taken from a variety of industries, here are some samples. See if these could be modified to your field of selling:

"So, if it were a choice between the lot size and having a spare bedroom, which would you feel was most important?"

"It seems to me we have three issues here. One is the total budget you will have for health insurance. Two is the spread of coverage you want for all employees. And three is whether you want to add dental care as an employee option. Where would you suggest we start as a top priority?"

"You have indicated that having more traffic on the first part of the week is one of your priorities, and yet you've said that table turn on the weekend is really where you make your profit. In terms of percentages, where would you divide the importance of each?"

"You indicated that fuel consumption was important in your selection of a tractor and that general maintenance of the machine was important. You've also indicated you wanted equipment that would pull a five-foot bush hog rather than the standard four-foot rig. To help me here get a hold on your situation, on a scale on one to ten, give me a value of these two things."

Whether it is corporate housing, company insurance, a restaurant chain or a city park department, in the case of all questions, no one person would make the decision. The final decision would be shrouded someplace in a loop.

When working such a group sale, or "working the loop," sellers can eliminate a lot of the fog or mist when they simply shift the "process" part of purpose-process-payoff to a three-P application.

That focus involves three areas: (1) Who are the players? What roles do they play in the selling situation? (2) What is their image of reality of the position? Is it urgency, gain, maintenance or euphoria? (3) What are their priorities?

Several points might be worth summarizing in this rather lengthy exploration of securing appointments, prospecting, qualifying and "working the loop."

1. As the skill level of selling goes up, the reliance on questions and getting the buyer to want to talk goes up.

2. Questions are not necessarily a means to gain control of the buyer. Rather, questions are a way to focus the direction of the meeting. It isn't the buyer the seller should control, it is the direction of the meeting.

3. The best way to learn to use questions is to write them down ahead of time. Prepare a road map of questions that will keep the customer or prospect focused on the issue at hand.

4. As skill with questions increases, the questions follow two paths of information: One of these is product needs, the other is personal needs.

5. There are two key techniques with this chapter on questions. Study them and do a little rehearsing. Both will pay rich dividends regardless of your present level of selling. Either you will get better or you'll sharpen the saw, or both.

As a final quest for complete information, the salesperson summarizes what has been agreed upon using recovery questions and confirmation questions. Phrases like "you said ... as I recall ... you made three points ... I believe you said your priority was ... you wanted a comfortable ride ... you gave me a budget goal of ... we agreed that February 15th was a reasonable date" provide a replay for complete understanding. The final question in the last step is probably a confirmation question, such as: "Did I describe our understanding from your point of view?" or: "Well, if we have agreement on that information, what do you see as the next step?"

In other words, the mindset of the fourth-level salesperson is: "I'm going into this stage of the sales process to get a decision." At the end of this stage of the process, the buyer is revealing the situation, his priorities and his values. What is the buyer image of reality and perception of probability? The salespeople will decide whether they understand what the buyer needs in terms of product and personal expectations. If they decide they understand what solution they are looking for, then they have successfully completed that phase of the process and are ready to move forward.

One final step is involved. They will jointly decide what the buyer will do next and what the salesperson will do next, and they will reach an agreement on that. In other words, there is a mutual commitment to action. Only then will the sellers have used questions as the tools they can be, to really penetrate the buyer belief system.

KEY TECHNIQUES OF HIGH-PERFORMANCE SELLING SUMMARIZED

"I saw this article in the Wall Street Journal and wondered if the point in the article would apply to your business."

Bridging from a news article or a trade journal is a key technique. Use general material, or news stories, or general research to bridge from a very general subject to a very specific subject.

This is a power technique because:

1. The open question about the general subject reduces the tension and sets the climate for more specific questions. You control the discussion.

2. You clearly establish that you are interested in the customer.

3. You set the stage for the client perception of "added value."

THE POWER IS IN THE TECHNIQUE. MODEL THE TECHNIQUE TO FIT YOUR STYLE. PRACTICE IT UNTIL YOU ARE COMFORTABLE WITH IT, USING YOUR WORDS AND YOUR PACING.

> "That's an interesting point and from
> your viewpoint, probably understandable."

A softening statement is several things. It is a verbal pause before you respond; it is a bridge between two possible different options; it is a gentle way to extend a little empathy; it is a great way to keep a discussion on a civilized level.

1. Recognize the other person's point of view or position. This can be done with short phrases like:

    "That's interesting."

    "I can understand your position."

    "That's certainly a point worth considering."

    "I can understand where you're coming from."

2. Avoid, when possible, the personal tie. Examples:

    "I know how you feel."

    "That always happens to me too."

"I can sure relate to how you feel."

There are two keys to this technique which will help produce high performance:

1.   It maintains the relationship and reduces the tension.

2.   It allows you to separate the people and the problem. You tend to focus more on the issue, the point and the position.

THE POWER IS IN THE TECHNIQUE. MODEL THE TECHNIQUE TO FIT YOUR STYLE. PRACTICE IT UNTIL YOU ARE COMFORTABLE WITH IT, USING YOUR WORDS AND YOUR PACING.

::

NOW WE'RE READY TO THINK ABOUT QUESTIONS

CHAPTER 14

NOW WE'RE READY TO THINK ABOUT QUESTIONS

E arlier we had intimated that questions are not the end-all in professional selling. Questions are not the issue. The issue is how to use questions to get the information you need to determine whether your product or service will fit the need, the expectation or the solution the prospect or buyer has in mind. Just asking questions will not help you locate the buyer belief system. Getting the right information, however, will help you do that.

Questions are tools. What kind you use is less important than how you use them. The wrong question at the wrong time can defeat your purpose. Your purpose is to find out what they have and what they want, to find out their attitude about the priority or importance of their want, and to learn if your solution will fit.

Let's go back to the matrix and see how the different levels of sales expertise might use questions. As you follow through the matrix, notice that while there is some increased skill in the kind of questions used, the real shift is in the way questions are used. Let's consider this process again in terms of PURPOSE-PROCESS-PAYOFF.

Beginners probably have little grasp of the use of questions if they are naturally high-tell people. Traditional sales training puts a further emphasis on presentation and telling. In fact, less-assertive sales types, those people who tend naturally to ask more questions, often were not hired because of the feeling they were not aggressive enough. When sales training began to teach the use of questions, there was another theory at work. How often have you heard this explanation?

SALES TRAINER: "When you ask a question, who thinks they are in control?"

SALESPERSON: "The buyer."

S.T.:   "Right! But who is really in control?"

S.P.:   "The person asking the question."

S.T.:   "Right, so when you want control, you ask questions, right?"

So, in reality, sales trainers were pushing questions in order to give salespeople a feeling of control. There is some truth to that, but not always a sense of direction.

Consequently, we have had many sales managers tell us something like this: "I have salespeople who really think they are consultants. They go out and ask more #!%$ questions and get more #!%$ information than they can ever use. And you know what happens to it? It sits on their desk and gathers dust. Nothing ever happens, that's what. I want sellers, not question-askers!"

And that is about what happens when people get forms filled out or just ask aimless questions. They come back with a collection of facts and opinions and really don't understand how to transform that collection of questions into information. This misconception probably goes all the way back to Socrates and the so-called Socratic method of teaching. He led people to form their own conclusions with a series of questions. From this came deductive reasoning and inductive reasoning and lots of knowledge taught in communication courses, and then seldom used.

The PURPOSE of questions is to gather information that fills a gap between what you know about a buyer and what you need to know.

The PROCESS of asking questions is to connect questions so that the buyer wants to reveal information, so the seller can learn both buyer product needs and belief system, or personal moods.

The PAYOFF for the seller is insight into the buyer's product needs and personal needs, which enables the seller to position the offering within the framework of the buyer belief system. That position will represent a solution for the buyer that fills both sets of needs — product and personal.

On the following page is the evolution of the use of questions as it fits in the concept of the matrix.

Tracking through this matrix can help you determine, to some extent, where your skill level is now. You can examine each of those four levels and figure out how you sell most of the time. We say most of the time, because it is possible that in any given situation you might be in any one of the four locations. Conditions of a

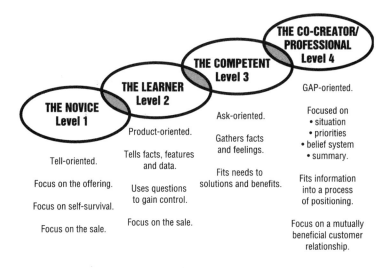

particular situation might demand that you sell in one of the four postures. For instance, in getting a first appointment, even seasoned professionals must go back nearly to the first level. They need to tell who they are and who they are with and the purpose of the call. That's tell-oriented. They need a credible business reason for offering their product or service; they need a good positioning statement. And their purpose, for that moment, is getting an appointment, which at that time is rather self-serving.

So, there is no static or rigid position in any of the four postures. The skill in selling is to be comfortable in any of the four postures and to be constantly pushing that customer connection into the higher level. Another way to look at the matrix is that it is a scale of selling expertise, and any top salesperson has the ability and skill to slide up and down the scale, depending on the circumstances.

Some buyers are somewhat abrasive and hurried and harassed. They are the Mad Hatter types, with places to go, people to see, things to do. They tell you in no uncertain terms that they want the facts, the price and be on your way. At that moment, you must position fast, shoot blind, pitch the heck out of your offering, summarize and do it all with the best pair of tennis shoes in town. You must have the adaptability and flexibility to shift with customer demands. That, or you need the courage to just walk out, which may not be win-win for you, them or your company. On the other hand, there is such a thing as business that produces a poor return.

Level two salespeople, the learners, generally use questions to gain and keep control. They have learned that asking questions is one way to get the buyer to talk to them. That it is generally true. Most people are more willing to talk about their businesses, their interests or themselves than they are interested in hearing about yours. This level of salesperson often manipulates the questions, right? They make a statement and close with a quick question, follow me? They will tuck in a fact and then ask: "Do you agree?" These are statements in disguise. Quite often, they are facts disguised as closed questions to which the other party can only respond: "Yes." Trial attorney types are good at this, right?

Still, at this level of selling, the objective is getting an order or making a sale. It is transactional selling. You have a need, I have a solution. Quite often, the sellers must guess what the buyers want or need. This type of selling also requires that the sellers be skilled at beating down objections. Their style is often a monologue with only a few check-in questions, like "OK?" And on they plunge. Then they ask for the order and the buyer says: "I'll think it over." Now the sellers are forced to open their "handling objections box" and get after it. Funny thing about handling objections this way: The more the buyer discusses his "objection," the deeper he embeds it into his belief system.

This explains why, if you want to manipulate the buyer a little, you turn the objection into a question. "So your question is ..." and back into the box for another fail-safe method of handling the objection. Level four or professional resource-type salespeople really don't encounter many objections. If they do, they probably anticipated them and are ready to align with the concerns and reservations of the buyer. More on that later. Back to questions and the third level of salesperson.

By this passage in a sales career, salespeople are probably much more ask-oriented than tell-oriented. They gather facts and feelings and make an effort to determine task needs and personal needs, so they can fit these against the benefits of their solution when they propose it. They see the sales process as locating a problem and see their role as finding or providing a solution to that problem. They are more focused on the customer and on customer product needs and personal needs. Their solution will involve both task appeals and personal appeals.

At this level of selling, the salespeople probably understand the uses of various kinds of questions. And they probably understand when and how to use them. They use questions to guide the call.

PERMISSION QUESTION:	Essentially a question that requests permission to ask questions. "Might I ask you about that, please?"
CLOSED QUESTION:	A question that requires a YES or NO answer. "Do you like what you are presently using?"
OPEN QUESTION:	A question that requires explanation. "Tell me what you like about what you are using."
FACT-FINDING QUESTION:	A question designed to get facts. "Tell me what models of machines you are using in your offices."
FEELING-FINDING QUESTION:	You are searching for an opinion, a feeling or perhaps an attitude. "What are the reasons you like your present advertising?"
CHECKING QUESTION:	A question that reaffirms you heard what you thought you heard. "Let me see if I understood your last point. You said you had mixed feelings about the neighborhood?"
RECOVERY QUESTION:	Provide mutual agreement. "Last time we visited, you said your budget was being reviewed and you wanted our proposal by the 18th. Is that still the case?"
PRIORITY QUESTION:	Used to establish a relative value. "So, would you say that early week traffic would be your No. 1 concern?"
OPINION QUESTION:	Often used as a substitute for feeling-finding questions. "So tell me, in you opinion, would our proposal appear to meet your needs as we discussed them?"
COMMITMENT QUESTION:	A question designed to test buyer readiness or willingness to do something. "It appears I have visited with all of your people in the decision loop. What would you advise as the next step?"
RESTATEMENT QUESTION:	A question that can tie down an issue for mutual agreement. "So, we have agreed that we will meet again on Tuesday, the 22nd, in the early morning. Is that correct?"

Third-level salespeople — the competent — can use any of these questions with comfort. They know when and how to use them. They are searching for needs, problems, opportunities, all seen through the eyes of the buyer. They are getting facts and feelings about areas that will allow them to fit task appeals and personal appeals to the final solution they recommend.

The fourth-level salesperson, the professional resource or co-creator, uses questions in a slightly different way. The search is more subtle. Often, before these sellers make the call that will result in a discovery agreement, they have done a considerable amount of research on the buyer or prospect. If it is a follow-up call or recontact call, they certainly have knowledge they gained in previous visits. Because of their perspective, they do not view a customer relationship as a static condition. They know that in today's world nothing is certain except change. If their search with the prospect or buyer is partially based upon what the buyer has and wants, they take that same approach with their use of questions. They use their questions as tools to secure different sets of information. We call this approach S E E S, a helpful acronym that helps you remember that the purpose of this call is to see it through the belief system of the buyer.

THE SEES FORMULA

There are four gaps of information the fourth-level salespeople want to fill. The first gap involves the situation. If they know what it was, they search for confirmation of what it was and then determine if it has changed. The gap they want to complete is their information on WHAT IS THE SELLING SITUATION NOW?

In this posture of questioning, they use recovery type questions. They want to verify facts they already have. In essence, they want to make sure they understand the situation, has it changed, who are the players, are there any new ones, are the buying practices still the same, will the specs be the same as we used last time?

But all these questions are focused on one specific area. The gap they want to fill in their information is DO I HAVE THE RIGHT INFORMATION ABOUT YOUR PRESENT SITUATION. And then, do I understand it correctly? The SELLING SITUATION is the focus.

Let's say you have taken over an account from another salesperson because of some territory adjustment or the other salesperson has advanced to another area. That person has provided you with some information. You now have a legitimate reason to review the situation: How has it changed, what will it be now? Let's say you are in real estate and you've been working with a wife and the husband comes to town for the weekend. Recovery questions become tools to see if the husband's view of the situation is the same as the wife's viewpoint.

Let's say you are working a sale where you have multiple decision makers. You are selling toxic waste systems and you have several layers of officials — state, country, EPA and private companies. As you move from party to party, you begin by recovering what information you have developed, but all focused on the present situation. You make sure that all parties are in general agreement on the problems, the facts, the specs, the data that will be involved.

STEP ONE: You use questions to determine THE SITUATION. The first S in SEES stands for SELLING SITUATION.

STEP TWO becomes an EXPLORATION. Here the search is a little more nebulous and the focus is more on opinions, attitudes and priorities. The reason for this search unfolds when you make the presentation. The solution you propose will be accepted, provided you cover two areas of needs for your buyer or buyers.

I'LL BUY IT BECAUSE ...

PRODUCT NEEDS:	PERSONAL NEEDS:
I like the model	Now is the time to trade
I like the color	I like the feel
I like four doors	I've always wanted a ...
I like the stereo	It's comfortable
I like the gas mileage	It will give me class
Facts, data, specs, features, tangibles	*Feeling, beliefs, opinions, instincts, intangibles*

We've used our illustration with an automobile because most people have some familiarity with the process of buying a car. On the left side are the product reasons our mythical person has used to justify the buying decision. Now, you might argue with their choice, and so might I, but they are using their belief system to justify their buying decision, not yours and not mine. Notice that in neither list was price a paramount consideration. If it had been, it might have been on the right side under personal needs and would have been listed as a "luxury car" or "an economy car." And what are they? Well, they are what we think they are, depending upon our belief system.

If you were a car salesperson, you could have gotten at some items on this list with your search for the present SITUATION.

What are you driving now? What do you consider some of its important features? How long have you had it? What do you like about it? Why are you trading now?

But, to get into the information on both lists, you need Exploration Questions like: "You've mentioned good mileage a couple of times. Tell me, what would you consider to be good mileage in a car today?" And then a follow-up question: "And, if you had a choice between a totally comfortable ride and getting more than 25 miles to the gallon, which would you prefer?" Or a question like: "Let me ask, in your mind, what are the status cars on the market today?" Or perhaps: "We haven't talked about color yet. Did you have something special in mind?" Responses to these exploratory questions will lead to the discovery of personal needs, opinions and buyer belief system. They uncover buyer personal needs. And, in most instances, the buyer is talking about perceptions. Not facts, but perceptions and images.

Now, an important point about these. When you search for the present SITUATION, you will probably use present tense questions. Words like "now ... still ... existing ... is ... are ... continue," and generally the responses are factual.

EXPLORATION questions are often futuristic. "What will happen if? What could happen when? What would be the consequences of that? What would you say would be realistic?" EXPLORATION questions also use words such as "explain ... tell me more ... what would be your reason for that ... what would you see as a reasonable time for that?" EXPLORATION questions also lead you into values, words like "too high ... too long ... too much ... not enough ... bad deal ... good deal" will be used in the conversation.

Let's pause here. How high is high? Well, it's as high as the customer or buyer says it is. We want their belief system, and within that system is their definition of "high," but we need to get at it through their eyes. Only they can tell us what high is. Or low. Or far away. Or short.

EXPLORATION QUESTIONS GET TO THOSE BELIEFS

The THIRD set of questions used by the professional resource or fourth-level salesperson we call EXPLICIT questions. The search here is for the payoff, the solution or specific benefit. Not a loose benefit, but a rather explicit benefit. How is this used? In the proposal, perceived value becomes added value.

Let's see how this works in real life for a level four real estate person. Early in the discovery, the salesperson focused on explicit questions regarding financial ability of a couple to make house payments. The salesperson found they were putting money into other investments. In the recommendation, the salesperson tucked in this statement:

"You said yesterday, I believe, Mr. Buyer, that you considered anything that would make more than 9 percent a good investment in today's market. This house will maintain property value in this location, but it provides another payoff for you. Property in this neighborhood has been appreciating in value every year at a rate higher than 9 percent. Two houses that were bought three years ago for $200,000 just recently were sold for $265,000. Both parties realized a return of their investment that was over the 9 percent you said you considered good."

The house had been positioned not only as a home but as an investment. The salesperson neatly tucked the home into the buyer portfolio, but to do so he needed explicit information.

There is an evolution in the use of questions that marks the growth of the salesperson. Novices often begin by using mostly closed questions. These create short answers. They almost work against the salesperson. Remember, the goal of questions is not to make the other person talk, but to make them want to talk. Open questions encourage the other person to want to talk. At the same time, they allow the salesperson to direct the focus of the meeting or dialogue.

At first, when level one and level two salespeople begin to use more questions, they sometimes feel out of control. They run into a situation where the other person does all the talking, tends to ramble and the dialogue loses focus. They need to learn to use RE-DIRECT QUESTIONS. We have listened to this skill in use by a high-performance salesperson, and it is amazing how you can interrupt a monologue with the use of a key technique: Letting the talker know that what he is saying is important.

To illustrate: The meeting is off the track. The salesperson wants to get it back on track. Start with a "softening statement": "Excuse me" ... or "Pardon me ..." PAUSE ... "could we go back to your point about the estimated budget for this, because I'd like to make certain I really understand that. Tell me again what you said about that." And bingo, you have re-directed the dialogue back to a focused point.

Now, to do this, the seller must have been listening in a very empathic posture! Explicit questions also take a special skill. Sometimes they need to be very pointed. Quite often, they involve money, the budget or the price the buyer has in mind. So again, the salesperson needs to be prepared to guide the dialogue.

Two techniques can help in this area of questions. The first technique is the use of BRACKET QUESTIONS.[1] The salesperson might say, for instance, in real estate: "So on the low side you might be thinking something like $115,000 for a home and on the high side it might be more like $150,000?"

This type of question does two things. First, it establishes a range. The salesperson needs to understand that most buyers will hear the low number and the high number might just slip by. So the salesperson might want to say, again in real estate: "That's important for me to know. I'll just make a note of that ... we said $115,000 on the low side and $150,000 on the high side."

The second thing this technique does is establish "elbow room" in the event there is the possibility of negotiation. And, the larger the dollars involved, the higher the odds are there will be some negotiation. If the sellers are working with a firm price, they will need to introduce other variables that could be open to negotiation. But now, they can be prepared to do that.

Another technique used by high-performance salespeople comes directly out of negotiation. In negotiation, we suggest that the seller will have three ranges. Again, we go back to ABC[2], but in a different sense. They have an "A," which is ASPIRATION; they have a "B," which is BE SATISFIED WITH; and they have a "C," which is COULD LIVE WITH.

To illustrate this technique in advertising, the salesperson might say to the buyer: "So, you're saying you would like to keep the budget in the neighborhood of $40,000 for your part of this promotion. That would be the best case ... you would be comfortable with $45,000 as the total cost and, if it was necessary, you could stretch to $50,000."

Each number is explicit, but by using ABC — ASPIRATION/BE SATISFIED WITH/COULD LIVE WITH — the salesperson has established a range and set up room for future give and take.

EXPLICIT QUESTIONS are often based on "what if" or "suppose" and attempt to put a specific value on the gap in the buyers' minds. This is their value, on the gap between what they have and what they want. Quite often, the explicit questions will deal with profits, increases, more efficiency, less waste, but the EXPLICIT QUES-

TIONS tie those payoffs to specific values, not vague values.

EXPLICIT QUESTIONS can be reversed into "What if you don't do this now? What would be the results? If we used conservative figures, what would the cost to you be?" Often, EXPLICIT QUESTIONS can be built around best case-worst case scenarios. Their purpose is to determine, if at all possible, explicit benefits, values or payoffs of the solution for which the buyer is searching. EXPLICIT QUESTIONS lead the seller to the value of the gap in the buyers' minds between what they have and what they want.

We gave you the acronym S E E S and, to this point, we have given you three types of gap fillers for the first three letters. The purpose of questions at the fourth level of selling is to determine the SITUATION, then EXPLORATION for the belief system and priorities, then EXPLICIT questions that get at specific values of the solution. The final S stands for SUMMARY.

SALESPEOPLE WORK WITH TWO GENERAL TYPES OF QUESTIONS:

OPEN QUESTIONS cannot be answered "yes" or "no." Open questions force, or allow, the other person to talk. Open questions are less threatening than closed questions. Open questions take longer to get a response. Open questions slow things down because the other person is likely to ramble.

CLOSED QUESTIONS are questions that can be answered "yes" or "no." They tend to make a conversation move faster. They can be threatening, as when the prosecuting attorney says to the witness: "Just answer the question yes or no."

Salespeople are more likely to use closed questions because they want to hurry things along. But, with the use of closed questions, salespeople can often trap themselves.

Open questions that lead a prospect or client to open up and really talk are not easy to come up with. Even seasoned salespeople have difficulty framing good open questions. They want the customer to open up, so they must avoid the possibility of a closed question. They want the open question to produce good information. So, good open questions are usually prepared in advance, they are written down and even rehearsed to see if they contain any traps.

We encourage salespeople to use articles from trade papers, newspapers, magazines and authentic sources. These articles can provide at least three key ways salespeople can build their credibility:

1.   They say, loud and clear: "I've been thinking about you and

clipped this."

2. They help produce the image of professionalism: "Your prob-
    lems interest me."

3. They can often be perceived as added value, something special
    the salesperson does for the client.

But, they have two more very important values to the professional salesperson. First, they make an excellent entry to get in to
see a higher person in the pecking order, to discuss the articles from
a general point of view. Then, they allow you to bridge into more
specific questions. The article becomes the bridging device.

And, from the standpoint of sales technique, that is the real
value to the salesperson. Follow this possible dialogue.

Sales: I saw this in *USA Today* and wondered if you thought it
            might be true in our market?

Client: Didn't see it. What's it about?

Sales: Says that Ford Motor Co. is making an effort to reach
            working women, putting more ambiance in their show-
            rooms.

Client: Well, we've been doing a lot more thinking about that,
            for sure.

Sales: So, what this article says might be true in your case, is
            that right?

Client: Let's see it ...

The salesperson bridged from a general question about a
national situation to a very closed, explicit question about the specific dealer's business. He had set the atmosphere for asking more
explicit questions, for really doing a discovery with the customer.

The technique will work with prospects, and it will work with
present customers. It can lead to more and better discovery work
by the salesperson.

KEY TECHNIQUES OF HIGH-PERFORMANCE SELLING SUMMARIZED

First, you tell about your information or your proof ... then show it.

High performance salespeople often use the "tell-and-show"[3]
presentation technique.

You first tell about the article or printed piece you are using.

Then you show the item to the customer or prospect. Instead of show and tell, it is tell and show.

This is a power technique because:

1.   By showing the printed piece after you tell the story, you tend to give the piece being used added credibility.

2.   Many salespeople just drop a piece of information on the buyer's desk.   Instead, this technique allows that salesperson to make the point two times, when they tell it and when they show it. The odds the buyer will remember go up a bit.

THE POWER IS IN THE TECHNIQUE. MODEL THE TECHNIQUE TO FIT YOUR STYLE. PRACTICE IT UNTIL YOU ARE COMFORTABLE WITH IT, USING YOUR WORDS AND YOUR PACING.

"So from this it seems to me we could be talking $40,000 on the low side and maybe something like $55,000 on the high side?"

The use of brackets can provide a low-pressure way to arrive at the buyer's sense of value. It can "get you in the ball park."

1.   We recommend you start with the low figure or low end of the value. If you are high with that, you will generally get a reaction.

2.   Step two is going to the higher figure or value. Don't be reluctant to push this one a little. You can always adjust.

This is a powerful technique because:

1.   It gets value into the selling situation and gives the salesperson an opportunity to test the water.

2.   It provides elbow space for the buyer without having to get into a firm price.

3.   It is a short step from this use of brackets into more explicit questions that can help qualify the buyer.

THE POWER IS IN THE TECHNIQUE. MODEL THE TECHNIQUE TO FIT YOUR STYLE. PRACTICE IT UNTIL YOU ARE COMFORTABLE WITH IT, USING YOUR WORDS AND YOUR PACING.

::

GETTING READY TO POSITION YOUR PRODUCT OR SERVICE SO THE BUYER OR PROSPECT WANTS TO MAKE A COMMITMENT TO BUY IT

GETTING READY TO POSITION YOUR PRODUCT OR SERVICE SO THE BUYER OR PROSPECT WANTS TO MAKE A COMMITMENT TO BUY IT

In the previous chapter, we introduced you to the S E E S concept of getting information. The end result of getting comfortable about securing information and using this concept is that you come to realize it is a very flexible tool. But, more than that, it provides a constant reminder that the situation is never fixed.

The S, the situation, may change from day to day. The information secured with the E or exploration questions may shift or be modified. Even the explicit or E question — which produced priorities, facts, margins or percentages — may change and shift.

The final S, or SUMMARY, tries to give the salesperson a solid hold on the buyer needs. The summary tries to provide the seller with the understanding of the buyer's IMAGE OF REALITY AND PERCEPTION OF PROBABILITY. It tries to produce a buyer-seller agreement, if only verbal, of what the buyer has told the salesperson about the selling situation.

Even at best, the summary agreement tends to be flexible and subject to modification. Now, let's add some substance to that generality.

Joel Arthur Barker has written a book, *Future Edge*, which ought to be in the library of every salesperson who is serious about moving through the levels and reaching high performance. It is essentially a book for leaders and managers, men and women who are searching for the answers to where their business will be tomorrow. If you are selling to these people, or their companies, isn't it logical you should know how they are thinking?

In the book, Barker deals with paradigms, those time-honored rules or policies that tend to provide such comfort because "that is the way we have always done it." He talks about the "Paradigm Pioneers" who were willing to anticipate and innovate.

He adds another phrase, "Paradigm Settlers," and uses the analogy of the Oregon Trail. The pioneers, those who first sought the way to Oregon, had no maps, only a sense of direction. They were novices, in a sense, because nobody had made marks for them to follow. When they had determined the way to achieve their objective, they were followed by "Paradigm Settlers." The settlers improved upon the early paths, profited from past mistakes or errors in judgment and moved the idea of immigration to Oregon forward.

Barker makes a point of the great risks the pioneers took, even if they were experienced mountain men. He makes a sly joke when he suggests the big question in the minds of the settlers was: "Is it safe out there?"

How often, do you suppose, in selling do buyers say to themselves: "Is it safe to do this?" How often, in their PERCEPTION OF PROBABILITY, are they weighing the odds of the success of your offering? Is it safe to buy this large an advertising campaign? Is it safe to buy this house? Will this policy really take care of the kids' education? The parallels are fascinating.

The parallels between Barker's stages of evolution, from pioneer to settler to what he calls the third phase or further development phase, bear a marked resemblance to our matrix of the evolution of selling skills. There is another fascinating resonance. The old paradigms of selling no longer fit the new game of selling. The old tried-and-true techniques no longer work as well. Getting appointments has become much more sophisticated. The buyer has become wiser, more knowledgeable and more sophisticated. There is a whole new set of dynamics at work.

Not the least of these shifting dynamics is the element of trust. It is entirely possible that few people ever trusted a salesperson initially. The job of the salesperson was to build that trust. This explains our great emphasis on building credibility. That shift in the dynamics of trust has accelerated into a whole other game! There is a new paradigm in selling.

Today, in too many instances, the game of selling has become very much like playing bridge. At least in bridge you know that each player was dealt 13 cards, but none of the players knows what is in the other hands until the top bidder gets the right to play the game. Their partner lays down the dummy, and the winning bidder knows what is in two hands, but not the other two. The opponents then try to deny the bidder enough tricks to make game.

In the old paradigm of selling, when there was a considerable amount of trust in the business world, the buying may have been a little more naive than today. A good salesperson could expect the buyer to be somewhat honest with him. As the selling situation developed, it was assumed the buyer and seller told nearly all or most of the truth, if not the whole truth.

Now, the question is this: Do buyers ever lie when they buy? The buyers say: "I'll think about it." Do you suppose they ever do? An advertising buyer tells a rep she wants certain demographics for a buy she is making. Are those demographics always reliable? A person tells the real estate agent he will work only with her, then buys a house directly from a seller, a house listed as "For Sale By Owner."

Why do buyers withhold information or not reveal all the information? To get a better price? To cut a better deal? To look good? Because "that's the way things are done today?"

In too many instances in today's marketplace, the buyer and the seller are in reality playing two different games. The buyer is playing with one deck of cards and the salesperson is playing with another deck that is stacked a little. If all this sounds a little unethical to you, it won't sound that way to others. That is the great paradigm shift in selling. Too often, information that would help salespeople do a better job of fitting their offering to the buyer's needs is deliberately withheld. The idea today is that it is OK for the buyer to take every advantage he can.

That is not meant to sound negative nor hostile. It is not meant to re-establish the idea that the relationship between buyer and seller is antagonistic. It is merely a reflection of a change or shift in attitude. It is a paradigm shift.

Add still another element to this marketplace change. The buyers want to know what the salespeople know. If the higher-level sellers have the credibility to make the contact, if their expertise in problem-solving gives them the perception of "added value," then what good buyer wouldn't want to extract information from the seller? Consultative selling can sometimes turn into unpaid consulting under these circumstances.

When you position this condition against another reality of the marketplace — namely the abundance of options and alternatives that most buyers have today — you have a need to sell with some type of system that allows you to constantly test the state of buyer readiness, their IMAGE OF REALITY and the PERCEPTION OF PROBABILITY. You constantly verify the status of your summary agreement, because it is this summary agreement that becomes the foundation for what we believe to be the key to high-performance selling. The summary agreement is subject to change and shift, but it, along with the game of playing with information that may or may not be totally valid, still represents the best way to position your offering so the customer wants to buy.

Transactional selling is based on leading with the product. The product will do thus-and-so. The product will solve this problem or that problem. Substitute the word service for product and the process is the same.

High-performance selling is based on leading with the summary agreement. You lead with the buyers' IMAGE OF REALITY and PERCEPTION OF PROBABILITY. You lead with what they want, what will close the gap between what they have and what they want, with their view of the selling situation. You lead with what they want as their payoff. Your solution becomes your promise.

The idea of PAPA was originally taken from a concept of TV and radio commercials used by David Ogilvy. He called it PROMISE-AMPLIFICATION-PROOF-ACTION, and claimed that any successful commercial that sold a product had these four elements of persuasion.

We have used the concept for presentations or recommendations in a modified form for many years. The steps were these:

This is the promise or the key payoff to you.

This is why and how the idea, system or concept will work (features, if necessary).

The proof of this is ...

Would you agree with this? Do you like this idea?

It makes a very neat way to actually get the promise up front and prevent the facts and data from getting in the way of the proposal or promise. But selling continues to evolve as the marketplace evolves. Fewer salespeople are selling products. More and more, they are selling solutions, concepts or systems. How a product will work is less important. The buyer assumes that all products will work to some degree or another. The key questions are how well it will work and for how long? And, how do I know that you, the seller, will be around to fix it if and when it doesn't do exactly as you promised?

So, the evolution of PAPA was natural. It has emerged as:

PROMISE	This is what you said you wanted (summary.) This is what our proposal will do to fix your problem ... it will give you what you want.
APPLICATION	This is how the solution will work.
PROOF	This is why we are so sure this will work.
ACTION	Would you agree? Or, do you see this as a fit with what you expressed as your priority? In your opinion, are we on target?

The payoff for salespeople who employ this process is in the last step. It can be used in a number of ways, but the idea of moving the sale along, of "closing the gap," is always present. That request for action is always available in this concept. It can be modeled as a close. It can be phrased as "are we ready to move forward?" It can be used as a trial question.

The payoff is the structure it provides as the salesperson shifts from recommendation to close. Properly used, it becomes a very powerful selling tool!

We have used the word "modeled" or adapted several times. More on that later as we approach closing from the concept of the four levels of selling.

These models aren't chiseled in stone or revealed in a burning bush. They are models for you to adapt, modify and massage so they fit your style of selling. They do work! Experiences of thousands of salespeople have proven that. But those people decided to try them. They experimented and polished their skills with the concept. They sharpened their saws! They cut more wood.

Returning to the matrix once more, let's summarize how the four levels of salespeople handle this presenting part of the sales process.

The novices lead with product facts, features and information. They may demonstrate them. They guess at what the prospect wants and use phrases like "everybody likes this feature" or "most people agree that ..." It is not uncommon for them to use a book of sorts when they do their pitch. In fact, World Book salespeople used to be taught to get husband and wife to sit together on a couch. Then the salesperson would build a wall around them on the floor, building each book into a brick in the wall as he stood them on end. The theory was the couple could not escape until they bought. And sometimes it worked! But can you imagine the information a World Book salesperson had to work with?

The second-level salesperson knows the product well, may even compare similar products or some competitive advantages that provide customer gain. But the focus is on the product or service. The presentation is highly tell-oriented.

The competent salesperson, or level three, usually leaves the cookies in the jar and presents more of the concept of what the solution will do for the prospect. The product advantages are used mostly to back up points made on how it works. Facts and product advantages are used to provide or document claims made about the solution. This level of salesperson will often use specific third-party references obtained from satisfied customers.

The professional resources salespeople position credible promises they have selected to fit into the payoff the prospect wants. They use product facts only to provide background or update the buyer on new developments. They see the product itself as almost generic. What is unique and credible is their plan, their concept for its use and its application. They fit explicit payoffs to the customer or prospect belief system. This is the way it looks on the matrix:

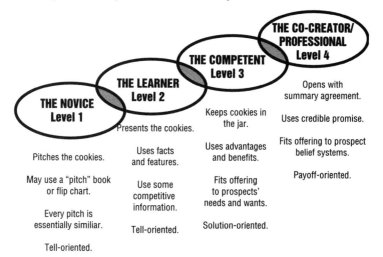

In other words, the salespeople do the sorting of the information for the buyer. They don't have to say: "So what this means to you is ..." or "The real benefit to you is ..." They position what they have in terms of credible strengths and advantages. Some people think of this library of advantages as "unique strengths." And, indeed, they may be unique. We think of them as PROMISES YOU CAN PROVE. Something can be unique, but you can't prove it! In fact, when you sell something brand new, you may spend more time educating the buyers than you do getting them to want to buy.

There is a story about the introduction of a new product that illustrates this point. More than 100 years ago, a dentist named Morton was working in his laboratory with nitrous oxide. He took a good sniff of the bottle and proceeded to pass out. When he came to, he realized he had no aftereffects. He had just been gone for a while. One day he had a patient who need a wisdom tooth extracted, a very painful process at best. He decided to use the bottle of nitrous oxide. The patient was out for the entire operation and came to with no aftereffects, just a very sore jaw. Morton couldn't wait to tell others the news. He spent the next six years "pitching his product," but nobody would try it. Finally, in a Philadelphia hospital, a doctor agreed to use it on a patient who was a pauper and needed a tumor removed. The operation completed, using the new product, the doctor took off his mask, turned to his interns who had witnessed the operation and said: "Gentlemen, this is no humbug!" And the age of anesthesia was born! No more patient agony, no more torture or shock. And, an old paradigm had been replaced!

Today, most salespeople don't have six years to get somebody to try their unique product with unique benefits and strengths. The benefits must have credibility. On the next page is an outline that can get you into this concept of selling credible strengths. It will fit precisely with the type of presentation you would make if you were on that fourth level of selling.

The outline on the next page can be used this way. Earlier, we discussed how the individual salesperson builds credibility fast in the opening phases of prospecting. We mentioned company reputation, other customers and previous experience as ways to do this. Take each of these three ideas and put them on the outline. Will they fit as a credible promise you make to a prospect or customer?

Your company reputation is the source of the promise. What can you say about it? Good, excellent, superior, proven? What might the other person say or think about that promise. He might say: "SO?" What would you then have available to prove your promise, to make it credible? You might supply names, show a letter, cite your customer base.

Where will you find these credible promises? Perhaps they are

Credible Promises I Can Make About My Product Or Service

Source	Promise	Challenge	Proof

advantages you offer that other competitors might not have, the ways your product or service can be positioned to allow you to provide that prospect or customer with a payoff.

You might want to start with your product. What credible, provable benefits will it offer? Product would be the source, your promise would be what it can do, the challenge might be the way a person would question that promise and your proof might be to quote a satisfied customer.

After you have considered the product, go to your people, your creative resources, your people with special expertise, your financing experts. What credible promises can you make about the people?

Now, consider some other areas. If you sell equipment, can you offer training that reduces time wasted in the changeover period? What have you learned from other customers that gives you expertise that could be applied to this situation? What about your delivery capabilities? Could you deliver goods or services in such a way that you would have an edge? What about your service? Are there aspects of this you can deliver that others cannot? What about the way you handle your accounts? Do you provide customer advantages in this area? Consider your technology. Does your company usually provide a leading edge? Can a new customer be comfortable that your product will continue to be updated? When innovations come along, can you provide these as options for the customer?

Examine your list carefully. Be creative, but always check that you have a credible promise, one you can prove and one you can deliver. Then, if you are like most salespeople we have taken through this list in a workshop, you say: "Why, this is added value!" This is what they are saying the customer wants today. This is what people are buying. They are buying "added value" or what seems, in their belief system, to be the promises they perceive their buying selection will produce for them.

So, the first step in any presentation would be the restatement of the summary agreement. P-A-P-A is positioned with the summary agreement, and P becomes the PROMISE OR THE PAYOFF. We have provided several reasons for use of this concept and the benefits that result.What proof can we offer for the value of this concept of selling?

We spoke earlier about the changing paradigms of the marketplace. We suggested that several ballgames had changed and cited as one example the trust bond between the buyer and seller. We suggested that in making a complex sale today, it is not uncommon for buyers not to show all their cards. The seller is playing with a new set of ground rules.

But the new rules of the game, the new paradigms of selling, also impact on the way information is presented and the way benefits and features are used. Earlier, we introduced the three edges of selling. We called these:

THE CRITICAL EDGE

THE COMPETITIVE EDGE

THE PERCEIVED EDGE

What often happens in a company or organization is that a designer or design team of a new product or service emerges from the conception stage very keen on their new child. After all, this person or team has sweated it out, and they should be proud of what the new idea can produce. This product or service pride carries into top management and marketing. Grand strategies emerge at the top. These are pushed down to the salespeople. The strategy becomes the marketing tactics. The result is features and benefits selling!

The reality of the marketplace today is that no product or service enjoys that critical or competitive edge very long. In fact, major companies are surviving very well in the high-tech world by giving another company the lead on a new product. Then they add a few bells and whistles, improve on the original model a little, put a new name on it and ZIPPO, they are ready to serve it as an alternative. Major buyers encourage this practice because they like more than a single source for their products. They can then use one source against another to avoid being at the mercy of a single supplier when it comes to pricing. It's the old law of supply and demand at work!

Something is marketed today, not so much as the result of strategy, but as the result of a series of tactics. Sales tactics are the results of positioning the unique or credible strength of a product, usually perceived, not critical nor competitive.

What's more, as selling major dollar investments moves more into team selling, the salesperson may not know the facts, data and specifics on a product. In fact, the buyer may not be interested in these. The decision maker will rely on expertise within the organization to devise the product specs. The decision maker wants to know what the results will be! What's more, the salesperson may bring resource people into the sale to focus on the facts and figures. This is often true in selling insurance, when a company is looking at a pension or annuity program for its employees. A single salespeople may not have the necessary expertise to dot all the "Is" and cross all the "Ts" and will bring in experts or specialists.

What's more, in some fields, products are changing so fast, the salesperson is hard put to keep up with all the product development. The bigger the line, the more this is true. A small company, selling a niche market, with a single offering, can more nearly expect its salespeople to be product experts. In fact, that may be one reason smaller companies are successful. Focused product information, well-presented, wins the marketing battle.

CAN TOO MUCH INFORMATION HURT?

Let's examine two things about information. First, how much information do people remember and for how long? From various sources we have assembled some research to make the point. Examine the four diagrams on pages 185 and 187. If you are really interested in the subject, after today you'll be able to recall about 72 percent of it, and after 30 days you'll remember only 30 percent. That says that if a salesperson unloads a full sheet of facts and features about a product to an interested person, one month later that interested person remembers only 30 percent of it. In fact, that person has forgotten 70 percent about the sales call!

Now, look what happens to material that is passed from one person to another. Less than 10 percent is "remembered," and 42 percent of that is "incorrect." Can you guess what happens to your proposal when it is presented by another person to a committee? WOW!

So much for how long most people remember information. Why should they? They'll have plenty before it's over! In our information age, there is so much information we are in danger of drowning in it. How often have you reacted to the statement: "Let me show you something new about that" by saying to yourself: "I've had enough of new today"? We receive information today through an increasingly critical filter. Something has to be really good, really informative, really interesting, or we simply don't let it through our filter.

The Classic "Curve of Forgetting MEANINGLESS Material" tells us:

- After 33 seconds, only 58% of what is learned is remembered.

- After 1 day, only 34% is remembered.

- After 6 days, only 25%.

- After 31 days, only 21%.

"Uber das Gedachtnes" — Ebbinghaus

While the "Curve of Forgetting

MEANINGFUL Material" shows:

- After 1 day, only 72% of what is learned is remembered.
- After 5 days, only 56% is remembered.
- After 10 days, only 47%.
- After 30 days, only 30%.

"Educational Psychology" — E.L. Thomdyke

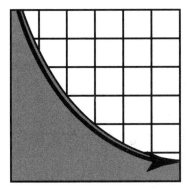

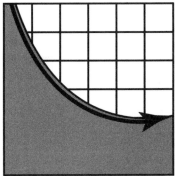

Now, let's look at another body of research on the subject. Can there be times when giving too much information becomes a turnoff? Absolutely. A story to illustrate this point. A young salesperson was calling on a shopping newspaper or shopper. He was selling a high-tech piece of desktop publishing equipment. His prospect was a crusty old codger who sent him first to the people who would use the new equipment. He showed them the machine, demonstrated "the mouse" and regaled them with features, facts and data. The users agreed to tell the boss they would like him to consider it. Then the salesperson started showing Old Crusty all the features. The gentlemen stopped him. "Look, son, I'm not interested in that stuff. Just tell me, can this machine get our paper out on time and save us man-hours?" Too much information nearly stopped the sale.

The value of features, benefits and advantages shifts as the size of the sale increases. Again, we have a matrix of sorts. When and how the seller uses data shifts.

Even if you could get your salesman invited — or make sure your media file was taken — into a planning conference, how well would this influence decisions in your favor at recommending, reviewing, revising, approving or buying time? Results of an experiment[†] — in which members of of the Cambridge Psychological Society wrote down all they could remember of a meeting held two weeks earlier — offer a clue:

OR CONSIDER HOW MUCH your prospect forgets after your salesman calls. Studies at Columbia University* reveal:

• After 1 day, 72% of a verbal message is remembered.

• After 1 week, only 52%.

• After 1 month, only 30%.

• Less than 10% of the specific points discussed were remembered by the average individual.

• 42% of "what was remembered" about these points was substantially incorrect.

* *"Educational Psychology" — E.L. Thorndyke*   [†]*"Facts And Fallacies" — Pelican Books, p. 405.*

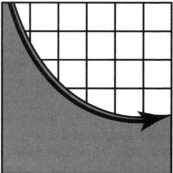

Advantages have a positive value in small-dollar sales. In a bigger-dollar sale, they are only marginally valuable to the salesperson.

But benefits and payoffs have a very positive value to the salesperson in both small-dollar sales and big-dollar sales. In the box that follows, that concept is outlined:

PURPOSE	PROCESS	PAYOFF	
		SMALL $	LARGE $
FEATURES: Give information	To provide facts, data about the product. What it is.	Marginally profitable	Neutral to negative
ADVANTAGES: How it is better	To show how features can be used or can help the customer.	Positive response	Marginally positive
BENEFITS: (Payoffs) What the advantages do for you	To show how the promise or solution meets explicit needs expressed by the buyer.	Very positive	Very positive

The chart shows the relationship of more traditional selling, which focused on FEATURES-ADVANTAGES-BENEFITS, in the climate or environment of selling in today's marketplace.

In today's crowded information marketplace, the facts and data about many products and services are viewed as essentially the same by the buyer. Features have neither an immediate sales impact nor a lasting remembrance with a buyer in either a large-dollar sale or a small one. In fact, in a large-dollar sale, too much data may impede the sale.

Advantages tend to have more value, especially if those values can be tied to applications. The implication with this approach is really that "the solution or promise will do this for you." The impact increases immediately, and there is a better remembrance factor.

The most powerful of the three elements is the benefit. Our concept takes the benefit one step beyond being just being a benefit and makes it a payoff for an explicit need. The presenting stage of selling has been directly related back to the discovery stage. If the discovery process developed explicit needs or payoffs, and was conducted properly, and was spelled out in the summary or recap agreement letter, those explicit needs can be picked out and placed in the presenting process. In the presentation, the promise is the payoff.

The solution becomes a promise. The promise is the payoff for explicit needs. The concept takes advantage of what is most important to the buyer. You begin with the P in PAPA.

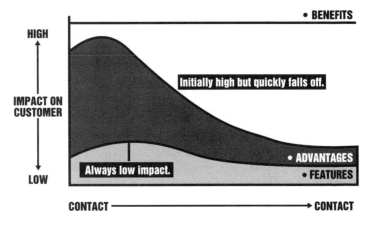

Another way to look at our concept is shown in the graph above, which was taken from the book *Spin Selling* by Neil Rackham. In that book, he explores this concept of explicit questions and needs, and the relative value of features, advantages and benefits, as "Type A Benefits," with Type A being general benefits and Type B being explicit benefits. His focus is on gathering complete information.

Notice that benefits maintain a high level of interest. Let's switch the term benefits to PROMISE. Remember, we introduced the idea that salespeople could use the phrase: "What this means to you is ..." when they began with a feature and advantage. To review, apply that to a salesperson selling a riding lawnmower. He might use the concept this way:

"This mower uses dual blades, which means increased cutting efficiency. It also allows the machine to cut a 48-inch swath where you told me your old mower was just a 36-inch model. *What this means to you* is that you'll not only get a cleaner cut on your lawn, but you'll spend about two-thirds the time you now spend mowing your lawn on a hot summer day."

We invert this selling style. In our concept of putting the promise up front, the dialogue would be a little more like this. Follow along with PROMISE-APPLICATION-PROOF-ACTION:

"You've said that mowing on a hot, muggy day wasn't a lot of fun. Well, this mower can reduce your time in the saddle about a third. You've got a 48-inch cutting blade working for you. Your old blade was only 36 inches wide. Plus, the twin blades, cutting together, increase the cutting efficiency and just give you a smoother lawn. I can provide you the names of customers who could give you specific figures on the time they have saved mowing their lawns. Tell me, would that have a value to you?"

In this case, the summary agreement was fairly simple. The buyer had said that mowing a big lawn on a hot, muggy day wasn't very much fun. Against this agreement, the salesperson positioned the promise. This mower would reduce time in the saddle about a third. He showed some blade amplification, some advantages and added the benefit of a smoother lawn — a little ego appeal, a personal win, a looks better. Then, for proof, he offered some names of satisfied customers and closed it out by asking for an opinion, a nice soft close that cost nothing in terms of moving the needle but did ask for some commitment to action. He gave the prospective customer every opportunity to want to buy.

To briefly summarize PAPA, leading a recommendation, written or verbal, with a promise or payoff allows the first focus to be on the customer needs. The P is followed by A — application. In this pattern, the application is more likely to strengthen the promise or payoff, will avoid too much detail and data, will focus more on benefit. For P, or proof of this, we offered two sets of research that provided reasons to focus on benefits rather than features and advantages.

This method of positioning a recommendation is nearly opposite from the style of leading with product, features and advantages. We feel that style leads to too much data and even confusion, and runs the risk of being forgotten quickly.

Why don't you try this style of positioning with your offering? You'll find closing falls naturally into place, and the number of objections you encounter will drop dramatically.

KEY TECHNIQUES OF HIGH-PERFORMANCE SELLING SUMMARIZED

"We have agreement on the benefits to you. It seems to me this could be an important decision to you, worth your undivided attention. Can you give us five minutes without interruptions?"

High-performance salespeople often use a control technique to handle interruptions.

1.   They first get agreement from the client on the importance of key benefits.

2.   They then get agreement that the benefits are worth undivided attention.

3.   They then ask the buyer, quite directly, for undivided attention.

This is a powerful technique because:

1.   The salesperson first reduces the tension in the close by getting agreement on easy or obvious areas, or key benefits.

2.   This sets up the direct request for undivided time. Discussion of benefits deserves the time.

THE POWER IS IN THE TECHNIQUE. MODEL THE TECHNIQUE TO FIT YOUR STYLE. PRACTICE IT UNTIL YOU ARE COMFORTABLE WITH IT, USING YOUR WORDS AND YOUR PACING.

Understanding How People Think Before You Put Together Your Recommendation

UNDERSTANDING HOW PEOPLE THINK BEFORE YOU PUT TOGETHER YOUR RECOMMENDATION

"Well, I'll think about it." The salesperson has just pitched her socks off and the would-be buyer pauses and then uses that phrase. Or, if you're selling automobiles or furniture, where the customer usually comes to the place of business, you get: "Well, I think we'll look around and we might be back."

In the first case, "I'll think about it" is really a nice way of telling the salesperson "No, thank you," but it avoids the need for complete rejection. Second-level salespeople often greet this response with a show of appreciation. "That's great," they will say, "I'm pleased to hear you say that, because that tells me I've said something that has you really interested. Tell me, what do you like about this enough that it will merit you thinking about it?" Slightly confronting? Yes, but it does work in a manipulative type of selling. They might even add: "The reason I ask that is I don't believe you are the type of person who would just tell me that if you really weren't going to think about it." Now they have created a high-tension situation by giving the other person a choice of revealing what they think or of admitting they are the kind of person who would do that. Does it work? Sometimes, if it doesn't create defensive behavior. And people generally won't really listen to other views or exchange information if they are in a defensive posture.

When we consider how people will react to a proposal, or how they will respond to a recommendation, we are, or should be, asking HOW WILL THEY JUSTIFY THIS? That would be the fourth reason people buy. Because they can justify it, or will justify it. And it's easy to come up with some quick answers: Because they are satisfied. Because they think they have gotten a special deal. Because the price was right. Because and because and because. But is this what they think, or what the seller thinks? Unless they tell us, we are never sure.

There are bodies of research that bear on this subject. One study was assembled by Dr. Jack R. Gibb at Stanford University. He did a series of studies, using grants from the Group Psychology Branch of the Office of Naval Research and published his findings in the *Journal of Communication* in September 1961. Gibb was interested in what generates defensive behavior. His study was directed at groups, but, of course, groups are composed of individuals, and while there are some shortfalls in applying his material to one-on-one interpersonal relationships, the dynamics are powerful enough to merit consideration. He published a table of comparisons between defensive climates and supportive climates. His research found that as defensive behavior is reduced, the receivers "become better able to concentrate upon the structure, the content and the cognitive meanings of the message."

DEFENSIVE CLIMATES	SUPPORTIVE CLIMATES
1. Evaluation	1. Description
2. Control	2. Problem Orientation
3. Strategy	3. Spontaneity
4. Neutrality	4. Empathy
5. Superiority	5. Equality
6. Certainty	6. Provisionalism

If you take the list of the left side of the page, you have old-style selling. The sellers judged what the customer wanted. They sold in a posture of control, they supplied the reasons why the customer needed the product. It was a clinical sale, and there was scant relationship. The salespeople made it very clear they were the experts and the customer didn't know much, and the sellers were certain about most of the issues. In fact, they had all the answers. Did this style of selling work? Yes, about 25 percent of the time. Therefore, salespeople in those days had to look busy and make tracks! They had deals coming, one in the fire, and one going at all times!

Now, consider the list of qualities (if that is a good word) on the right side. Description is both giving and getting information. Problem orientation is an understanding of what you have and what you want. Spontaneity is a series of adult "Aha's" or "well, that could be's." Empathy is seeing it from the other person's belief system. Equality is being neither humble not arrogant, but credible and according that same quality to the other person. Mutual respect is another way to say it. And, finally, provisionalism is the quality of considering options and alternatives and accepting the possibility that an idea may not be the only idea, or it may not be absolutely the best idea, but it's worth a shot.

We would summarize this finding as it applies to selling this way: If you want a defensive customer or prospect, sell on the left side of the page; if you want a supportive customer, sell on the right side.

Therefore, when you consider your recommendation, consider the tone, the quality, the perception of the supportive climate. Your buyer is more likely to be both receptive and supportive.

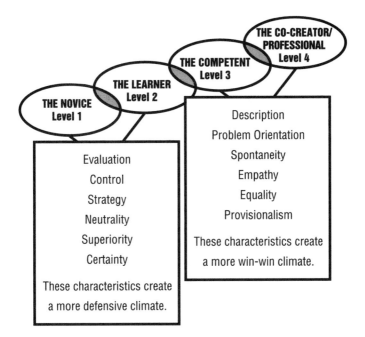

THE CO-CREATOR/ PROFESSIONAL Level 4

THE COMPETENT Level 3

THE LEARNER Level 2

THE NOVICE Level 1

Description
Problem Orientation
Spontaneity
Empathy
Equality
Provisionalism

These characteristics create a more win-win climate.

Evaluation
Control
Strategy
Neutrality
Superiority
Certainty

These characteristics create a more defensive climate.

Notice how the two climates seem to settle in with the paired levels of selling. It seems to be an almost natural order. How you sell creates a climate. But that's a one-sided view of selling. Look at it from the buyer side and switch the four levels of selling to the four levels of buying. Where do you think most buyers start? What would be logical in terms of no credibility or no need-no payoff-no justification? Isn't part of selling pulling them from no mutuality to mutuality, from no need to need, from no benefit to a payoff and from no justification to justification?

Another body of research that applies to this subject of the tone or the quality of the recommendation was assembled by Dr. J.P. Guilford, a psychologist at UCLA, in his book, *The Nature of Human Intelligence*. It bears on this issue of how people think. Guilford's material has a resonance with John Dewey and problem solving. Dewey said: Identify the problem, consider the alternatives, pick the best alternative, test that against your resources and then act. Guilford focuses on three types of thinking, which he calls Cognition Thinking, Divergent Thinking and Convergent Thinking. Let's apply that to selling:

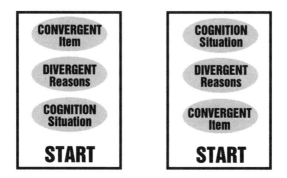

Guilford calls the first type of thinking "cognition." Cognition involves gathering facts, the data, the information. Call it a recognition process. As it might apply to sales, salespeople might think this way when attempting to assess the SELLING SITUATION. They sort through a lot of information and decide what fits and what doesn't. They evaluate their information, find possible applications of data, locate possible fits to find a pattern.

Divergent thinking then involves pros and cons of the situation. Some people are described as "thinking with a one-track mind," or maybe as "having a closed mind." These are people who probably have trouble with divergent thinking. They would have trouble understanding that an old paradigm may no longer have an application. Divergent thinking involves the skill or the discipline to consider more than one possible answer. In the sequence we have set up with the circles, we put DIVERGENT THINKING in the middle circle and called it reasons. The intent was to describe the state of considering options or possibilities.

Convergent thinking is the sort of thinking that produces choices, priorities or decisions. It becomes a sort of focused integration of information, facts, data or situations and begins to narrow possible choices to a course of action.

In our use of the matrix, level one and level two salespeople would probably deal more with a process of thinking that went from Convergent thinking to Divergent thinking to Cognitive thinking. The pattern might be ITEM/PRESENTATION/BENEFITS/REASONS to JUSTIFY. This type of selling would tend to produce a rather passive listener/buyer ... strong emphasis on benefits and advantages and push the Divergent thinking into the close. At this point, the salesperson encounters all types of objections in the close, because the client or prospect is trying out all sorts of options or alternatives against the offering on the table.

Even if the opening of the presentation had begun in a supportive climate with non-defensive buyers, the buyers would usually become defensive of their views and opinions. So, what can salespeople do that will make even a defensive buyer want to buy? They need to make an offer so attractive that even a defensive buyer can't refuse. Price becomes the primary reason for justification.

Now, examine the other pattern of thinking and the application to selling. It begins with the examination of the situation. We have described this step as a "joint venture." The buyer provides necessary information. The salesperson searches for the state of buyer readiness. Is the selling situation one of discomfort or hurt, hope or gain, maintenance or euphoria?

Together, the salesperson and the buyer explore options and possibilities. The salesperson then, based upon what has been developed to that point, presents a possible solution we call THE PROMISE. Both seller and buyer end up using Convergent thinking.

Much has been said in selling that "people buy emotionally, but they think logically." That may be a paradigm that is no longer valid. If it is a big sale, lots of money involved, a very serious decision, there may be a little emotion involved. That's where the level four salesperson adds that PERSONAL WIN. But in a complex sale, whether to an individual or a group, the odds are that justification will be based on thinking and logic.

Therefore, even a limited knowledge of how buyers think or are thinking could be very helpful. What's more, the system of selling we are recommending, which we see being used by high-performance salespeople, follows this track. Our point in enlarging this topic in this chapter is not necessarily to prove its value to you, nor is it to justify the case for our concept of selling by basing it on persuasive theory. Rather, the purpose is to encourage salespeople to understand both the theory and the application of good fundamentals, so they can improve their skills and their knowledge of selling. Another purpose is to shake salespeople out of the old ruts and habits of selling. The old paradigm of selling isn't working as it once did.

To summarize from our opening analogy borrowed from Joel Barker: High-performance salespeople have already found the road to Oregon. The payoffs are there. It now seems safe for the settlers to head in the same direction, to improve upon the path, to take full advantage of the opportunity.

We have tried to summarize this chapter with the diagram[1] that follows. First, it shows how level one and level two salespeople tend to follow one process of selling which results in what we call transactional selling. Level three and four salespeople tend to use a reverse process in terms of the steps in the process. They spend more time in the Discovery stage and less in the close.[1]

Overlaid on this diagram we would ask you to mentally place the research we have discussed and consider how the processes

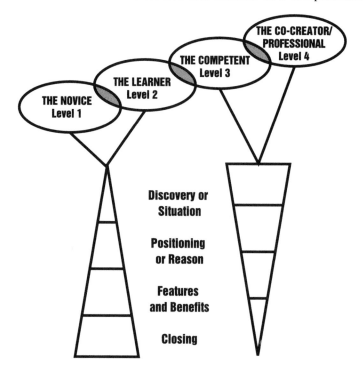

apply to creating defensive buyer behavior and the type of thinking that will be involved.

If we tied accepted research on the way people think to the specifics of selling, we arrive at some conclusions. One would be that you can sell with either a transactional approach or a consultant approach, because people do think both ways. Transactional selling forces the buyer to make the connection between the situation and the offering. Consultant selling fits the solution to the situation.

Another conclusion would be the amount of time spent in the various stages of the sales process. If you find, in the closing stage, that you need to go back and review features and benefits and, in effect, to again present your offering, then you are probably selling at level one and two. If, on the other hand, the close goes smoothly, there are minimum objections and the buyer seems to want to move forward, then you are probably selling at level three and four.

Larger and more complex offerings are usually sold today at level three and four. The reason is not entirely the skill of the salesperson. Another possibility is that their method fits more naturally into the way people think and buy today.

KEY TECHNIQUES OF HIGH-PERFORMANCE SELLING SUMMARIZED

When you are getting small agreements, nod your head in a positive way. This small bit of body language helps affirmation.

Combining body language and mini-contracts is a positive technique.

When you are using the "mini-contract," small agreements, as you present, add positive body language. Just nod your head slightly up and down.

This is the power technique because:

1.   You secure agreement as you proceed. Closing comes more naturally.

2.   You draw the buyer into the presentation.

3.   You build a positive atmosphere.

THE POWER IS IN THE TECHNIQUE. MODEL THE TECHNIQUE TO FIT YOUR STYLE. PRACTICE IT UNTIL YOU ARE COMFORTABLE WITH IT, USING YOUR WORDS AND YOUR PACING.

::

PRESENTING RECOMMENDATIONS AND UNDERSTANDING THE FOUR POSSIBILITIES OR OPTIONS

PRESENTING RECOMMENDATIONS AND UNDERSTANDING THE FOUR POSSIBILITIES OR OPTIONS

If we go back to the concept of four levels of selling, how sales-people step from one level to another, we can apply that concept to the stage of the sales process in which we make a recommendation.

The straight product pitch fits the novice level of selling. You knock on the door and sell the cookies. Or, you plug in the vacuum cleaner and demonstrate how it picks up dirt and dog hair. Or, you ring the bell, introduce yourself and start pitching cosmetics. Any of these approaches is novice selling or the straight product pitch. Does it work? Sure, if the sellers stay pumped up in spite of all the rejection they take. Some people survive and even prosper. And this is not to say that there aren't times when even the professional will be required to make a straight product pitch. The message we're trying to send, and hope will be received, is KNOW WHEN YOU ARE SELLING WHICH WAY and understand the pitfalls and the limitations.

Level two sellers, the learners, will use more features and benefits of the product. They may even offer a test drive, have a Tupperware party, present an Amway-like line of products and do some picking and choosing for the customer. Their presentation, if it is written, will rely heavily on showing why their offering is superior or costs less. And, quite often, in closing, they use a special offer or some limited opportunity to create a feeling of urgency. Does it work? Sure it does. If we were to estimate the way selling is done in the United States today, we would say that 60 percent to 70 percent of all selling is done in a transactional way. That is certainly true of smaller-dollar sales.

When we use that percentage, we're thinking of the number of sales, not necessarily the dollars involved. The irony of selling is that there is always the pull of the benefit of selling more, the challenge of more income, more prestige, peer group recognition. The further irony is that there are only two ways to sell more. Either you make more sales or you make bigger sales.

Many years ago, a wise old salesman — in those days they were mostly male animals — was passing out advice, which he liked to do. "Son," he said, "I've tried the system every way it can be tried. I've won with it and I've tried to beat it, and I keep coming back to one cardinal rule. If you want to move up in this game, you either sell more or sell bigger. I happen to think bigger is better."

There is no research for the statement that 60 percent of all sales are made today with transactional selling. In total numbers, that would probably be a decent estimate. Likewise, there are probably very few big-dollar sales made in the transactional selling posture. In total dollars, 60 percent of the dollars involved in selling are probably sold in the consultant posture. That figure may even be higher. It is certainly true in advertising, insurance and real estate, heavy machinery and high-tech.

Level three selling, or counselor selling or competent-level selling, produces that transition from talk to listen. There is a major shift in the presentation from a shotgun sort of selling to more of a rifle shot type of selling. Now, the needs of the customer are the focus. More information has been gathered, and the process of developing that information is more comprehensive. The conversion of information to recommendation involves more thinking, matching and creativity.

There is another major shift in the third level of selling. If transactional selling is done with a single decision maker, then consultant-type selling is more often done with multiple decision makers. More buying influences or decision makers are involved. There must be more tailoring to each person's needs.

On the following page, you will find a diagram. It is our version of the counselor sales approach for selling radio advertising, but it could apply easily to any kind of advertising sales. It has two words in it that are unique to broadcast sales, the word "ratings" in the upper righthand box and the letters "RAB" in the middle lower righthand box.

Ratings refer to the measurement systems used in broadcasting to determine audience size. But ratings could be cost-per-thousand figures, and then would be applicable to any form of advertising. In other words, these are the standards of measurement or standards of performance. If we were selling engines, we would have horsepower criteria as the standards and compare our motor to the standards.

Counselor Sales

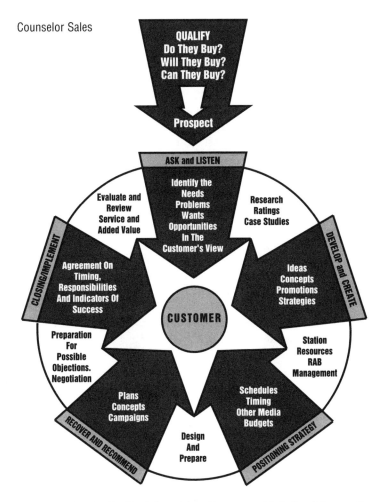

RAB is the Radio Advertising Bureau, which furnishes radio stations with information about different categories of business. Nearly all industries have such a resource. We have adapted this diagram to a number of different industries and it has always fit, with only minor modifications in words.

The diagram visually tracks the high-performance selling approach. It begins with a qualified prospect. That is the ask-and-listen stage. Then it moves to the creativity stage, then the positioning strategy, the recovery and recommendation stage, then decision and implementation, concluding with service and added value.

The fourth level of selling involves two shifts or changes from consultant selling. The professional or co-creator salesperson is more like a partner, and the sales process is really more of a partnership. Don Beveridge, in his materials, refers to this level of selling as "being the unpaid person on their staff." In other words, at times it seems almost as though the salesperson is working for the client. Any salesperson who has been IBM-trained will have been indoctrinated with this idea of added value and service for the customer. We call this type of selling the co-venture type and position it one step beyond consultant selling. They virtually live with that account and often become part of a planning session when new technology is in the offering or when a new ad campaign is being planned.

Now, for a person who has been a transactional salesperson all his or her life, this kind of selling might seem a bit like Star Wars. We often encounter resistance: "That is big-dollar stuff and it won't work around here." But consider for a moment that it does work in the insurance industry, it is working more in the financial world, it works in accounting, and then consider how Mary Kay or Vivian Woodard have shifted their salespeople to "beauty consultants." Both companies start the sales process with complexion analysis or skin analysis and then position a range of products designed for this special customer.

What's more, many of the very salespeople who pooh-pooh the idea of consultant selling, of partnership selling, will have a few customers with whom they have developed that sort of relationship. Unconsciously, they have literally walked up the steps of selling with their bigger and better customers.

The fourth level of selling, joint venture selling, often puts the salespeople on the line for results. Because it is a longer-lasting relationship, a true customer relationship, the sellers are around to see if the promise produces the results it was supposed to. They are often a part of that evaluation. They may be part of fixing it, if there is a problem.

Notice that in the matrix on the next page, in addition to the customary four levels of selling, we have added the images the buyer has of the seller. The image describes a style of selling. We call them:

THE DOOR KNOCKER

THE PRODUCT PRESENTER

THE CONSULTANT

THE PROFESSIONAL or CO-CREATOR RESOURCE

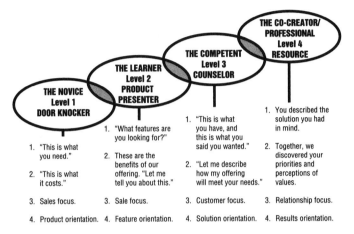

Again, Don Beveridge uses very similar terms when he speaks of the "evolution of salespeople"; he calls them the Commercial Visitor, the Product Peddler, the Consultative Salesperson and the Sustaining Resource. He uses the concept to illustrate styles of selling.

We use them in a slightly different context. We say the way you sell results in an image. When you leave a call, you leave an impression. When potential customers on the floor walk away, you, as a salesperson, have left an impression. They will evaluate the salesperson if it is an important buying decision. Words we might use are "hustler, quick-hitter, egomaniac, pitched it and moved on" for that first level if the impression was unfavorable. Or we might have said: "Must be new, tried hard, seemed OK, nice-appearing young man or she was cute in her Girl Scout uniform" if the impression was favorable.

For the second level, there is a different set of impressions. We might say: "Hard-sell dude, really into features, told me more than I ever wanted to know," or "really knew his office machines, had a good grip on comparative values or handled herself well" if the impression was favorable.

Levels three and four produce a different impression. We might feel the salespeople are more interested in us, that for some reason we could trust them more. We probably told them more about our situation, they seemed to be more credible and professional. We might even have thought of them as problem-solvers.

In many instances, if not in all, we form our final opinion of the sellers from the way they make their presentation. Do they assume we like cookies and pitch the peanuts out of them, or do they consider what we think? How do they position their offering? Do they present it as a product, or do they make it part of a solution we have in mind?

Quite often, the presentations used by the novice and the learner are fairly rigid. In real estate selling, that level of salesperson will show a number of houses, all in the price range the buyers have indicated is their range. They pitch houses until they hit a nerve. The professionals will show two or three houses, usually after some careful listening and some creative searching for the house that fits the buyer image. But they show those houses for reasons. The reasons are not theirs. The reasons are the buyers'! In other words, they not only know their houses (product), they know their buyers and the belief systems of those buyers. They use price as a guideline, not a primary consideration.

Thus, the recommendation for the consultant or the professional is much more flexible and customized.

We're going to provide you two models of presentation. One is a model for a product sale. The other is a model for a solution sale. First, you'll find the model for the product sale outlined on the following page. At the end of this unit, you'll find a model designed for you to adapt to your selling needs, if you choose to do so.

Both models assume you are selling something that will require a written presentation. However, both models can easily be adapted to a verbal or even an audio-visual type presentation. Both adapt to many uses. The basics apply to many forms. It's just a case of determining where you are in your development as a salesperson, where you want to be and how soon. The models will help you get there.

TECHNIQUES AND MODEL FOR PRODUCT PRESENTATIONS

WHEN TO USE:

1.   When you want to present the same idea to a number of prospects or clients.

2.   When you need to make a number of calls.

3.   When you want to prospect with a specific offering. (If they tell you "no," you can often do a very fast discovery of why they said "no.")

HOW TO USE:

1.   Keep the product presentation simple. Make it easy for buyers to say "yes" or "no."

2.   You control the presentation. You track logically.

3.   Use the visual material to reinforce your verbal presentation, even to using just key words or points.

FOR WHAT?

1.   Special offerings or promotions. Special events.

2.   Specific packages or offerings.

3.   Visually oriented prospects, people comfortable with print.

THE ELEMENTS

PAGE 1:   CUSTOMIZE (Use the prospect or client name when possible) "This concept was designed for (their name)."

PAGE 2:   THE ATTENTION-GETTER (What makes this special!)

PAGE 3:   BENEFIT TO THEM

ADVANTAGE

ADVANTAGE

PAGE 4:   THE PLAN — MECHANICS — IMPLEMENTATION

(How It Works)

PAGE 5:   SPECIFIC BENEFITS

A. Traffic   B. Tie-In   C. Contest

D. Sales Incentive   E. Extra Values

PAGE 6:   THIS IS HOW YOU PARTICIPATE

(Include the deadline here: You must decide by ...)

VERY STRONG CLOSE — You go for "yes" or "no."

Be prepared to give the prospect a single sheet that contains the information. Leave your business card. If they have asked for "time to think it over" and that fits your deadline, set a specific time to call back for their decision.

This is copyright material and may be reproduced only with express permission of Greenwood Performance Systems.

TECHNIQUES AND MODEL FOR SOLUTION PRESENTATIONS

WHEN TO USE:

1. When you have done a thorough discovery and have a solid summary.

2. When you are doing a group decision maker sale.

3. When you are seeking major dollars and important decisions.

HOW TO USE:

1. In a personal presentation, if at all possible.

2. Adequate copies for all decision makers or buying influences.

3. Use narrow margins when possible and double space if possible. People may make notes on the presentation.

FOR WHAT?

1. When you are serious about getting a serious decision about a serious piece of business.

2. See number 1, just above.

THE ELEMENTS

PAGE 1:   OPENING STATEMENT.

PAGE 2:   STATEMENT OF SOLUTION OR PROMISE. THIS IS (P)

PAGE 3:   POSITIONING OF PROMISE. (REVIEW OF SUMMARY AGREEMENT)

PAGE 4:   VERIFICATION OF SOLUTION. (HOW PROMISE FITS SUMMARY)

PAGE 5:   APPLICATION AND AMPLIFICATION OF PROMISE. (HOW SOLUTION WORKS) THIS IS (A)

PAGE 6:   PROOF. (DOCUMENTATION, GUARANTEE, EXPERIENCE) THIS IS (P)

PAGE 7:   ACTION. (DECISIONS NEEDED, NEXT MOVE) THIS IS (A)

As outlined in the previous chapter, this concept of solution selling is built around the acronym PAPA. That is the easy way to remember it. The elements in more detail fall into place this way:

We have suggested that page one of the presentation be a positioning statement. That statement will contain words like: "This unique plan ... specially designed for ... concept has been customized for ... ." The idea is to make it very clear that this is a solution, or concept or plan. It is not a product. They can compare your product with any other. This plan will be much harder to compare in terms of product features.

Page two becomes your promise, your solution, the payoff the buyer specifically asked for. This is the P of the acronym.

Page three is the verification of the solution. Here you tie your summary agreement with the solution. You will use words like "after discussion, we concluded that you want increased efficiency ... after our study, we concluded your field people wanted more ... we had agreed your top priority was faster delivery, and this plan will increase delivery at least 25 percent." This stage takes the buyer's concept of the solution as developed with the summary and uses both product positioning and personal positioning to verify the relationship between solution desired and promised payoff.

This page may review the people who were involved or consulted. If this is the case, the last sentence of this page should contain a line such as: "Was there any buying influence whose opinion we have not considered?" This is the safeguard that protects the salesperson against a late decision maker who appears in the buying loop. So you check, especially if the presentation is verbal or audio/visual. In essence, have we touched all the bases to this point? You want to be seriously sure of this point. You are asking: If this fits, are we ready to make a decision? Have we included everybody who needs to be included?

The next page includes the application and amplification. If you use printed specs or data here, underline or mark with yellow highlighter the important points. Make it easy to follow. You outline features and credible benefits application. You outline research applications, how data and research fit. You outline time span applications, budget applications, being careful not to get into specific pricing. You get into added value and those applications. You outline who-what-when-where and how.

NOW, you add proof on the next page. Here you might show how you have met specs, offer comparisons to those systems currently in place and perhaps use testimonials or list satisfied customers who would serve as references. You remove as much element of challenge as you can with your proof.

The next page is the action page. Here you outline implementation, delivery, installation or a schedule of events. You include a date for approval in your schedule. You use realistic dates and time frames. You show whose responsibility it is for certain and specific things, you show what you or your organization will do and what the buyer needs to do. You show training, orientation, pre-marketing plans, etc. In other words, you push your recommendation into the future and ASSUME CONSENT.

Your last page outlines pricing or investment. You may choose to do this in terms of "provided we reach agreement by a certain date, these rates would apply." Or, "the investment quoted here will be honored until (a specific future date)." In other words, you put a fuse on it and put some sense of urgency in the recommendation. You've offered a valuable solution. It deserves consideration. You can't hold the offer open indefinitely.

Now, there are some reasons for this particular sequence in preparing this type of recommendation. There are some nuances in this concept. First, the use of the fuse. If they question the time limit, be prepared to negotiate something that more nearly fits their schedule. If the pricing can provide for some options and alternatives, you have left room for negotiation.

Remember, the odds are excellent that, if the decision is major and the dollars are major, there will be some negotiation. Again, product selling tends to be more rigid in these areas than consultant or partnership selling. In fact, it is not unusual on some major sales that the parties involved will emerge with some form of joint venture. They may share in initial research or even development of the concept. They may turn to a leasing arrangement instead of a purchase agreement. And, in some very complex sales, they may even share legal expense when they know the lawyers will eventually be involved in the recommendation.

What's more, in today's world of marketing, it is entirely possible that three or more companies may join in a partnership or joint venture. For instance, in the Frequent Flyer programs, there are hotels, rental cars and airlines all sharing in the concept of the program. You have amusement parks, airlines and tourist destinations all sharing in a mutually beneficial promotional concept. Increasingly, supermarkets are marrying various food vendors in leveraged promotional plans. More and more products that are perceived as being pretty much the same by the consumer are being combined or married to other products to provide a unique offering for the public.

The pure product solution is becoming less of a reality. The need for level one and two types of selling is lessening. The need is for more level three and level four salespeople. Demand for their skills and expertise if growing. Opportunities for this kind of selling are growing. As Wayne Dyer says in his book *You'll See It When You Believe It*: "It is not a case of looking at the apple and wondering how many seeds it contains; rather, it is a case of looking at the seeds and wondering how many apples they contain."

The difference between the two types of presentations on the following pages provides a good opportunity to make other points. There is no question that the solution presentation requires more work. It requires more probing, more research, a better understanding of the buyer, more creativity. It requires not just more work, but more smart work.

Let's go back to the pea game we used as the analogy to help you remember the way to determine the state of buyer readiness. We painted a word picture of four shells lined up, all unmarked, and titled them Discomfort-Hope-Maintenance-Euphoria. If the seller can identify great urgency-pain-discomfort or great gain-hope-potential and has an offering with a unique competitive edge, the straight product pitch can still work. Often, this is a case of a salesperson being in the right place at the right time. But, in either case, we have provided a model to fit your need.

PRACTICE MODEL FOR A PRODUCT PRESENTATION

ACCOUNT NAME FOR CUSTOMIZED FIRST PAGE

PAGE 1:   This presentation has been prepared especially for

_____

YOUR ATTENTION-GETTER

PAGE 2:   This special offer will _____

_____

_____

BENEFIT TO THEM.

PAGE 3.   The special benefits of this are _____

_____

which provides the advantage of _____

_____

and the advantage of _____

_____

THE PLAN ... THE IMPLEMENTATION ... HOW IT WORKS ... MECHANICS ... SPECS ...

PAGE 4.   _____

_____

_____

SPECIFIC BENEFITS. (Limited offer ... time limit ... tie-in values ... leverage.)

PAGE 5.   _____

_____

_____

THIS IS HOW YOU PARTICIPATE. REQUEST FOR ACTION OR DECISION.

PAGE 6.   The deadline for this is _____

and the requirements are _____

_____

YOU USE A VERY STRONG AND DIRECT CLOSE. YOU ASK FOR A DECISION. YOU TELL THEM IF THEY HAVEN'T SAID "YES," THEN THEY HAVE, IN REALITY, SAID "NO."

Be prepared to leave a one-sheet description of the offering. Leave your business card. Be very specific about the deadline.

PRACTICE MODEL FOR A SOLUTION PRESENTATION

OPENING STATEMENT

POSITIONING PROMISE (Brief review of summary agreement)

THE PROMISE (This is the proposal/recommendation/solution)

*VERIFICATION OF PROMISE OR SOLUTION. (How promise fits summary)

APPLICATION AND AMPLIFICATION OF PROMISE (How your solution will work)

PROOF (How you prove, document or make credible your promise)

ACTION (Steps to be taken, what we will do, what they will do)

YOUR FUSE (Deadlines or expiration dates of offer)

*This is optional, depending upon circumstances.

The odds today are that buyers are more likely to be in the posture of maintenance or status quo. If what they presently have is working reasonably well, they will be less likely to jump on an alternative, because of the "cost of switching." The cost of buying a house isn't just the house. It costs to move, to change insurance, to hook up appliances. In advertising, it costs to shift from one medium to another, if only for the reason of the cost of switching production. The radio commercials must be replaced with television announcements.

The more a product is regarded as generic, the more an offering is seen as essentially the same as other offerings, the less chance of the presence of "switching costs." If a buyer has many options, and sees them as pretty much the same, the selling situation is absent the cost of switching and probably is transactional selling. It becomes a utility sale. The product is presented as a utility. The lowest price will usually get the sale.

When you make your presentations using P A P A, whether you become skilled at following the steps verbally, in written form or a combination of the two, you are forced to present something more than a utility! What's more, what you put into the "solution offering" can initially help eliminate the hidden objections to the "cost of switching." The direct comparison of product to product is more difficult to make.

Carry that thinking one step further. Suppose that, in your original presentation, you really did offer a promise, you showed the advantages of the application and you proved the value of your offering. You asked for the business and you got it. Now you have a customer. You have an opportunity to sell more, sell up, improve the relationship, to really position yourself and your offering to the customer. You build a co-venture.

Now, you are no longer the hunter looking for business. You are the hunted, the offering that other salespeople are taking shots at. You are the standard for comparison. Now, ask yourself this question: "How easy would it be for my customer to switch the business they are doing with me to another source?"

So, selling at the higher level isn't just a case of reward for the immediate sale. That is the short-term gain. But, if P A P A is used correctly initially, and if the follow-up service is there, if the sales-person builds and maintains the high-level relationship, the long-term gain is even more substantial. There is less chance to lose business in the long term.

::

SOMETIMES THERE ARE ROADBLOCKS TO COMPLETE AGREEMENT, AND HOW DO WE HANDLE THOSE OBJECTIONS?

CHAPTER 18

SOMETIMES THERE ARE ROADBLOCKS TO COMPLETE AGREEMENT, AND HOW DO WE HANDLE THOSE OBJECTIONS?

O ld-style selling usually had a format that could be simplified into three stages: PRESENTATION, OBJECTIONS and CLOSING.

Presentation might have been embellished a little in the training sessions with some discussion of developing rapport with the prospect, but the central idea was how to get and keep control. The theme was that the salesperson dominated the buyer. In fact, the words used, such as "get attention" or "beat down objections" or "put the close on them," all revolved around a relationship between buyer and seller that was almost antagonistic, adversarial or competitive.

Objections then fit neatly into this package. You presented; they raised objections. You handled the objections and you closed. They raised another objection, you turned it into a question and you closed. In the scheme of understanding the sales process, objections fit neatly between the pitch and the close.

As the marketplace grew more sophisticated and customers became better-educated and better-informed, it was only natural that selling would adapt to those changes. Salespeople began to ask: "How do I handle the objection to an appointment?" When a buyer declines to set an appointment with a salesperson, it really calls for some skill to handle that objection.

These developments were troubling to sales trainers, because now they were less certain where to put the subject of objections in their material. Other developments also came into the picture. Some sales courses began to talk about a "trial close," or testing the water to see if the state of buyer readiness could be determined. Other books on sales began to advocate a series of questions during the presentation that would check buyer understanding. "Is that point clear?" "Do we have an understanding so far?" In our material, we call this technique "mini-contracts," or getting little agreements on the points of the presentation as you move along, so there won't be one big request for agreement at the end of the presentation.

In essence, all these techniques were methods for reducing objections. Depending on the level of sophistication of the technique and the level of development of the salesperson, there would be varying degrees of acceptance and understanding of these techniques.

We suggest that each of the four levels of sales expertise recognizes objections differently and probably handles them in different ways. The minds of the salespeople change, the words they use change and the methods change and evolve. We believe that no part of the sales process is better explained by the sales matrix. It shows the evolution of the skill of handling objections.

This evolution of the skill of handling objections begins with direct confrontation and an adversarial relationship. It progresses to a much higher level that is really more conflict management than it is handling objections. In fact, the principle we advocate is taken right from leadership training and works as well in management conflict as in sales conflict.

If you check the matrix in this unit, you'll see that in level one and level two, the focus is either on the salesperson or the product. In these two levels, it is an inward focus. The novice feels any objection is personal rejection. He is being rejected. The level two sellers feel their idea, product or service is being rejected. They transfer the

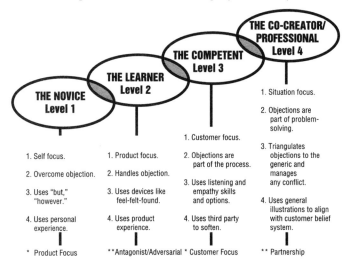

objection from personal to product.

In levels one and two, the atmosphere is more adversarial. At one extreme, the salesperson sees the encounter as "either I win or you win." You may have heard that old phrase: "In every encounter somebody makes a sale. Either I do or they do." That goes back to the idea of win-lose or lose-win types of selling. If such an encounter could have been worthwhile for both buyer and seller, and no agreement is reached, it results in lose-lose.

Out of this climate or mindset comes the idea that you "overcome objections." We've seen sales sessions where a sales manager throws common "objections" out to the salespeople and they are supposed to overcome the objection. These experiences tend to embed the idea into the minds of salespeople that objections are barriers to be overcome.

Listen to beginning salespeople respond to some objections and the odds are excellent they will use either the word "but" or the word "however." The exchange might go like this:

Buyer: "That's all very nice, but I can sure buy it cheaper from several other sources."

Seller: "But, will you be getting the quality we are offering?"

Another scenario:

Buyer: "The other people are giving me one case free with every 12 I order."

Seller: "However, wouldn't you agree that when we pick up shipping charges, that's worth a lot more than a case of goods?"

Quite often, you will hear a personal reference in the objection handling:

Buyer: "You mean I need to make a 12-month commitment to get this price?"

Seller: "Well, I don't like to make long commitments, either, but in this case, it is a pretty safe buy considering our reputation.

Signs of level one salespeople working with objections often include body language. There is hardly a pause between the buyer objection and the seller response. In fact, it often appears they are merely waiting for the objection so it can be handled. Or, the opposite may be true, they brush right by it, intent on their presentation and paying little attention to buyer response.

Level two salespeople begin to use devices and techniques. Often, they will have a favorite way to handle an objection. For instance, they might use something like "FEEL-FELT-FOUND." Let's say the field is insurance.

Buyer: "Well, as you know, we are looking at several different plans or options, and I'm just not sure what you are offering is in the ballpark."

Seller: "I can understand you feeling that way, because quite often when a person is looking at several different options the comparison can be a little confusing. Just last week, I was working with a client in the same situation and they felt a little confused and maybe even overwhelmed. We looked closely at all the features in our plan, especially the long-range advantages, and they decided to put value ahead of price. Could we use a similar approach in your case?"

Here, the seller switched from the word "found" to "decided" or had massaged the original concept around a little bit. Another thing about this FEEL-FELT-FOUND is that it begins with what we call a "softening statement" or an empathizer.

The softening statement puts a nice pause in the dialogue before the seller gets to the point. Instead of the immediate "but" or "however," there is that phrase: "I understand how you feel."

There are many types of softening statements, such as:

"That's an interesting comment."

"I can see the logic of what you're saying."

"That certainly is a valid concern."

"Really ... yes ... of course ... looking at it from your point of view."

Let's put a softening statement together with a FEEL-FELT-FOUND in another scenario. Let's say you are in a furniture store, looking at a sofa and you casually flip over the price tag and see a very big number there. Unconsciously, you say: "Wow!"

Seller: "You're looking at the price tag?"

You: "That's a fairly heavy price!"

Seller: "Well, your reaction is fairly normal. Many people feel that way when they consider an investment in an

important piece of furniture, and a piece like this usually sets the tone for the whole room. Some of my best
customers originally felt like this line was overpriced.
You'll notice something else on that tag. That's the
name of the manufacturer, Yield House. Not many
stores are qualified to carry their line ... been making
beautiful furniture up in New Hampshire for over 100
years. So, when folks take that into consideration, how
long this line retains its shape, the styling that can last
a lifetime, the reputation that backs up every piece they
make, well, people found enough good reasons to justify their choice. They were pretty comfortable they
were making a sound selection."

Now, there is FEEL-FELT-FOUND in the hands of a pretty fair
country salesperson. In fact, he is just about at level three. In fact,
in this scenario, he would move right on up when he began to ask
some questions:

Seller: "Tell me, because it seems you are attracted to quality,
               would a sofa be for a new home? Are you remodeling?
               What is your situation?"

And, with that question, he moves from transactional selling to
consultant selling and to high-performance selling.

Level three salespeople, the competent, consider objections
part of the sales process. Often, in their call planning, they will do
a little brainstorming or visualizing and anticipate objections they
might encounter. They plan their presentation to eliminate as many
objections as possible. But the strength of this level of selling rests
in the discovery of what the prospect or customer wants. By the
very nature of the presentation, it is positioned into what the
prospect or customer said they had and what they wanted. The
salesperson takes this information and builds around it.

When objections are raised, the objections often become resistance. Quite often, the resistance is to change. The status quo or the
comfort zone of the buyer is a very powerful pacifier. Think of it this
way: Neither the push of discomfort nor the pull of hope is sufficient
to create action or motivation.

Evidence of this is sometimes articulated by the buyer with
statements like: "Well, I'm just going to have to think this one
through," or "Well, I really just don't know what to say at this time."

At the second level, the salesperson will throw darts. "Is it the
price?" "Is it the timing?" "Is it the terms?" "Is it the model?" Or the
buyer may say: "Well, I'll just have to take this one to the client."

Or, even more mysterious: "Well, it will take a few days to get a decision from the committee."

How often have you heard even an experienced salesperson say: "I never could figure out why they didn't buy it?"

A level two salesperson can seldom handle resistance to buying. So, how do the level three or level four salespeople handle this situation? They put all their listening skills to work to hear both what the other person is really saying and what he is not saying. They probe to understand, but not to challenge. They introduce as much empathy as possible with complete focus on the buyer. They shift to third-party stories.

They create a problem-solving atmosphere. They shift to options and alternatives with phrases that begin with "what if" and "suppose." If a concession is involved in the "suppose we could" statement, it is a very small concession. They involve the other person in the problem-solving, searching for a possible solution. They avoid confrontation. They make it as easy as possible for the other person to change his or her mind, because only the other person can change his own mind or modify his position. The image created by the salesperson is one of understanding and adaptability. It becomes a joint venture.

In advertising sales, you might hear salespeople say, very carefully: "You'll notice there is a deadline in this proposal. Actually, there is room for only two more sponsors in this plan, and I would sure like to see you be one of those." That's pushing the buyer a little in the direction of discomfort. They might miss a good offering.

In real estate selling, the salesperson might say: "I can understand you not wanting to move too fast. I was working with a couple last week and they were looking at a house that was a wonderful value. Of course, those houses don't stay on the market that long, and you can guess what happened."

Turn either of these scenarios around and make it the pull of hope. The advertising salesperson says: "Actually, we are down to having room for just one more sponsor. Some of the ideas we're working on with other sponsors are rather exciting. In one case ... (AND THEY SITE A SPECIFIC SITUATION)." And now you are working with hope to get the response off center, out of status quo and into hope. You are trying to move the pea under a better readiness shell.

In the case of the real estate scenario, it might go: "I can certainly appreciate your reasons for not wanting to move too fast. Not long ago I was working with the nicest couple and they were really in that undecided position. I stressed the value of the house and they made the decision to move ahead. Now they are so busy and so excited about their new home they can't wait for the closing. You might want to consider those benefits as you think this over." Here is the push of hope, because moving into a new home can be exciting and very satisfying.

In each of the situations we have given you as a word picture, we have tried to illustrate how level three salespeople handle resistance and objections as a natural part of the process. They use listening skills. They give the buyers room to change their minds. They are careful to avoid confrontation, giving the buyers room to amend and modify their resistance or objection. Seldom do they ever paint the buyers into the corner. There is genuine empathy for the buyer position. This is conveyed with heavy use of the third-party story.

Said another way to make the point, at levels one and two, salespeople like to put the monkey on their back. They want to handle the objection. They want to overcome the objection. Level three and level four salespeople really don't want the monkey on their back. They bring along their satisfied customers, their happy clients, and they let those folks carry the monkey. That's the use of the third-party story.

Think back again to when you made an important buying decision in which a good amount of money was involved. How were you guided to the stage where you bought? Was it some silver-tongued salesperson? Or was it a third-party reference?

Moving to the fourth level of selling and some of the skills employed by the professional person who will function more often as a co-creator: We have suggested that consultant and co-creator selling have a different context from transactional selling. Transactional selling puts the focus primarily on the product. The upper levels of selling have a double focus: One on the product needs of the buyer, the other on personal needs. One is the business end of the process and the other is the people end. So the upper-level sellers make a conscious effort to separate the product and the people. They send that message by the words they use. The method is important.

This is the way a model of this method would be visualized. In the left circle, you have the other person, them, the buyer. In the right circle, you have me, the seller, us. In the third circle, you have the objection, the issue, the reservation.

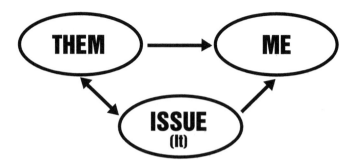

In this concept of dealing with objections, the issue is without ownership. It is not the buyer problem or the seller problem. It is neutral. The salesperson shifts to third-party language. Phrases like: "So the reservation is the length of time for delivery, is that it?" Or perhaps: "The issue here seems to be one of change, and change often is difficult." The implication is clearly made that the issue, the problem, the reservation (all words used instead of objection), is a neutral problem that we ought to consider.

At this point, the sellers turn to another system for dealing with the objections. There is an issue here, they almost think to themselves at this point, and I wonder how it FITS ... and FITS, the acronym, introduces another system. This is the way that model looks:

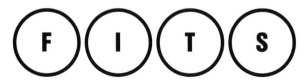

The (F) stands for focus and calls for focused listening and focused probing. But the probing is done in the third party. The sellers probe the issue, not the other person. They use third-party language, neutral language, as much as possible. This reduces the tension and allows them to manage a difference of opinion or conflict.

The (I) stands for identify. Identification consists of using another triangle. That triangle looks like this:

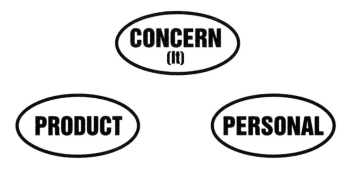

Is the issue one of product, implementation, specifications, or is the issue a personal concern? Is it a belief system concern? If it is a belief system concern, it will involve:

POWER

PRESTIGE

ACCEPTANCE

RESPECT

Notice that in the (I), or identify step, we have changed issue to concern. Whether an objection is really resistance in disguise is often a matter of semantics. Whether the objection is to the product or doesn't fit the belief system, both are concerns. One says: "I don't think your product will do the job" and the other says: "For personal reasons, this isn't the solution I had in mind." In either case, they are concerns. The fourth level of selling recognizes them as such and will often, in dealing with either objection or resistance, use that very word.

Usually, in this stage of the sales process, when the concern is lack of information, that concern will be stated by buyers as a question. That concern may come before they have made a decision, or when they have sorted through the options and have decided your solution is not the best one. It is possible that from the time you put together your solution or recommendation, their needs have changed. It's possible the buying influences or players have changed. So, until you can identify that concern, the buyer is not likely to give you a commitment.

This leads to questions or probing, to identify the concern, product or personal. A concern can be a tip-off to any of the following:

1.   The needs have changed.

2.   There are new, or additional, needs not uncovered previously.

3.   There has already been a decision made against your offering.

4.   You may need to revise your solution.

The salesperson needs to identify why the concern exists and make the connection between that concern and how it will affect the buying decision. What's more, the salesperson needs to be responsive to that concern, unless there is reason to do otherwise, at that time.

For instance, suppose you were selling advertising for a Shopper that also offered a marriage mail opportunity. You were making a recommendation to a medical clinic. In a previous call, you had determined the prospect wanted to reach professional and upper-income people in specific zip zones. The location of the clinic would save them time and there would be no long waiting for doctors. You had recommended they run rather glossy, upscale inserts in the Shopper. The prospect has considered your recommendation and now he says the following things. Which statements would identify the concern and which statements would identify a need for you to revise your recommendation? Use (C) for concern and (R) for revisions.

1. _____   "I don't think your publication is right for our clinic this quarter. I think we can expand our business by using upscale magazines."

2. _____   "So far, we have concentrated our advertising on upscale, local magazines, but I'm just not sure the time is right for us to consider a broader market."

3. _____   "I just don't know about your idea. We really need to reach an upscale market, and you've got a lot of clutter in your paper each week."

4. _____   "I don't think your publication will help us. We are pretty well satisfied with what we are doing now."

Statement No. 1 is concern. What is the key word in that statement? How does the publication not fit this prospect's concern? Statement No. 2 is also a concern and would not require revising the proposal. Statement No. 3, upon further probing, might indicate a need to revise the proposal. The salesperson might want to emphasize another location in the paper itself. And Statement No. 4 is also open to further probing because the solution apparently has not closed the gap between what they have now and what they see as an alternate solution. Probing for the root of the concern will provide IDENTIFICATION. So now we have Focus and Identification.

The (T) stands for triangulate, or the use of a three-legged stool. The sellers are careful to keep the issue — even if it is personal — triangulated. They keep the issue neutral with the use of a third-party analogy. They guard against putting the belief system of the other person on the line. Remember, they can't change a buyer's mind — only the buyer can do that. The search for the FITS involves "what's in it for them?"

That question leads directly to the (S) or the search. The seller searches, with questions, for the solution to the objection.

When they believe they have located that reason or reasons for the objection, then — and only then — will they position a possible solution. Always, it is a mutual search, using such phrases as: "So, suppose we look at that issue and see what options might be available." Again, the language is neutral. The issue still has no ownership.

The dialogue of such a situation might go something like this:

Buyer: "I like your recommendation here very much. It has some good points, but a cash outlay at this time of that amount is just out of the question."

Seller: "You're referring now to the upfront amount or to the total investment?"

Buyer: "Well, probably both. The upfront requirement would make my present budget look like a war zone."

Seller: "Yes, that's a valid point from your view. Budgets have a way of being rather rigid at times." (The problem is not the buyer or the seller. The third leg of the stool has been added. It is the budget. That is the impersonal issue.)

Buyer: "I could agree with that statement." (They just bought the third leg.)

Seller: "So, what would happen if we did this? Suppose we leave that issue for the moment. Let's look at what is positive in the other areas of your analysis of this recommendation and then come back to it. Perhaps we can work out some alternatives."

The key technique here involves these steps:

FOCUS: Really listen and focus on the buyer or the buying influence making that statement.

IDENTIFY: Was the budget issue real? Was it personal? Notice
               they referred to it as "my budget," but it wasn't a total-
               ly rigid position. They called it a "war zone." It had a lit-
               tle play in it. What is the belief system of this buyer?
               What do you know about them to this point?

TRIANGULATE: The salesperson got out the three-legged stool
               and handled it as a budget issue. He triangulated the
               issue. It was now a generic issue that called for reso-
               lution. This is conflict management.

SEARCH: The salesperson chose to let the issue sit for the
               moment. It was there, it had been identified. It was a
               problem to be solved, perhaps as the last difference
               standing between the salesperson and buyer commit-
               ment. They would mutually search for a way to resolve
               the issue.

In the opening chapter of this journey, we led you through what happens to the minds of the salespeople as they pass through the different stages of sales development. Not all salespeople will reach the level of a professional. However, any person inclined to sales can reach that level of competence with commitment, good self-talk and effort. It is their choice.

To move to the third and fourth level of selling, salespeople must learn to negotiate the troubled waters of objections. If levels one and two require a strong ego, then three and four require strong empathy. Self-actualization of both buyer and seller becomes a factor. Buyer Images of Reality become stronger, and the seller encounters more powerful people. As the size of the sale increases, the skill and expertise of the buyer is also likely to increase. For these reasons, we are convinced that the ability to handle objections is likely to be the last skill the advancing salespeople will add that will allow them to reach the higher levels.

The buyers also have self-actualization as a part of their belief system. This dimension is present for both the high-level salesperson and the high-level buyer. Both have a set of needs. For the seller, that set of needs revolves around money, psychic challenge and self-actualization. Thus, the high-level salesperson can slip into the role of partner much easier than can the novice. The same is true of the buyer. The buyer has that same set of needs, such as money or income (I want to keep my job), psychic challenge (I want power, prestige, acceptance or respect) and wanting to feel good about the process of buying, the final commitment and the results to be obtained from that commitment.

For most buyers, psychic challenge is the top priority. And now we come again to the idea that people buy because a product fits their needs, and because of what that product will do for them — the solution or promise — fits their belief system or the psychic challenge conjured up by their belief system. They want a personal win.

Our summary of this subject of objections would be this: Objections are a fact of life in selling. They are present for all four levels of selling. In the first two levels of selling, both novices and learners handle objections in a rather frontal way. They may even believe they can change the other person's mind. In the third and fourth levels of selling, the salespeople come to understand they cannot change another person's belief system. They can, at best, modify it or, more likely, help the buyer change his own mind.

The skill of handling the objections grows with each level. As the understanding of the complexity of the issue grows deeper, respect for the process also grows. If the novice uses a shovel to cover up an objection, then the professional uses a scalpel to make as small an incision as possible, so the patient suffers no pain.

We have provided a number of ideas, illustrations and models for consideration. Study all of them. Pick the one or ones you feel fit your stage of professionalism, your career passage. They all have a place.

PRACTICE IN USING F-I-T-S

We will provide a number of fairly common objection statements. We suggest you read the statement out loud to yourself so you really hear it. As you begin the focus step, open that with a softening statement, such as: "I see" or "Yes, that's an interesting point" or "I understand."

Then write your response as you focus, identify and triangulate into the three-legged stool. Keep it impersonal or third person. Then, design at least two probe questions that would maintain the issue in neutral. Avoid the words "I" and "you," if at all possible.

STATEMENT: I'm not real sure. That's sounds a little risky to me.

FOCUS: _____

_____

_____

IDENTIFY: _____

_____

_____

TRIANGULATE: _____

_____

_____

SEARCH: _____

_____

_____

STATEMENT: I'm really not in that big a hurry right now.

FOCUS: _____

_____

_____

IDENTIFY: _____

_____

_____

TRIANGULATE: _____

_____

_____

SEARCH: _____

_____

_____

STATEMENT: That price seems a little high to me.

FOCUS: _____

_____

_____

IDENTIFY: _____

_____

_____

_____

TRIANGULATE: _____

_____

_____

SEARCH: _____

_____

_____

STATEMENT: Does the price drop if we increase the size of the order?

FOCUS: _____

_____

_____

IDENTIFY: _____

_____

_____

TRIANGULATE: _____

_____

_____

SEARCH: _____

_____

_____

Now, go back and check yourself. In looking at your responses — and in some cases you may have been using a little imagination — do you find phrases like these:

FOCUS: I see. That does sound like a concern.

Oh, really. That might be something that should be looked at.

I understand. In your opinion, the problem is the color.

IDENTIFY: Could we talk about that a little more?

In that regard, your point is ...

Perhaps you could explain that a bit for me ...

TRIANGULATE: So, the concern in this instance would be ...

That issue seems important, and we ought to consider it.

Color is usually a personal thing that needs consideration.

SEARCH: Can you explain that for me?

Tell me more about your point on this.

Would this be important to you?

Are you thinking of how others would view this?

Are you saying this would break a normal buying pattern?

Would this be more of an issue than the ...?

Could you clarify the reasons for that for me, please?

KEY TECHNIQUES OF HIGH-PERFORMANCE SELLING SUMMARIZED

"I can certainly understand your feeling on that, and other folks have felt the same way. When they weighed the pluses against the minus, they found that ... "

This technique is the first step in handling objections.

1.   It is the basic method of handling an objection by introducing FEEL, FELT and FOUND.

2.   I understand how you feel.

3.   Others have felt the same way.

4.   Upon further examination, they found ...

This is a power technique because:

1. It uses obvious empathy as the first step.

2. It uses the "third party" to handle the objection.

3. It adds the credibility of previous experience by the third party.

THE POWER IS IN THE TECHNIQUE. MODEL THE TECHNIQUE TO FIT YOUR STYLE. PRACTICE IT UNTIL YOU ARE COMFORTABLE WITH IT, USING YOUR WORDS AND YOUR PACING.

::

... It Also Depends Upon The Personality Of the Buyer Or Buying Influence, And Their Needs

... IT ALSO DEPENDS UPON THE PERSONALITY OF THE BUYER OR BUYING INFLUENCE, AND THEIR NEEDS

We said that in top-level selling, the professionals handle an objection by using focused listening, identifying the issue, triangulating, then searching for solutions to the issue. They are not so much interested in handling an objection as they are in resolving a concern.

The model we provide, F I T S[1], will work on a variety of people. Exactly how it is used will depend upon the buyers and their belief system. We skimmed by four needs in the previous unit: power, prestige, acceptance and respect. Those certainly aren't the only elements in a belief system, but they have been used in several bodies of knowledge to identify needs and expectations. Our organization happens to use the Wilson Learning material, specifically their Social Style material.

Social Style is, in reality, a two-dimensional way to look at needs and expectations — why people respond to other people as they do. The two dimensions are assertiveness and responsiveness. Assertiveness is the horizontal dimension. People on the left are ask assertive and people on the right side are tell assertive. Those are the new words now in use at Wilson Learning in their copyrighted version of Social Style. Responsiveness is the vertical dimension. Below the center line are those people who are people responsive, and above the line are those who are task responsive.

This results in four quadrants (see Placement Diagram A on the next page). In the upper righthand box is the DRIVER. They are task responsive and tell assertive. They want control and autonomy. In the lower righthand box is the EXPRESSIVE. They are people who are responsive and tell assertive. They want recognition. In the lower lefthand corner is the AMIABLE, people responsive and ask assertive. They want approval. In the upper left box is the ANA-

LYTICAL, task responsive and ask assertive. They want respect. (See placement Diagram B.)

This concept was probably rooted in Carl Jung and his definitions of Thinker, Feeler, Sensor and Intuitor. Jung had two other dimensions in his research, the introvert and the extrovert. Social Style dropped these from the concept.

Placement

Diagram A

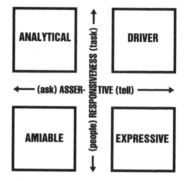

As you can see, you now have four quadrants. Approximately 25 percent of the universe would be in each quadrant. This concept emphasizes that there is no best social style and no right place to be in the quadrants. Each style has strengths and weaknesses. Each style has needs and expectations. When you learn to recognize the social style of a prospect or customer, you can tailor your sales process to those needs and expectations.

Placement

Diagram B

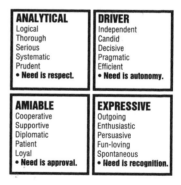

In Placement Diagram B, we have listed the basic characteristics of each of the social styles. These characteristics also could be defined as needs and expectations. For instance, the analytical will relate best with a salesperson if that salesperson is logical, thorough, serious, systematic and offers facts, data and information.

The best way to deal with people of each social style is to meet

their needs and expectations. The analytical likes respect, the driver likes autonomy, the expressive likes recognition and the amiable likes approval.

There has been a spate of this material in the world of sales lately. First of all, it's a pleasant ego trip to find out how other people view you. The material also has some basic application. But when you carry it to some extremes — word descriptions of buyers such as zealots, autocrats, plutocrats, gamesmen, sharing-caring people — it can get a little confusing to a salesperson faced with an abrasive buyer who has just saddled him with: "You're asking what? You must be out of your gourd!"

Novices or level one salespeople really aren't into this. They just want to find a person who will listen to them and who might buy something. They play the odds without much regard for investigating the buyer's belief system. By the time they are in the Learner stage or level two, they begin to figure out that they have to find a decision maker or nothing much will happen. The Learner spends a lot of time pitching to somebody who really can't make a buying decision. By the third level of selling, or when the salesperson begins asking questions to determine that gap between have and want, the salesperson becomes more conscious of finding a decision maker.

At this level of sales expertise, they have recognized three types of buyers. They categorize them as the people who have the power to say "yes," the people who have the power to say "no" but can't say yes and the buying influences, or people who can't say "yes" or "no" but can influence the people with the power to say either. The third-level salespeople go a step further when they divide the belief system into product and personal. Now they ask: Why will my buyers say "yes" if they can and why might they say "no," and how do I position my offering within their belief system? Does the buyer want control, recognition, approval or respect?

An understanding of social style helps identify that personal agenda. It helps in all phases of the call: questioning, recommending, handling objections and closing. It helps locate the belief system or personal agenda. Thus, the third-level salesperson working with a group of decision makers will develop the sales strategy for the solution or promise and will then consider the tactics that will work with each individual involved. The analyticals in the group will want respect and detail. The drivers will want autonomy and choices. The expressives will want recognition and the concept. The amiables will want approval, safety and a feeling of teamwork with

the salesperson. Social Style thus helps the salesperson locate and provide the personal win.

This brings us to the fourth level of selling, the professionals. They follow the same initial steps. Can the prospect say "yes"? Can they say "no"? Can they influence the buy? Then they ask themselves a second question: Who really will make the decision? And what tactics will be used with this person? What is their belief system and what is their need? Autonomy or control, recognition, approval or respect? They then identify each person in the decision-making group.

They build something into their solution, if they can, what will appeal to each of the decision makers. Sound a little complex? Not really. In real estate, how may times have you heard an agent say: "I had the wife sold but the husband didn't like the location?" Or perhaps it was: "Everything was perfect, that is until the kids saw it and it didn't have a big enough pool to suit them." The kids couldn't say "yes' or "no," but they sure were buying influences.

In actuality, any time a seller has more than one person in the buying loop or in a buying decision posture, the dynamics are present for multiple appeals to each buyer or buying influence. With each person, the salesperson must locate the situation, the priorities and the explicit benefits that person expects and needs.

In group selling, the person who can say "yes" is your prime prospect to be the advocate or the partner for your solution. The tactic, then, is to cultivate that person without alienating the other players. Consider this tactic used by a professional working on a major sale:

He had his recommendation finished. He took a risk. But then there is always more risk when the reward is greater. He called his identified decision maker. He had counted on this individual's need for both power and prestige. He asked for an appointment. He got it. This was his positioning for his move.

"I realize this may seem a little unorthodox, bringing you our proposal before some of the people in the group see it. But, I have the sense you will be an important voice, if not the final voice, in the ultimate decision. (APPEAL) This is the final proposal and this is the synopsis on this page. I'm asking you to review it briefly. Then, I would like your opinion. Not a decision, just an opinion. If we are in the game, as you see it from your vantage point (APPEAL), I'll go back and follow the usual channels. But I would appreciate your perspective on this." (APPEAL)

In essence, he said: "I need a partner at the top. If you like this, will you help me?"

If the tactic used by third-level and fourth-level salespeople is to cultivate the "yes" sayers, then their tactic with the "no" sayer is to neutralize them as nearly as possible. They have been identified as influences who can kill a proposal, but can't approve it. Quite often, these people actually see themselves as screens or buffers, and their job is to find some reason something can't be done. It is not unusual to find them in accounting or the business office, where they have made the budget a holy grail. They will often pick at details, finding the lint in a proposal.

It may take time to neutralize them and remove their doubts, step-by-step, if necessary. Neutralizing may require research, data, detail and point-by-point analysis of strengths and weaknesses of your proposal. Often, professional salespeople will point out a weakness before they do. They may speed up the credibility of both the sellers and the proposal. You don't try to win every game with these people. You focus on winning the set and match. These people don't like to be beaten 6-0, 6-0 and 6-1.

Now, we come around again to handling objections and why they are easier for level three and level four people to handle. First, they know the situation, the priorities or belief system and the explicit benefits. They understand who can say "yes" and who can say "no" and who can influence the decision. And this gives them insight into how to handle objections.

If the belief system of the buyers revolves around power and control, you listen, identify, triangulate and, in the search for resolution, you use options and alternatives. You give them control. If the belief system revolves around prestige, you repeat the steps to the search part and you do some brainstorming or play with possibilities. The buyer may find the answer. If the buyer needs acceptance, you factor in safety and mutual problem-solving, and you go slow. No hurry with these folks. And with the person who wants respect, you treat any objection as valid. You search with care, being sure of detail.

In the early stages of selling, the Novices and the Learners will use just about any way that works to handle an objection. That's fine. They need to learn how to handle them, need to learn to stand their ground. But as they develop, as their careers begin to evolve, they need to add the polish, and the skill of modeling in the way they handle an objection, to the belief system of the buyer. They learn to do this when they begin to focus more on the personal needs of the buyer. As they do this, they will find themselves becoming more flexible and being more comfortable.

High-performance selling today almost requires an understanding of how to give the buyer a PERSONAL WIN. Level three salespeople often do this unconsciously. You'll hear them use phrases like: "I don't think anybody could second guess your decision on this." Or something like this when they describe how they sold it: "Harry likes to look good to the client, and this proposal gave him plenty of opportunity for that." Or it might have been something like: "Linda is really the power behind the throne, and I played to her ego whenever I could."

If this is an unconscious skill at level three, it becomes a conscious skill at level four. How to provide the PERSONAL WIN is built right into the sales strategy. Social Style provides a handy system for the Conscious-Competent, high-performance salesperson.

KEY TECHNIQUES OF HIGH-PERFORMANCE SELLING SUMMARIZED

The classic objection of "I'll think it over" fits nicely with any discussion of the social styles. The first step in handling this objection is the positive reaction by the salesperson: "That's understandable. I'm glad to hear that." Then comes the application of the social styles.

For the Driver ... the probing should center on the results they want.

For the Expressive ... the probing should focus on their recognition of a good value.

For the Amiable ... the probing ought to focus on the safety of the offering.

For the Analytical ... you review the logic, then take the logic step-by-step.

"I'm glad to hear you say that. That indicates to me we have some value here, or you wouldn't consider it. Tell me, what did you like about this?"

There are two keys to this technique which produce high performance:

1.   The softening statement and the positive reaction. This reduces the tension.

2.   This sets the stage for follow-up probing, which can

then focus on results, recognition, safety or logic.

This is a powerful technique because:

1.   It allows the salesperson to control the tension. It is a positive reaction to delay. This reaction encourages the buyer to open up.

2.   The key then becomes the probing, the purpose of which is to put the process into a forward motion.

3.   It provides for a review of the offering, a view of the total concept.

THE POWER IS IN THE TECHNIQUE. MODEL THE TECHNIQUE TO FIT YOUR STYLE. PRACTICE IT UNTIL YOU ARE COMFORTABLE WITH IT, USING YOUR WORDS AND YOUR PACING.

Additional Reading On Social Style:

Social Style/Management Style (New York: American Management Association) Robert Bolton and Dorothy Grover Bolton Door.

::

AND IF YOU REALLY WANT TO BE SUCCESSFUL IN SALES, YOU WILL FOCUS ON THE GAP ... NOT THE GOAL

AND IF YOU REALLY WANT TO BE SUCCESSFUL IN SALES, YOU WILL FOCUS ON THE GAP ... NOT THE GOAL

"That," we have been told, "is downright heresy!" Or, by a sales manager or two: "You're trying to mess up the heads of salespeople!" Probably no person talking about selling has ever achieved 100 percent conversion to advice. Even preachers have trouble hitting that number.

So, before you dismiss that statement as just a catchy title in a book about selling, read this part carefully and consider it. If you will try the method, if you practice it for just 30 days, you'll find yourself on the GREEN BRICK ROAD TO SUCCESS. You'll find it enhances your earnings. You'll find it improves your closing ratio. You'll find it provides a simple way to correct course until you do reach that goal.

First, let us make it abundantly clear that no person in sales can be successful without goals. Don Beveridge uses an analogy in his workshops that gets this point across very nicely. He tells of getting on an airplane and, as he passes through the door, the pilot is standing there greeting passengers. He asks the pilot if this is the flight to Tampa. "Oh," says the pilot, "we'll be close to there. It may not be exactly Tampa, but we'll be close. Trust us!" You see, not hitting a goal wouldn't work very well for flying. If the pilot had only a vague idea of where he was going, if he missed the runway by a couple thousand feet, it might not please the passengers.

Can you imagine the voice on the speaker in that plane? "We realize you have choices when you fly and we appreciate you picking TENSION AIRLINES. We realize that Sarasota is not exactly where we planned to land, but it's close and we certainly did the best we could."

Too often, salespeople set big, long-range goals for themselves. They want to fly coast-to-coast. They forget one little detail.

They forget to file a flight plan. They do not consider what a pilot has to when he takes off. He has a flight plan! What's more, he can, depending upon time, weather and traffic conditions, modify that plan to fit the situation. What's more, he has certain check-in spots that provide a direction of flight. Radio landmarks lead him from one GAP to another. In essence, that pilot, to reach his goal exactly, will focus on the gaps and not the goal! He takes the plan one leg at a time.

In this material, we have used that word GAP several times. We used it as a guide or marker on the use of questions. For instance: "What is the SITUATION now and what do I know about it?" Then: "What else do I need to know about the SITUATION?" How do I go about filling that gap? We have suggested that buyers have a gap between what they have now and what they want. The solution provided by the salesperson will, we hope, fill that gap.

And when we discussed objections, we used the acronym F I T S. The objection was a gap that needed to be closed. The sellers have a gap between presentation and buyer commitment. What is it? So they focus, identify, triangulate and search for a solution to that objection.

We have also suggested that a sale is a process. The buyers make commitments all along the process. It may not take very long, but first the buyers make a commitment to give time, to reveal information, to talk and listen. Then they make a commitment to consider, make a decision, justify that decision and finally make a buying decision. If you use a horizontal line to visually show that process, it would fit nicely into a one-through-ten process.

Many people focus on the sale or the goal. Too often, that sale is not only in the distance, it requires checking in with a number of markers along the way. Sometimes, there is a need to amend a flight plan. You can't do that unless you know where you are at that time. To use a football analogy, too often the salesperson tries to score a touchdown every time he gets the ball.

Very few touchdowns are scored with long plays. Some are, and they are spectacular. More often, the touchdowns come as planned

results from a series of plays. More touchdowns are scored by moving the ball for first and tens. The long run or the long pass delights
the crowd, but the odds are against the big play.

So, our concept of selling involves a mental picture of moving
a needle from the start of the sale through ten stages to the goal,
which is the sale. That doesn't mean ten calls, or even ten specific
events. But the idea will be the same. Roughly, it breaks down this
way: You'll move the needle from one to three when you qualify or
uncover the buyer or prospect. Can they buy, do they have the
resources, is there a fit? At that point, they move into a "yellow light
phase" as a possible. From four to six or even seven, they are possible, or in neutral — maybe "yes" and maybe "no."

This may be the most important stage of the selling process. It
may also be where the salesperson loses the sale. At this point, the
steps would involve a solid discovery to determine the situation,
explore priorities and values, find the product need and personal
need, locate explicit benefits or promises and then fit this information with your credible buying reasons. It is a time of inspection,
investigation, problem-solving and creativity.

The constant question involved is WHAT DO YOU NEED TO
DO NEXT? WHAT DO YOU NEED TO DO TO MOVE THE
NEEDLE? Who else should you see? Who are other buying influences? Who is the decision maker? Are we sure of budget figures?
When you learn to use the system for whatever you sell, you may
see five as the presentation stage. For instance, your presentation or
recommendation may need approval by several layers of decision
makers. Who else will be involved? How do you get action from
them? How do you move the needle from five to six or seven?
Always, the question is: WHAT DO I NEED TO DO TO MOVE
THE NEEDLE, to get it to ten?

Maybe eight in the real estate process is reducing the agreement
to contract, nine is getting signatures from both parties and ten is
closing. Maybe nine is arranging the financing. You know your selling patterns and can simply fit the concept to your sales process.

Using this technique fits several ways into high-performance
selling. First, let's consider you. It absolutely changes your attitude!
Every time you make progress, you move the needle. Every time
you move the needle, you have gotten a step closer. The question
becomes: "What do I need to do next?" There is the psychic satisfaction of completing a phase of the process. You can enjoy a picnic. If the goal is the banquet, then every stop along the way can be

a mental picnic. You'll find this is a powerful psychic motivator. It forces the salesperson to be progress-oriented, not goal-oriented. You become proactive.

But each step provides an indicator. And if you know there are certain steps in your process, certain bases you must cover, then missing one of those steps or bases becomes less likely with this system. There is less chance something will fall through the cracks. Your attitude shift includes another very subtle part of the sales process. You are less likely to focus on where you have been and more likely to focus on what you need to do to move the needle.

There is another powerful benefit to this system. When the concept is adapted by a sales organization, the language used between salespeople and the sales manager changes. Too often, especially in smaller sales organizations where there's almost daily pressure to make something happen, the sales manager ends the day with a "report session." Crew selling involves this type of reporting on daily activity. The only problem is, the sales manager is not interested in a report, he or she wants a report of sales. The favorite phrase is: "What did you get today?" And, if you didn't get anything, you end the day in the dumper. The idea behind this is to put the full peer group pressure on each person as he reports. The fear of looking bad in front of the group is the stimulus for selling something, selling anything, that day.

This style of management leads almost automatically to the daily, morning meeting, where the sales manager attempts to wind up all the salespeople tight enough they won't run down before the day is over. Does this method focus on the goal, or the finalized sales work? Yes, it can be made to work, but the results are predictable: high sales turnover and salesperson burnout.

Compare this approach for managing salespeople to the more positive question: "Where is the needle on this one?" The salesperson can respond with an estimate of where the needle stands on any given piece of business. Then the follow-up management question can be: "What do you need to do to move the needle?" Again, this becomes positive reinforcement, not negative reinforcement.

SALESPEOPLE ARE OFTEN PROGRAMMED FOR FAILURE; THEY WERE DESIGNED FOR SUCCESS.

We have used that phrase several times, perhaps without explaining it fully. We really do believe that salespeople are designed for success. Salespeople are very special people. In the first place, nothing much happens in the world of marketing until somebody sells something. That's an old phrase that was designed to make salespeople feel good about themselves, but it has more than a ring of truth in it.

We like salespeople because they are generally independent souls who bet on what they can do. They bet on themselves. Most of them put their egos on the line every day, facing rejection and disillusionment. Most of them are competitors. They like to win, they like to beat last year's figures, they like making goals. Most of them have the belief that what they sell will provide a benefit for a client or customer. Sure, there are some "tin men" out there who sell only for a living. But most salespeople believe in their product.

Most of the salespeople we have met and worked with are decent people. They are honest and have a streak of integrity. Some will tell you they have walked from a sale because it wasn't the right thing for the prospect. Some will tell you they couldn't do business because the ethics of the situation bothered them.

In nearly all instances, these people are designed for success. They are intelligent, don't mind hard work, they laugh, they cry, they fail, but they try again. They were designed for success. The good Lord did not make failures. He designed successful people.

But, too often, salespeople are programmed for failure. I didn't realize it when I was a kid. I sold eggs door-to-door for my uncle who had a chicken farm. Eventually, I sold a case of eggs Wednesday afternoon after school, every week. That's 24 dozen in an afternoon. But how many doors in the block did I knock on to sell a dozen eggs? Five ... six ... block after block. "Good afternoon. My uncle has a chicken farm. He raises his own chickens. These eggs were gathered yesterday. They are fresher than you could ever buy at the store, and I sell them for five cents less than you would pay at the store. I'm wondering if you would like to buy some honest-to-goodness farm fresh eggs?"

"We never buy from door-to-door salesmen." "We don't eat eggs." "My wife does the shopping and she isn't home." "I don't have the money right now." "You look cold out there. I don't need any eggs but would you like a cup of hot chocolate?"

Going door-to-door, I was programmed for failure. The insurance salesperson walks through the valley of the shadow the first year. He is programmed for failure. The ad salesperson who starts with no accounts is programmed for failure. The salesperson who works for the sales manager who "came up the hard way and nobody ever helped me" is programmed for failure.

Small wonder that so many salespeople look back at the way they started and shudder. They were programmed for failure. The situation dared them to succeed! But they made it! Because, you see, they were designed for success! That's why we so strongly suggest to salespeople that they focus on their success.

Of all the concepts we have offered salespeople through the years, perhaps none has been as powerful, none has been as successful as the very simple concept: YOU FOCUS ON THE GAP ... NOT THE GOAL.[1] What do you need to do to make something happen? How do you move the needle? What's the next step? This is proactive selling.

Take that rule and combine it with this one: YOU NEVER LEAVE A CALL WITHOUT A COMMITMENT TO ACTION. That is also proactive selling, high-performance selling. You leave with a commitment. You will see them again on a certain date. They will consider your offering and you will call them Tuesday. You will be back next week with a proposal for them. You will meet next week and, in the meantime, you will have talked to the partner involved. You leave with a decision!

Both concepts are congruent. Both are proactive. Both are focused on a gap and what needs to be done to close it!

Again, to emphasize: Nothing in this concept is meant to suggest that selling is a ten-step process. If your focus must be on "What did you sell today?" it does not have great application. But if you are selling larger dollar units, if you sell a product or service that has a longer buyer cycle, if you are in an environment where there are multiple buying influences, then this system will work for you. It can lead you to higher performance.

You will learn in time where you can condense steps to make the process move faster. When you see the needle at the same place over a period of several weeks, you know that situation calls for action or examination. You may even see the needle move backward sometimes. That happens.

When it does, what do you need to do to get it moving forward again? You keep in mind that you focus your attention on the needle and what you need to do to move it, to close that gap, to arrive at ten.

YOUR FOCUS IS THE GAP, NOT GOAL. When you close the gap, you've reached the goal. They key is to always ask, after every call, after every meeting, after any presentation: "Where is the needle?" You are no longer focused on where you have been. You are focused on where you need to go in order to score.

If the GAP concept is a pipeline and you are moving business through that pipeline in order to reach that goal, then consider these words of caution:

Caution No. 1 would be to always remember this: The closer you are to hitting the goal, the closer you are to missing it. The closer you are to winning a sale, the closer you are to losing it. The concept of the gap helps keep you focused on priorities, and you move the nines to tens!

Caution No. 2 would be to always be aware of the front end of the pipeline. Too often, salespeople tend to focus on the middle part of the pipeline. That isn't where you focus. You focus on what needs just a gap or two closed to get to ten and then ... then ... you make certain there is new business in the pipeline. The middle seems to take care of itself without a lot of pressure.

But forget the front and you wake up one day and there are no gaps. You forgot to put some business, some new prospects, some new possibilities in the pipeline. Now, there is trouble in River City. The skill of using this concept is to focus on 8-9-10 and 1-2-3. That takes the slumps and valleys out of selling.

In the evolution of selling, salespeople begin by learning how to prospect, find new business, locate new opportunities. And they say to themselves: "Someday, I won't have to go out door-knocking." And as they add business, they begin to live off their established business and they spend less and less time looking for new opportunities. Their skills improve, their customer list improves and their income improves.

They no longer have the push of discomfort or the pull of hope, and their world becomes one of status quo. From there, it is just one short step to euphoria!

The surest way to high performance is to always have some 1-2-3 accounts in the pipeline. And, again, our matrix works here. The level one salesperson finds business anyplace he can! High activity begets some opportunity. The level four salespeople find new business from present accounts, and we have described the techniques they use in an earlier chapter. The point is, they are never out of the prospecting posture. They exercise constant maintenance of their pipeline.

EXERCISE FOR CHAPTER 20

There is another application of the idea of focusing on the gap and not the goal, and it applies to your personal goal. We have dubbed the four stages of evolving into a high-performance sales-person as follows:

NOVICE

LEARNER

COMPETENT

PROFESSIONAL

We have suggested that every salesperson is in one of those four levels; that every salesperson, having reached the level of the professional, has evolved through the first three stages to reach the level of high performance. Some few salespeople have the ability to move fast and suddenly vault into that top level. Or, they believe they have reached that top level, only to discover, when their sky rocket has burst, that they have not learned all there is to know about selling. Then, they often find they need to go back and re-learn many of the lessons they bypassed on the road to fast success.

Where you think you are, as a salesperson, depends a great deal on your attitude toward your profession and toward yourself.

If you work in an environment where you have management providing appraisal, you have the help of performance evaluation. If you do not have this resource, then you provide your own evaluation. Your personal perception of your sales performance may or may not be accurate.

On the following page, we have provided you with a series of questions and optional responses to create a helpful self-appraisal. This introspection can tell you where you are now. You then might decide where you want to be. If there is a gap, focus on the gap of what you need to do to move your personal needle to reach your goal, at whatever level that goal might be.

At the end of Chapter 21, you'll find a key that will enable you to compare your answers and score yourself, if you so choose.

SALES INVENTORY

Directions: Identify the behavior you are most likely to exhibit in each sales situation. Read each of the four statements for each item carefully. Think about what you would do in each circumstance. Then circle the letter of the alternative action choice that you think would most closely describe your behavior as perceived by prospects or clients. Circle only one choice. Answers on page 262.

1. Call Opening

    A. You need to get attention, get control, maybe dazzle them a little.

    B. I let them know I'm there as a possible resource. The relationship is important.

    C. I tell them why I'm there, what I might do for them and how that fits them.

    D. The buyers will set the pace for the call. They buy if they are ready.

2. Discovery Questions

    A. I search for needs and interests so my presentation fits their concern.

    B. If they need something, they'll tell me without me bugging them with questions.

    C. I keep them talking and eventually they'll tell me things about their business.

    D. I believe I know my product and what's best about it for them.

3. Presenting

    A. My job is to show how our product will provide benefits and opportunities.

    B. I present the recommendation and let the buyers draw their conclusions.

    C. I work with facts and claims until I get a yes or no.

    D. I focus on a good relationship and let the product fall into place naturally.

4. Handling Objections

    A. I gloss over objections and take no chances with a good relationship.

    B. I bury the objection before it buries me.

    C. There is no way to really change their minds; I try to show pluses and minuses.

    D. I try to understand why they have objections and remove those doubts.

5. Closing

    A. If the customers are ready to buy, they'll tell me so.

    B. I sum up the presentation, treat objections as questions and ask for the sale.

    C. I keep the pressure on until I get a yes or no. I keep closing.

    D. There is a key time to suggest the presentation fits them.

6. Basic Premise of Selling

    A. If you make the right presentation, the buyer will perceive benefit.

    B. To make a sale, you must control the buyer and the situation. You must win.

    C. You can't create sales out of nothing. Make the calls and you'll sell some.

    D. You make the sale when you prove your product makes the buyer better off.

7. Thoroughness

    A. I investigate facts in-depth and personally satisfy myself as to their accuracy. No one is going to catch me short when it comes to facts.

    B. I concentrate on learning the positive facts and tend to rationalize negative facts to diminish their importance.

    C. I collect and validate both negative and positive facts, continuously updating them, so that I can give the customer an objective basis for a sound decision.

    D. I take facts given to me at face value. When asked for them, I pass them on without embellishment.

8. Involvement

    A. It is a coincidence when the customer wants what I offer.

    B. Customers sell themselves whenever I am able to get them to be active in thinking about, trying out or experiencing a demonstration.

    C. I am involved in selling the customer, whom I expect to listen and to take my advice.

    D. Being actively interested in customers as people allows them to feel secure in evaluating the products I offer.

9. Convictions

   A. I go along with opinions, attitudes and ideas of customers and others or avoid taking sides.

   B. I listen for and seek out ideas, opinions and attitudes different from my own. I have clear convictions but respond to sound ideas by changing my mind.

   C. I stand up for my ideas, opinions and attitudes, even though it sometimes results in stepping on toes.

   D. I prefer to accept opinions, attitudes and ideas of customers and others rather than push my own.

10. Conflict

   A. I try to avoid generating conflict. When it does appear, I try to soothe feelings and to keep people together.

   B. When conflict arises, I try to cut it off or to win my position.

   C. When conflict arises, I try to remain neutral or stay out of it.

   D. When conflict arises, I try to identify reasons for it and to resolve underlying causes.

11. Energetic Enthusiasm

   A. I know what I want and pressure others into acceptance.

   B. I support, encourage and compliment others on what they want to do.

   C. I direct my full energies into what I am doing, and others respond enthusiastically.

   D. I put out enough to get by.

12. When I lose a sale, my normal response is:

   A. When I appear to be unsuccessful with a customer, I come back with alternative approaches. I don't let one failure diminish the prospect of success with another customer.

   B. Whether I fail or succeed, I feel every turndown can result in a learning experience.

   C. Failure doesn't affect my enthusiasm. There is always another prospect around the corner.

D. When I am turned down by a prospect, I approach the next one with the fear that I might be rejected again.

13. Decisions

A. I place high value on getting a decision that makes the sale.

B. I place high value on maintaining good relations.

C. I place high value on getting sound creative decisions that result in understanding and agreement.

D. I accept the decision of customers and go to the next call.

14. Temper

A. When aroused, I contain myself, though my impatience is visible.

B. By remaining sure of my product, I rarely get stirred up.

C. Because of the disturbance tensions can produce, I react in a warm and friendly way.

D. When things are not going right, I defend, resist or come back with counter arguments.

15. Humor

A. My humor fits the situation and gives perspective; I retain a sense of humor even under pressure.

B. My humor is seen by others as not always funny.

C. My humor is hard-hitting.

D. My humor aims at maintaining friendly relations or, when strains do arise, it shifts attention away from the serious side.

BRIDGES OVER ANXIOUS WATERS —

(not troubled, just anxious)

Here are two lists of words. Psychological testing indicates that some words tend to be restful words; they invoke a relaxed atmosphere, a favorable reaction. On the other hand, there are words that invoke stress, a sharp reaction. For the most part, the restful words are soft-sounding words. The unfavorable words are sharp, often hard words. In the closing stage, use stroking words, not striking words.

FAVORABLE WORDS FOR CLOSING

Approve	Agreement	Authorize	Safety
Comfort	Deserve	Discovery	Proven
Evaluate	Fun	Guarantee	Understand
Easy	Results	Save	Love
Health	New	Right	Let's
Proud	Profit	Happy	Value
Trust	Value		

UNFAVORABLE WORDS FOR CLOSING

Contract	Deal	Sign	Sell
Cost	Decision	Buy	Try
Decide	Failure	Hard Pay	Signature
Price	Lose	Hurt	Cheap
Death	Bad	Fail	Angle
Obligation	Worry	Liable	Difficult

Make it ... "If you'll just authorize this agreement." ... Not ... "Just sign where I made the X."

Make it ... "If you'll just approve this above where I've noted." ... Not ... "If you'll just sign this deal where I marked it."

Make it ... "I believe you'll discover this is a very profitable advertising investment." ... Not ... "Don't worry about this not being a good decision, it can't fail."

THE SINGLE MOST IMPORTANT WORD TO USE IN A CLOSING IS THE BUYER'S NAME. OF ALL THE WORDS IN OUR ENGLISH LANGUAGE, THE NAME DOES MORE TO PRODUCE A POSITIVE, RELAXED, COMFORTABLE ATMOSPHERE THAN ANY OTHER THING THAT CAN BE SAID. IT IS DIFFICULT TO USE IT TOO OFTEN.

ANSWERS

Not every response fits the question perfectly for every person. There may have been instances where you would say to yourself: "Not any of these really fits me." Hopefully, you picked the one that most nearly fit you. However, the 15 questions will provide a profile that is at least relative. It will provide you with some insight of your own mental attitude.

More importantly, it will provide a basis for deciding what level of selling you now employ or exhibit. Keep in mind, there is nothing terribly wrong with any of the postures of selling. There is a time and a place for each. Every salesperson has used all four levels of selling, if their skills and attitudes have risen to the top level. The important idea is that all salespeople, at some time in their career, have passed through these levels, certainly the first two levels, in order to reach a high-performance level of selling.

Here are the scorings of the inventory:

Take the original pages and transfer your circled answers to the scoring sheet below. You then have four columns of letters you have circled. You might have circles in only three of the four or, if you are very new in sales, you might have circled letters in only two of the columns.

Add up the number of circled letters in each column. That will give you some relative idea of where your attitude toward selling is now.

	Door Knocker	**Product** Peddler	**Counselor** Representative	**Professional** Resource
#1	D	A	C	B
#2	D	B	C	A
#3	C	B	A	D
#4	B	A	C	D
#5	A	C	B	D
#6	C	B	A	D
#7	D	B	A	C
#8	A	C	B	D
#9	D	C	A	B
#10	B	C	A	D
#11	D	A	B	C
#12	D	C	B	A
#13	D	A	B	C
#14	A	D	B	C
#15	B	C	D	A

::

HOW CLOSING, GETTING A COMMITMENT TO ACTION AND GETTING DECISIONS ARE ALL WOVEN TOGETHER

How Closing, Getting A Commitment To Action And Getting Decisions Are All Woven Together

It is interesting that the more you learn about selling, the more you understand that closing is not something which happens at the end of the sales process. That may be how the Novice or level one salesperson will look at the process, but it does not represent the view of the level four or Co-Creator salesperson.

DIFFERENCES IN CLOSING:

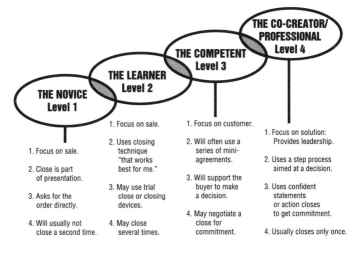

THE NOVICE Level 1

1. Focus on sale.

2. Close is part of presentation.

3. Asks for the order directly.

4. Will usually not close a second time.

THE LEARNER Level 2

1. Focus on sale.

2. Uses closing technique "that works best for me."

3. May use trial close or closing devices.

4. May close several times.

THE COMPETENT Level 3

1. Focus on customer.

2. Will often use a series of mini-agreements.

3. Will support the buyer to make a decision.

4. May negotiate a close for commitment.

THE CO-CREATOR/ PROFESSIONAL Level 4

1. Focus on solution: Provides leadership.

2. Uses a step process aimed at a decision.

3. Uses confident statements or action closes to get commitment.

4. Usually closes only once.

If we briefly tracked this process through the matrix, we would see that attitude shifting. The Novices do see the close at the end of the process. They really don't realize that when a prospect decides to hear them, give them time, to look and listen, that prospect has already been "closed" three times. He has made three decisions.

When the Learners pick up the idea that they open their

appointment with a technique that involves a permission question, they have made their first close if the prospect says they can ask some questions. To illustrate that, the salesperson says something like: "I was thinking about meeting you and what you might like to know about me and I wrote down some questions. Would you mind if I asked you those questions?" First, the salespeople raise their credibility with the prospect by being prepared with written questions. They also get their first close when the prospect gives them permission to ask their questions.

When the Competent sellers learn to handle their recommendation or solution with a series of checking questions as they go through the proposal, they get a number of closes or decisions. They might ask: "Are those points clear?" Or, they might ask: "Do you like the benefits in this idea so far?" And each time they ask and get agreement, they have a close or a decision. When they ask: "Should we consider the next step, then?" they have a commitment to further action.

When the Co-Creators ask: "Have we included all the decision makers in our needs analysis?" they are asking for a decision and getting a close.

When selling is transactional, there is obviously more emphasis placed on closing. In level one and level two training, there ought to be some explanation of the fundamental of closing. Salespeople ought to learn the three fundamental types of closes. These are:

1. The Direct Close

> Example: "Would you like to buy this model?"
>
> "Can we do some business together on this?"

2. The Trial Close

> Example: "Based on the several plans we've looked at here, which seems to best fit your needs?"
>
> "If you were to utilize this package, when would you be starting your schedule?"

3. Assumptive Close

> Example: "Would you like to have me wrap this for you?"
>
> "How would you like to take delivery?"

Nearly all the other storybook closes are based on these three basic closes. Interestingly enough, most of the standard closing "techniques" really do fit the first two levels of selling but are seldom used in the top two levels. Add to these closes still other variations:

The Subtle Close

> Example: "You really do like this, don't you?"

The Alternate Close

> Example: "Do you like the blue one or will you want the pink one?"

The Colombo Close

> Example: "It seems that you like this idea but aren't buying it."
>
> "Where in my presentation did I go wrong?"

The Hot Item Close

> Example: "This is the last one of these we have. They have been very popular. Better act now."

If I Can, Will You? Close

> Example: "If I can help you find financing on this house at 8 percent, would you consider going to contract today?"

And the list goes on, with each type of close suggesting that the seller can lead the buyer to water and make him drink. If one won't work, maybe another one will. It all fits in level one and level two, and it fits the high tell style of selling. Does it work? Yes, it does work, especially in smaller sales. Especially in sales where the seller has only one opportunity to sell. You can get people to buy because most people do like to buy things. We are a marketplace-driven economy and people will buy.

What, then, are the downsides of level one and level two closing? Your odds of closing are lower if the sale is a big-dollar sale. The odds are higher it will be a one-time sale and not a customer relationship. The odds are better there will be buyer remorse. And, some people in the business office would tell you, the salespeople who sell almost exclusively this way will have a higher track record of takebacks or credit problems if financing is involved.

The key mind shift in closing that takes place between level two and level three is with the action of the buyer. In levels one and two, they buy because you ask them to buy. In levels three and four, the offering has been so positioned that they want to buy. Closing becomes a natural process.

Through the years, I have been asked this question many times by bright-eyed, bushy-tailed salespeople: "If you could use only one close in every sale, what would you say?" My answer is very simple:

ARE WE READY TO MOVE FORWARD?

Study this phrase carefully. First, it fits every level of selling. Depending on how the offering has been presented, this close will fit. Study it some more. Notice it is both a trial close and a direct close. If the response is something like: "I'm not sure we're quite ready yet," the salesperson has a number of responses.

Picture the line from one to ten again. Remember the concept of closing the gap. You were trying to go from eight or nine to ten. They've just indicated they are still at eight or nine. A direct close — "Would you like to buy this?" — puts you back at one or gets you to ten. Your gap has become much greater.

A negative or less-than-positive response means the buyer isn't ready for ten. So, the salesperson's response, depending on the situation, might be: "Is there some point we ought to review?" Or, it might be: "It sounds like there might be a small reservation. Can we talk about that?" I have heard on a call with a skilled level four salesperson just the phrase "Oh?" and then a pause, and the buyer took it from there to pinpoint the issue.

Notice, too, the inclusion of empathy. "Are we ... " It is a relationship of buyer and seller. Subtle? Perhaps. Effective? You bet!

Anytime we ask for an opinion, a commitment for further action, for a decision or an agreement, we are closing. Closing becomes moving any idea or concept, any product or service presentation, toward completion.

There is another dynamic at work in this process.

When the dollars involved are small and the decision is not important, a salesperson can ask for the order more often than when the dollars are big and the decision is important. Big dollars do not always mean a big close. When there is a group of decision makers, it is very possible that one or more of those buying influences won't want to make a big decision, because of the impact it might have on their career, their advancement or their present job. They view the offering as something where they have very little to gain personally and everything to lose. To them, it is a big decision that will impact on them personally.

But when you have just bought a suit, and the salesperson suggests a nice tie for the man or a matching scarf for the lady, that salesperson can ask for a buying decision several times for the add-on, and the customer really doesn't mind. The tension is down, they've made the major decision about how they will look, and the add-on item really doesn't call for a lot of justification. And how many times has a tie been purchased because "it went well with the suit?"

But if the decision had involved a college education for a child, and perhaps how insurance fit into a total estate plan, then you have much more than a decision about a matching accessory. Both the total dollars involved and the far-reaching consequences of the decision mean the salesperson will probably have an opportunity to use just one close and it must be made at the proper time in the sales process.

So the semantics of closing change and shift as the dollars get bigger and the importance of the decision gets bigger. This requires a shift in the attitude of the salespeople on closing, or they will never reach that level of high performance.

We used the word tension earlier, and there are two times in the selling process when tension is a factor. When the seller and buyer first meet, there is tension. The job of the salesperson is to build mutuality, commonality and credibility as fast as possible. This reduces the tension to a comfort level for both seller and buyer. Sometimes, seasoned salespeople will chuckle a little at the idea of tension when they meet a new person. But that means they have forgotten how it was when they started selling and that feeling of discomfort was present. It's a little like it was if you ever went on a blind date and you wondered what he or she was going to be like. The first few minutes were a little uncomfortable until you got acquainted. You either decided the blind date wasn't your cup of tea or nature took its course.

The second time in the sales process during which tension is a factor is in the closing stage. A person making an important decision is under some pressure. The hard closer will actually put the buyer under more pressure when he presses for the decision. Quite often, a buyer in one situation is a seller in another situation. These people have also studied selling, and they can see the clever technique coming before the arm lock is ever put on them. Today, the buyer is just more sophisticated. We've all heard the adage that we may like to buy but we hate to be sold.

Closing doesn't need to be mental battle or an arm-twisting situation. The Competent-level salespeople begin to understand this and shift the closing into much more of a cooperative process, where they are actually helping the buyer make a good decision. They make it clear in the whole process that their purpose is to help the buyer make a valid decision the buyer can fully justify. They make it clear they don't want just to sell something, but rather they want a customer relationship that provides for future mutually beneficial business. It becomes a case of providing the buyer with enough information, fitting a solution to their needs, both product and personal, and making them comfortable with their decision.

Selling them becomes a step-by-step process of getting commitments. We measure the progress of the sale by the commitments and agreements the buyer is willing and able to make.

The salesperson paces with the buyer. At the third level of selling, salespeople will often make use of a trial close. They will ask for a decision on a minor point before moving to a total commitment. Usually, these requests for a decision will be leading questions to move the process along. Here are sample questions used by level three salespeople:

"Are we ready to consider possible financing options on this house?"

"Would you like to see some financing choices available on this car?"

"Could we schedule an appointment next week with your group?"

"Do you like this idea well enough that we should consider how we would implement the plan?"

"Do you see anything we have missed, any information you would need, that would help you make your decision?"

Every one of those trial closes has two elements. In every statement there is a request for a minor decision. There is also a forward motion in each question that will lead to the next step.

The third-level salespeople have also learned one other important thing. There is nothing harder to live with than not knowing where they stand. By now, they have learned a few simple rules of selling. Those look something like this:

End the sales call with the best commitment you can get. "Maybe" or "I'll consider it" is not a commitment. Leave with an understanding of what you will do and what they will do and when you will meet again for a decision.

It is better to get "no" than be up in a hang glider. "No" allows you to move on.

Have some backup alternatives you might be able to get a decision on if you feel the timing is not right for a final commitment at this time.

Know where the needle is, where the gap is and try to move the needle as near the close as possible. You may summarize the present situation and agree with the buyer on what still needs to be accomplished. You get a decision on this.

If you sell with low expectations, that message comes through to the prospect or buyer. Make it clear you have high expectations for a decision.

Third-level and fourth-level salespeople also know they can open a presentation by closing. Here are some samples of this technique we have heard used or seen employed:

Level two salesperson: "The reason, (their name), I'm here today is to help you buy our (product). Naturally, you'll make that decision yourself, but after I ask you a few questions and tell you some interesting things about (product or service), you should be able to do that. Does that sound fair to you?"

This statement leaves little doubt about the purpose of the meeting, the process of the look and listen, and the desired payoff.

Level three salesperson selling advertising: "There is something you should know up front, (name), and I tell you this because I know you always consider price an important part of the decision. This special offering has no flexibility on pricing. So, if price is an issue with you, let's not take each other's time. Will price be an important issue?"

That calls for an important decision up front by the buyer. Will they haggle over price, or will they make their decision on this offering based upon value?

Fourth-level salespeople open a group meeting with this statement: "Well, ladies and gentlemen, I believe we are together today to reach a decision on the recommendation we have made to your organization. I believe we have covered all the issues and concerns in previous meetings, and I believe we have general agreement that our revisions have removed those concerns. Would that be your consensus at this time?"

Clearly stated and to the point. We are gathered together to make a decision. That opening also makes it rather difficult for a negative player to inject last-minute questions. That word "consensus" is rather powerful.

Compare these closing statements used as opening statements with some of the closes used by the Novice and the Learner. Here are some samples:

Alternate Close

> "Would you like the X model or the Y Model?"

Assumptive Close

> "What is your mailing address?

Minor/Major Close

> "Could we agree on a closing date so we can arrange for the buyer and seller to meet at that time?

Leading to a Ben Franklin Close

> "Let's look at the pluses and the minuses on this and then you decide."

A Worst Case/Best Case Close

> "What do you see as the worst case scenario if you decide to go ahead?" "What do you feel would be the best case result of this decision?"

Notice the technique in these last two and the slight touch of manipulation. When you use the BEN FRANKLIN, you use a piece of paper. The seller helps the buyer with all the pluses, then gives him the paper and asks him to list the minuses. Which list do you suppose will be longer? And in the case of the WORST CASE/BEST CASE close, notice you always lead with the down side. You finish with the up side. Which will have front-of-mind awareness?

This leads to a final point on closing or getting a commitment. Level four or Co-Creator salespeople seldom close, as such. Their objective is to get a decision, but they want their promise or solution to work for the buyer, to be good for the buyer, to be totally justifiable for the buyer. They have put their best thought, creative ability and work into the recommendation. They really believe it is the best course of action. So, not only will they enter that commitment stage of selling with credibility, they will enter it with confidence. And this will involve the last shift in attitude and getting the commitment. They provide a certain type of leadership. You'll hear requests for commitment phrased more like these:

"It appears to me we are ready to move forward on this."

"I have provided a very simple agreement here and will need your approval where it is indicated." (NOTICE THEY DO NOT USE THE WORD "SIGN," NOR DO THEY USE THE WORD "CONTRACT." BOTH WORDS RAISE TENSION. THEY USE PARTNERSHIP WORDS.)

"It looks like the next logical step would be for me to call our people and have them process this recommendation."

And you may hear them use what we would call a SUMMARY CLOSE. These would be the steps:

SUMMARIZE: "Let me do a brief recap here to sum up where we are. You said you wanted ... and that ... was a priority. It appears those needs have been met."

PROMISE: "When we use (solution), these are the results you can expect. It will provide ... in the following ways. Is that a reasonable summary? (TRIAL QUESTION)

COMMITMENT:"I'll need both of you to approve this where it has been indicated and we will have your plan in place."

So, the process has moved through the four levels of selling, from the Novice, who takes a deep gulp and asks for the order, to the Co-Creator, who leads the buyer into making a justifiable decision. Closing fits into the attitude of the salesperson. Is a sale the goal? Or, is the goal to get a justifiable decision? From a direct close, such as: "Can we do business together?" to a statement close, such as: "It seems to me the basic decision here is whether you use a balloon payment on the end or whether you will use standard financing?" From a question, such as: "Can we start next week?" to a statement, such as: "Well, it seems we're ready to move forward."

A closing question leaves the entire decision to the buyer. A statement close makes it a partnership decision. If the decision is truly a major one, top-level salespeople use what we call a PILOT CLOSE. It would go like this in the world of sales training:

SALESPERSON: "It seems to me we have general agreement here on a worthwhile investment, but your principle concern is the implementation of the plan in your organization. Let me suggest we start with the sales managers and use them as a pilot program. We can evaluate as the training progresses, and if you then believe the results

> justify the investment, we can implement the total plan. Let's schedule the sales managers for the February date you said was feasible. I believe we can justify your confidence."

Notice that there is no question in this close. It calls for an agreement, but provides for a failsafe decision. It is stated in a very justifiable way.

Getting a commitment is the final leg of the journey for salespeople. Depending upon their level of expertise, they will move from poor closing ratios to high closing ratios. They will move from small-dollar sales to big-dollar sales. They will grow from getting smaller decisions to getting big decisions. Along that journey, they will have learned to use the four steps we have outlined. They will build credibility, because that is the first step to high-performance selling.

They will have learned to help the prospects or the buyers find their need, that gap between what they have and what they want. They will have learned to discern the stage of buyer readiness. They will have learned positioning and how to position their promise, their solution, their concept to meet the product needs and the personal needs of the buyers. And, they will have learned how to help the buyers justify their decision, so that decision fits the buyer Image of Reality.

Now, we have come full cycle. We leave you with these questions:

WHERE ARE YOU NOW?

WHERE DO YOU WANT TO BE?

HOW WILL YOU GET THERE?

Perhaps the concepts you have learned, or been exposed to in this book, can help you on your career path. We sincerely hope they do.

::

CHAPTER 22

"If You Ain't Been Throwed, You Ain't Been Ridin'"

"IF YOU AIN'T BEEN THROWED, YOU AIN'T BEEN RIDIN'"

S ales managers often say to me: "I have the funny feeling you are spending a lot of time training salespeople to do things on calls they never make." And I respond: "That's an interesting point of view and sadly seems to be shared by some sales managers. It's like a fellow told me the other day when we were talking about training. 'You know,' he said, 'I'm not sure any of us can train sales-people. You train dogs. I'm not sure you can get salespeople to retrieve. Maybe the best any of us can do is to encourage them to try ... to give it their best shot ... and when they make a good ride, hey ... you give 'em a pat on the back and tell 'em they did good.' I'm sure there is a lot of truth to what he said. Maybe it's that you have to keep trying to get people to try."

Walking back from that meeting, I got to thinking about a story I often tell salespeople. It is a sort-of-true Oklahoma story. In Oklahoma, you sort of take any story with a grain of salt, especial-ly if a politician tells it. But the sort-of-true story has a good point to it, so it is passed along when the timing is right, often at the end of a workshop or seminar.

It was a hot, early July afternoon, a Saturday. Oklahoma has a lot of small towns and these small towns have small rodeos. Just west of Checotah, Oklahoma, is a small grandstand and an area they drag everything now and then to produce a dirt arena. There was a crowd gathered: pickup trucks, horse trailers, noise and dust.

I walked over to a rail at one side of the arena and just stood and watched and, about then, a chute opened and a young fellow came out riding a bronco who jumped around like he had an upset stom-ach. He spun around a couple of times, let out a snort or two and off sailed the cowboy and into the dust he fell. He got up and started walking, dusting off his jeans with his hat as he walked. He passed right by me, and this was our visit:

Me: "Quite a ride."

Him: "Yep, Ornery animal."

Me: "They have a purse for this event?"

Him: "Yep... not very big, though."

Me: "Can you make any money in rodeos like this?"

Him: "Ah, if you're lucky, you pick up a couple of thousand dollars in a summer. Not much money unless you're in the really big rodeos."

Me: "Why do you suppose people do it, then?"

Him: "Well, like me, I just like to think I can ride any animal they give me."

Me: "The challenge, maybe. When you do it well you feel good?"

Him: "Somethin' like that. And you pick up a few bucks and see your frens."

Me: "What...tell me... do you think about when you're picking yourself out of the dust?"

And, for the first time, he really looked at me. Our eyes really looked at each other for the first time. And then he shrugged.

Him: "I don't guess I think much. If you ain't been throwed, you ain't been ridin'." There was a pause.

Me: "Thank you, my friend. You have just given me a powerful connection. Much obliged and thanks for visiting."

Him: "You in rodeo work?"

Me: "Nope, mostly I'm in sales work. But it holds there, too. If you ain't been throwed, you aint been ridin'."

It was about then, I guess, that writing this book seemed worthwhile.

::

EPILOGUE

T his book has been nearly 20 years in the making, maybe more. It has evolved in many ways, much as the professionalism of selling has evolved. What was new and fresh one year was obsolete the next year. In fact, today, as you read this, the profession of selling may be at yet a higher level, a fifth dimension, so to speak.

There are many resonances in selling techniques and in the transmitting of those skills from one person to another. I suspect, in one way or another, that all teachers of any art or craft feed off each other. It may be, as you explore this book and its contents, that you will find things said by others in a slightly different way than I have broached the idea.

They say all speakers or trainers go through an evolution with their material. When they start out, at the Novice level, they quote their sources rather openly. There is a considerable amount of attribution, because this gives the speaker or presenter a certain amount of credibility. As time passes, their sources become a little hazier and they may say something like: "Somebody once said ... I've forgotten who it was," and then they deliver the message.

The third stage is when they begin to believe that all of the material is theirs and they forget to mention any source whatsoever.

You'll find names in this book such as Don Beveridge, Larry Wilson, even Willy Loman and Willy Gayle. Beveridge is a living person, a dynamic presenter and a forerunner in advocating "consultative selling." Larry Wilson is the Wilson of Wilson Learning, who pioneered consultant selling in the insurance business. For several years, Wilson Learning material was a staple in what our company offered to the radio industry, as well as other categories of business. I'm sure their ideas have meshed into mine in many ways.

To carry this concept of resonance one step further, it wouldn't be logical if the philosophy of people you know and admire didn't show up in your work.

I have never met Stephen Covey. I learned of him one day about seven years ago when, during a break at a workshop, a longtime friend came up to visit and asked me if I had read Covey's book, *The Seven Habits of Highly Effective People.* "Well," said my friend, "you ought to, because a lot of your stuff sounds like what is in his book." And then he added: "You'll find a lot about habits in his book, because it is about habits."

That, of course, was his reference to my analogy of the "barrier reef" and what was in the belief system of salespeople that kept them from realizing full potential. I wrote the title down and faithfully promised I would locate the book. Several years filled with good intentions passed, and then I learned of another Covey book called *Principle Centered Leadership*, which I read with great interest. In this book, I found a reprise of the seven habits of highly effective people, and I remembered my friend's suggestion.

These are Covey's seven habits:

1. Be proactive.

2. Begin with an end in mind.

3. Put first things first.

He sees these first three steps as "private victories," the steps that take a person from dependence to independence. In other words, there is the suggestion of evolution in this, much as we offer the stages in the evolution of the growth of the salesperson. We suggest "purpose-process-payoff" as the steps in selling. To ask yourself: "What is my purpose" obviously is a proactive mental process. To say the second step to yourself is to mentally rehearse the steps, the tactics, the strategy, the plan, the agenda. This is being proactive.

We use the phrase "focus on the gap, not the goal." In other words: "What do I need to do next to close the gap and get me to the payoff." That would be another way to say "put first things first," although this is not exactly the context in which Covey uses it.

But all of these habits, or steps to independence as a salesperson, would fit the concept of the first two levels of selling, the Novice and Learner. There is a great deal of resonance here.

Covey uses three more habits:

4. Think win-win.

5. Seek first to understand and then to be understood.

6. Synergize.

If you look at our concept of the evolution of the salesperson into the Competent and the Professional levels, there is again a considerable resonance. We believe the seller and the buyer begin, together, to find mutual benefits. This is certainly true at the "Co-Creator" level. We point out that the communication style shifts from a "tell" posture to a "listening" posture. In other words, salespeople seek first to understand before they begin to suggest any solution. ("Be understood.")

His seventh and last habit is "sharpen the saw." This suggests continued growth, ever learning, ever open to new ideas and concepts. This whole book is about growing into the high-performance levels of selling, becoming the self-actualized salesperson.

Toward the end of his book, Covey creates his own analogy, bringing in another friend we have never met in person, but who we have met many times in shared moments in his books and articles. Darned if Covey doesn't get into trout fishing and bring in Gene Hill, he of the world of hunting and fishing and, more than that, insightful peeks at nature.

For many years, I have been a devout supporter of Ducks Unlimited, The Nature Conservancy and other organizations committed to wildlife causes. Many times I have been asked: "How in the world do you reconcile selling and management training with conservation?"

I see all the reason in the world to connect the two. I am committed to the idea that conservation is the skilled management of natural resources. I am equally committed to the concept that leadership is the skilled management of human resources. As a human being, I bear an obligation, a stewardship, for the natural resources. I can't quite bring myself to be a preservationist. As Alston Chase put it in his book *Playing God In Yellowstone*: "... what good is the cathedral if the congregation cannot use the building?"

But, surely, we can find a balance that allows us to harvest natural resources and allow for their replenishment. Surely, there must be something called "principled conservation" that can allow for a harvest without threatening a species with extinction.

As a human being, it is entirely logical to me that I, too, am a fitting subject for conservation. I am my own steward. If my chosen profession happens to be selling, then I have a responsibility to use my personal resources in such a fashion that I find a balance for the reasonable consumption of those resources. I should avoid either extraction of those resources or total preservation of those resources of time, energy and expertise. As a conservationist, I have the responsibility of stewardship to my community, my job and myself. I am, like the duck or the goose or water, or the forest or the prairie, a resource that ought to managed and used wisely.

Gene Hill talks about hunting and fishing in a very retrospective way. Ponder his words on trout fishing: "Consistently successful anglers are not locked into fixed responses to situations; rather, they are flexible, constantly reading the water to discover the best place from which to cast into each lie. They, in fact, learn to think like a fish. Often, they will approach the water slowly, keeping a low profile, perhaps even casting from a kneeling position."

Ah, my friend Hill is talking about selling, not trout fishing. Let's see how it fits:

Consistently successful salespeople are not locked into fixed responses to situations; rather, they are flexible, constantly reading the customer to discover the best place from which to fit customer needs or problems to their offering. They, in fact, learn to think like the buyer. Often, they will approach the situation slowly, keeping a low profile and asking rather than telling.

Another comparison. This is Hill on trout fishing: "Match line, leader and tackle to the type of fishing you do, taking into account such things as the speed of the current, the depth of the water and the rate of retrieve. If you fish different waters, have more than one line. And give careful thought and attention to the leader, the most important link in the tackle system."

Isn't that a beautiful analogy for high-performance selling? If you have accepted the concepts of this book, you'll draw all sorts of fascinating connections!

How often have I stood and watched one of my skilled trout fishing friends patiently coax a small fly across the water, at times dance it away from the unseen fish, thus making the quarry a little more anxious to take the fly. And how often have I watched a high-performance salesperson quietly say to a prospect: "Well, it may be that this just isn't the right time for you to consider this proposal. Maybe we should just put the idea on hold." And the response came back so quickly: "No, no, I didn't mean that at all. I'd just like to know a little more about how the billing will be handled."

If the offering was in reality not good for the client or prospect, then the tactic is not valid. But if the offering is legitimate, valid and of actual value to the buyer, then is it not my job to help them want to buy — not make them, but help them want to buy?

Through the years, it has been my privilege to represent many fine products and services. I don't believe I have ever helped any-body buy something that did not produce the end results of helping them. Many times there was a long period of delayed gratification. And then, at some point in time, there would be a comment like: "I'm really glad you helped me make that decision. It has really worked out well."

A sales trainer, a teacher of skills and techniques, a mentor, lives with that same time span of delayed gratification. Oftentimes, it is a stewardship of faith. You feel you have done the right thing, shown the right technique, modeled the right path. And then, one day, you hear the words: "You remember that time when you got me to try to use more open questions to get people to want to talk to me? Boy, has that idea ever paid off in rich dividends for me. In fact, you made quite a contribution to my career. Thank you."

And I say: "No, thank *you*."

∷

CREDITS

CHAPTER 33 PAGE 33   1. This model was acquired from Wilson Learning and is used with their permission.

PAGE 36   2. This idea came from Zig Ziglar's book, *See You At The Top*

CHAPTER 4 PAGE 41   1. The "Pattern Game" was adapted from Wilson Learning material and is used with their permission.

CHAPTER 5 PAGE 49   1. References made with permission of Wilson Learning.

CHAPTER 7 PAGE 67   1. These edges were originally developed in Greenwood Performance Systems material and are used with their permission.

PAGE 73   2. This concept is used by Wilson Learning as Purpose-Process-Payoff. Used here with their permission.

CHAPTER 8 PAGE 79   1. The concept of P-A-D-A was an original part of Selling Radio, a sales course offered by Greenwood Performance Systems. It is used in this book with their permission.

CHAPTER 9 PAGE 87   1. These two terms are also used by Norm Goldsmith in his management workshops. Used by permission.

CHAPTER 10 PAGE 98   1. Taken from Counselor Selling, a sales course offered by Wilson Learning. Used by permission.

PAGE 106   2. Taken, in concept, from Wilson Learning material and their "Ben Duffy" technique. Used with permission.

CHAPTER 14 PAGE 168 [1.] Originally used in Selling Radio, a sales course offered by Greenwood Performance Systems. Used with permission.

PAGE 168 [2.] Originally used in Negotiation, a sales seminar offered by Greenwood Performance Systems. Used with permission.

PAGE 170 [3.] Originally used in Selling Radio, a sales course offered by Greenwood Performance Systems. Used with permission.

CHAPTER 15 PAGE 128 [1.] Originally developed for Greenwood Performance System in the course, Selling Radio. Used with permission.

CHAPTER 16 PAGE 198 [1.] We were first introduced to this description by Don Beveridge. The concept is his and is used with permission.

[2.] This term was first used in Selling Radio, developed for Greenwood Performance Systems. Used with permission.

CHAPTER 19 PAGE 239 [1.] This model was acquired from Wilson Learning and is used with their permission.

CHAPTER 20 PAGE 254 [1.] The concept of "You Focus on the Gap, Not the Goal," was originally developed for Greenwood Performance Systems and is still a part of their offerings. Used with their permission.

INDEX

INDEX

A

A Worst Case/Best Case Close 272
acceptance 9
action 212
activity............................98, 101
actual criteria........................23
added value 80, 100
advantage 91
advantages.............12, 81, 187
adversarial relationship 12
advocate 150
agency buyer 53
Alternate Close....................272
alternate close.....................126
Amiable................................91
Analytical 91
application 211
appointment........................126
appointment letter 130
appointment letter model 130
aspiration 168
assumed consent 212
assumed consent letter 133
Assumptive Close 266, 272
atmosphere 24
attitudes 165

B

Babe Ruth.............................98
Barker, Joel Arthur......175, 198
be satisfied with 168
belief system
   ...8, 22, 44, 45, 60, 68, 141
benefit.............................77, 91
benefits 187
Beveridge, Don
   ....25, 206, 207, 249, 279
Bolton, Robert and Dorothy
   Grover Bolton Door.....245
bracket questions.................168
bridging 102
bridging articles 145
buyer...................................53

buyer belief system 166
buyer-focused.......................12
buying criteria
   ....22, 23, 27, 79, 85
buying process 105

C

call 97
call proficiency.....................25
calls 97
Changing The Game: The New
   Way To Sell.......................7
Chase, Alston 281
checking questions......140, 163
closed questions..140, 162, 163
closing.............18, 21, 219, 265
coaching 11
co-creator.............................10
cognition thinking 196
comfort...............................140
Commercial Visitor.............207
commitment 8, 32, 140
commitment questions 163
commitment to action .154, 254
commodity buying 79
commonality.........................31
competence 8, 31
competency 32
competent.............................2
competitive edge.....67, 78, 183
concept 11
conflict management...........220
conscious-incompetent..........33
consequences.........................44
Consultative Salesperson 207
convergent thinking 196
could live with 168
counselor 21
counselor sales 204, 205
Counselor Salesperson..........49
co-venture...........................206
Covey, Stephen 280
credibility.....31, 45, 52, 62, 63,
   ....140, 143, 146

credible business reason
................143, 148, 161
credible promises 182
critical edge..................67, 183
culture..............................35
customer 53
customer connection 130
customer needs analysis......140
customer relations 26

D

dead plant 102
Death of a Salesman............139
decision 104
decision makers......................26
defensive behavior 193
defensive climates...............194
designed for success ...145, 253
Dewey, John........................196
DINKS 69
direct customer......................53
direct mail 130
discipline 8
discovery 8
divergent thinking 196
Driver 91
Dyer, Wayne........................213
Ducks Unlimited 281

E

efficiency........................53, 54
ego 19, 32
ego strength.....................19, 32
empathic listening 114
empathic technique 113
empathy......................8, 22, 32
empowerment......................150
establish buying criteria........26
euphoria................................70
expectations..........................35
experience 8
expertise 22
explicit questions 166, 168
exploration questions..165, 166
Expressive 91

F

F I T S 250
fact-finding questions .140, 163
fear 21
features..........................12, 187
features and benefits 21, 183
feeling-finding questions
....................140, 153, 163
fiddler on the roof 20
first turndown......................128
focus..................................9, 10
focus of the call..................162
focus on the appointment....126
focus the direction..............154
four stages of learning 41
fully leveraged present customer
....................................146
fuse 212
Future Edge........................175

G

gain 70
gap 250
gatekeeper 150
Gayle, Willy 279
general request 127
getting the contact................18
Gibb, Dr. Jack R................194
giving information 32
goals......................................11
group decision....................150
Group Psychology Branch,
    Office of Naval Research
....................................194
group selling........................150
Guilford, Dr. J.P. 196

H

Hierarchy of Needs..............13
high-tech field 27
high activity..........................21
high tell 21
Hill, Gene..................281, 282
Hill, Harold 139
human behavior....................42

I

I don't know 125
I made a mistake 125
IBM 206
If I Can, Will You Close 267
Image of Reality....................87
implementer 150
inside game 8

J

joint venture 100, 212
joint venture selling 206
Journal of Communication .194
judgment..............................114
Jung, Carl 43, 46, 240
justification 51, 53

K

Kasarda, John D. 35
Kenan Institute of Private
        Enterprise 35
key accounts.........................23

L

leadership 272
Leading To A Ben Franklin
        Close 272
Learner 2
leveraging accounts...............26
listening 18, 20, 111
Loman, Willy 11, 139, 279

M

main point...........................114
maintenance 70
making a connection 126
Maltsby, Maxwell 43
marketing concept.................27
marketing cycle 1
Mary Kay 206
Maslow, Albert....11, 13, 43, 45
McDonald's............................77
Merrill, David 18, 46
mini-contracts.....................220
Minor/Major Close 272
model the buyer 62

models of presentation 208
money.......................................9
Morton.................................181
move the needle 251

N

Nature Conservancy............281
Nature of Human Intelligence
       196
need 50
needs of the customer 204
negotiation 22, 148, 168
negotiators.............................14
never take no from a person
        who can't say yes 150
new offering 141
no comfort................49, 50, 55
no help...................................49
no hurry 49
no justification 50, 55
no need 49, 55
no payoff 50, 81
no trust..................................49
Northwestern Mutual Life
        Insurance.......................69
Novice 2

O

objections 18, 22, 219
Ogilivy, David....................178
open mind............................114
open questions 140, 163
opinion questions 153, 163
opinions 165
opportunity 100
options and alternatives 23
overcome objections 221

P

P A P A (Promise-Application-
        Proof-Action)
        ....178, 188, 211
P A P A Model.......................79
P.S. 130
Paradigm Pioneers 176

Paradigm Settlers 176
paradigms 175
paraphrase...........................114
Pareto....................................7
participation in an event 142
pattern game........................41
payoff73, 77, 98, 142, 146, 187
pea game 70, 213
peer group 9
peer group acceptance...........10
people skills 18, 22
perceived edge 68, 69, 183
perceived value 166
perception of probability 87, 88
permission questions...140, 163
perseverance..........................18
persistence........................8, 18
personal 60
personal needs.............162, 166
Personal Styles and Effective
    Performance 46
personal win 62
pilot close 273
pitchman.............................139
plan 73, 98, 146
planning calls 21
players 151
Playing God In Yellowstone
   281
position...............140, 141, 152
positioning...........................141
positioning statement..143, 161
post-sale implementation 31
post-buy..............................105
posture 106
potential..............................33
presentation.............18, 22, 219
presentations.........................10
price..............................79, 165
Principle Centered Leadership
   280
priorities 152, 165
priority questions 163

proactive.............................252
proactive person 36
proactive selling 254
product.................................60
product-focused....................12
product needs 165
Product Peddler...........139, 207
product presentations 208
product sale 208
professional 2
programmed for failure
    ....145, 253
promise 211
promised..............................100
promises you can prove 181
promotional activity 27
proof...................................212
prospecting.....................21, 99
psychic challenge 9, 11
psychic satisfaction 251
Psychological Types.............46
psychology 42
pull of hope 72
purpose 18, 73, 98, 146, 147
Purpose-Process-Payoff 159
push of discomfort 72
pyramid 13

Q
qualifying 21
qualitative selling 79
questions 18, 20, 139, 153

R
RAB 204, 205
Rackham, Neil....................187
Radio Advertising Bureau
    ....204, 205
ratings................................204
readiness..............................72
readiness to buy 50
ready, willing and able...........8
recovery questions 163, 164
re-direct questions...............167
reference........................99, 100

references 106
referral letter........................131
rehearse 19
Reid, Roger 46
rejection...............................10
Resolution Trust Corporation
....81
response...............................53
response rate.........................130
responsive listening.............114
responsive technique...........113
restatement questions..........163
result..................................77
results 53
return on investment 22

S
Sales Inventory....................256
sales letters 129
sales managers 17
sales process.........................219
Sales Sonics 49
sales strategy 150
S E E S....................164, 169
S E E S model......................32
selective listening................113
self-actualized......................11
self-actualized individual......13
self-appraisal 256
self-discipline 18
self-esteem 32
self-focused 19
selling 21
selling situation 71
Seven Habits of Highly Effective
    People, The 280
sharpen the saw.....................13
single decision makers........150
situation......................164, 169
social style 12, 18, 91
Social Style/Management Style
....245
solution presentations 210
solution sale 208

solving problems.................142
South Africa 115
special purpose....................131
special reason 126
specific time 127
Sperry Corporation..............118
Spin Selling 188
Stanford University.............194
status quo 71, 77
staying organized 18
Steil, Dr. Lyman K. 118
Stimulus-Pause-Response ...115
strategic planning...........25, 26
strategic selling 150
summarizes..........................113
summary.....................169, 175
summary agreement....175, 178
Summary Close.................273
supportive climates 194
suppose................................168
survival................................8, 9
Sustaining Resource......14, 207
synergizers...........................14
system..................................11

T
tactical sales strategy 22
task needs 162
teaching 11
team leaders.........................14
telephone prospect calls......128
tell me..................................140
tension 269
The Alternate Close 267
The Colombo Close 267
The Direct Close 266
The Hot Item Close.............267
The Subtle Close.................267
The Trial Close....................266
third party............................53
third-party reference
..............99, 142, 143, 146
tie it down 127
time management.............8, 18

time span 102
Toward a Psychology of Being
....45
trade talk..............................147
transactional 31, 203
transactional selling 31, 162
trial close....................219, 270
Type A Benefits...................188
Type B Benefits 188

U
UCLA...............................196
unconscious-competent
..............................33, 70, 71
unconscious habits 33
unconscious-incompetent......33
urgency.................................70
user 150

V
verbal feedback 113
verification of the solution..211
versatility..............................23

W
Wal-Mart 89
want to buy..........................268
want to talk..........................167
what if 168
will you help me?................125
Wilson, Larry....7, 49, 148, 279
Wilson Learning 18, 49, 279
Win 89, 91
Win-Win 70, 77, 78, 148
Woodard, Vivian 206
work the loop 150
working on the phone 147
working the loop.................153

Y
You'll See It When You
    Believe It 213
Your Personal Listening
    Profile...........................118

Z
Ziglar, Zig 101